"In *The Knowledge Illusion*, the cognitive scientists Ste
bach hammer another nail into the coffin of the rational individual . . . positing that
not just rationality but the very idea of individual thinking is a myth."
— *The New York Times Book Review*

"Sloman and Fernbach offer clever demonstrations of how much we take for
granted, and how little we actually understand. . . . The book is stimulating, and
any explanation of our current malaise that attributes it to cognitive failures—
rather than putting it down to the moral wickedness of one group or another—is
most welcome. Sloman and Fernbach are working to uproot a very important
problem. . . . [*The Knowledge Illusion* is] written with vigour and humanity."
— *Financial Times*

"*The Knowledge Illusion* is at once both obvious and profound: the limitations of
the mind are no surprise, but the problem is that people so rarely think about
them. . . . In the context of partisan bubbles and fake news, the authors bring a
necessary shot of humility: be skeptical of your own knowledge, and the wisdom of
your crowd."   — *The Economist*

"A breezy guide to the mechanisms of human intelligence."   — *Psychology Today*

"In an increasingly polarized culture where certainty reigns supreme, a book advo-
cating intellectual humility and recognition of the limits of understanding feels
both revolutionary and necessary. The fact that it's a fun and engaging page-turner
is a bonus benefit for the reader."   — *Publishers Weekly*

"Utterly fascinating . . . Anyone engaged in the work of nurturing healthy and
flourishing communities will ultimately have to wrestle with the questions posed in
this book. Sloman and Fernbach help us to do so gracefully, acknowledging the
truth of how little we know, and finding hope in this precarious situation."
— *Relevant* magazine

"The message at the heart of this book is simultaneously humbling and inspiring: We
don't know very much individually, but what we know collectively is astounding."
— *Mindful* magazine

"Between Sloman and Fernbach they have provided an insightful and thought-
provoking read on how much the individual knows in relation to the community of
knowledge."   — *Nature Partner Journals*

THE KNOWLEDGE
illusion

Why We Never Think Alone

STEVEN SLOMAN

AND

PHILIP FERNBACH

RIVERHEAD BOOKS

NEW YORK

RIVERHEAD BOOKS
An imprint of Penguin Random House LLC
375 Hudson Street
New York, New York 10014

The Library of Congress has catalogued the Riverhead hardcover edition as follows:

Names: Sloman, Steven A., author.
Title: The knowledge illusion : why we never think alone / Steven Sloman and
Philip Fernbach.
Description: New York : Riverhead Books, 2017. | Includes bibliographical
references and index.
Identifiers: LCCN 2016036297 | ISBN 9780399184352
Subjects: LCSH: Thought and thinking. | Knowledge, Sociology of.
Classification: LCC B105.T54 S56 2017 | DDC 153.4/2—dc23
LC record available at https://lccn.loc.gov/2016036297
p.   cm.

First Riverhead hardcover edition: March 2017
First Riverhead trade paperback edition: March 2018
Riverhead trade paperback ISBN: 9780399184369

Printed in the United States of America

Book design by Ellen Cipriano

Contents

THE KNOWLEDGE
illusion

Introduction:
Ignorance and the
Community of Knowledge

Three soldiers sat in a bunker surrounded by three-foot-thick concrete walls, chatting about home. The conversation slowed and then stopped. The cement walls shook and the ground wobbled like Jell-O. Thirty thousand feet above them in a B-36, crew members coughed and sputtered as heat and smoke filled their cabin and dozens of lights and alarms blared. Meanwhile, eighty miles due east, the crew of a Japanese fishing trawler, the not-so-lucky *Lucky Dragon Number Five* (*Daigo Fukuryū Maru*), stood ondeck, staring with terror and wonder at the horizon.

The date was March 1, 1954, and they were all in a remote part of the Pacific Ocean witnessing the largest explosion in the history of humankind: the detonation of a thermonuclear fusion bomb nicknamed "Shrimp," code-named Castle Bravo. But something was terribly wrong. The military men, sitting in a bunker on Bikini Atoll, close to ground zero, had witnessed nuclear detonations before and had expected a shock wave to pass by about 45 seconds after the blast. Instead the earth shook. That was not supposed to happen. The crew of the B-36, flying a scientific mission to sample the fallout cloud and take radiological measurements, were supposed to be at a safe altitude, yet their plane blistered in the heat.

All these people were lucky compared to the crew of the *Daigo Fukuryū Maru*. Two hours after the blast, a cloud of fallout blew over the boat and rained radioactive debris on the fishermen for several hours. Almost immediately the crew exhibited symptoms of acute radiation sickness—bleeding gums, nausea, burns—and one of them died a few days later in a Tokyo hospital. Before the blast, the U.S. Navy had escorted several fishing vessels beyond the danger zone. But the *Daigo Fukuryū Maru* was already outside the area the Navy considered dangerous. Most distressing of all, a few hours later, the fallout cloud passed over the inhabited atolls Rongelap and Utirik, irradiating the native populations. Those people have never been the same. They were evacuated three days later after suffering acute radiation sickness and temporarily moved to another island. They were returned to the atoll three years later but were evacuated again after rates of cancer spiked. The children got the worst of it. They are still waiting to go home.

The explanation for all this horror is that the blast force was much larger than expected. The power of nuclear weapons is measured in terms of TNT equivalents. The "Little Boy" fission bomb dropped on Hiroshima in 1945 exploded with a force of sixteen kilotons of TNT, enough to completely obliterate much of the city and kill about 100,000 people. The scientists behind Shrimp expected it to have a blast force of about six megatons, around three hundred times as powerful as Little Boy. But Shrimp exploded with a force of fifteen megatons, nearly a thousand times as powerful as Little Boy. The scientists knew the explosion would be big, but they were off by a factor of about 3.

The error was due to a misunderstanding of the properties of one of the major components of the bomb, an element called lithium-7.

Before Castle Bravo, lithium-7 was believed to be relatively inert. In fact, lithium-7 reacts strongly when bombarded with neutrons, often decaying into an unstable isotope of hydrogen, which fuses with other hydrogen atoms, giving off more neutrons and releasing a great deal of energy. Compounding the error, the teams in charge of evaluating the wind patterns failed to predict the easterly direction of winds at higher altitudes that pushed the fallout cloud over the inhabited atolls.

This story illustrates a fundamental paradox of humankind. The human mind is both genius and pathetic, brilliant and idiotic. People are capable of the most remarkable feats, achievements that defy the gods. We went from discovering the atomic nucleus in 1911 to megaton nuclear weapons in just over forty years. We have mastered fire, created democratic institutions, stood on the moon, and developed genetically modified tomatoes. And yet we are equally capable of the most remarkable demonstrations of hubris and foolhardiness. Each of us is error-prone, sometimes irrational, and often ignorant. It is incredible that humans are capable of building thermonuclear bombs. It is equally incredible that humans do in fact build thermonuclear bombs (and blow them up even when they don't fully understand how they work). It is incredible that we have developed governance systems and economies that provide the comforts of modern life even though most of us have only a vague sense of how those systems work. And yet human society works amazingly well, at least when we're not irradiating native populations.

How is it that people can simultaneously bowl us over with their ingenuity and disappoint us with their ignorance? How have we mastered so much despite how limited our understanding often is? These are the questions we will try to answer in this book.

Thinking as Collective Action

The field of cognitive science emerged in the 1950s in a noble effort to understand the workings of the human mind, the most extraordinary phenomenon in the known universe. How is thinking possible? What goes on inside the head that allows sentient beings to do math, understand their mortality, act virtuously and (sometimes) selflessly, and even do simple things, like eat with a knife and fork? No machine, and probably no other animal, is capable of these acts.

We have spent our careers studying the mind. Steven is a professor of cognitive science who has been researching this topic for over twenty-five years. Phil has a doctorate in cognitive science and is a professor of marketing whose work focuses on trying to understand how people make decisions. We have seen directly that the history of cognitive science has not been a steady march toward a conception of how the human mind is capable of amazing feats. Rather, a good chunk of what cognitive science has taught us over the years is what individual humans *can't* do—what our limitations are.

The darker side of cognitive science is a series of revelations that human capacity is not all that it seems, that most people are highly constrained in how they work and what they can achieve. There are severe limits on how much information an individual can process (that's why we can forget someone's name seconds after being introduced). People often lack skills that seem basic, like evaluating how risky an action is, and it's not clear they can ever be learned (hence many of us—one of the authors included—are absurdly scared of flying, one of the safest modes of transportation available). Perhaps most important, individual knowledge is remarkably shallow, only scratching the surface of the true complexity of the world, and yet we often don't realize how little we understand. The result is that we are often overconfident, sure we are right about things we know little about.

Our story will take you on a journey through the fields of psychology, computer science, robotics, evolutionary theory, political science, and education, all with the goal of illuminating how the mind works and what it is for—and why the answers to these questions explain how human thinking can be so shallow and so powerful at the same time.

The human mind is not like a desktop computer, designed to hold reams of information. The mind is a flexible problem solver that evolved to extract only the most useful information to guide decisions in new situations. As a consequence, individuals store very little detailed information about the world in their heads. In that sense, people are like bees and society a beehive: Our intelligence resides not in individual brains but in the collective mind. To function, individuals rely not only on knowledge stored within our skulls but also on knowledge stored elsewhere: in our bodies, in the environment, and especially in other people. When you put it all together, human thought is incredibly impressive. But it is a product of a community, not of any individual alone.

The Castle Bravo nuclear testing program is an extreme example of the hive mind. It was a complex undertaking requiring the collaboration of about ten thousand people who worked directly on the project and countless others who were indirectly involved but absolutely necessary, like politicians who raised funds and contractors who built barracks and laboratories. There were hundreds of scientists responsible for different components of the bomb, dozens of people responsible for understanding the weather, and medical teams responsible for studying the ill effects of handling radioactive elements. There were counterintelligence teams making sure that communications were encrypted and no Russian submarines were close enough to Bikini Atoll to compromise secrecy. There were cooks to feed all these people, janitors to clean up after them, and plumbers to keep the toilets working. No one individual had one one-thousandth of the knowledge necessary to fully understand it all. Our ability to collaborate, to jointly pursue such a complex undertaking by putting our minds together, made possible the seemingly impossible.

That's the sunny side of the story. In the shadows of Castle Bravo are the nuclear arms race and the cold war. What we will focus on is the hubris that it exemplifies: the willingness to blow up a fifteen-megaton bomb that was not adequately understood.

Ignorance and Illusion

Most things are complicated, even things that seem simple. You would not be shocked to learn that modern cars or computers or air traffic control systems are complicated. But what about toilets?

There are luxuries, there are useful things, and then there are things that are utterly essential, those things you just cannot do without. Flush toilets surely belong in the latter category. When you need a toilet, you really need it. Just about every house in the developed world has at least one, restaurants must have them by law, and—thank goodness—they are generally available in gas stations and Starbucks. They are wonders of functionality and marvels of simplicity. Everyone understands how a toilet works. Certainly most people feel like they do. Don't you?

Take a minute and try to explain what happens when you flush a toilet. Do you even know the general principle that governs its operation? It turns out that most people don't.

The toilet is actually a simple device whose basic design has been around for a few hundred years. (Despite popular myth, Thomas Crapper did not invent the flush toilet. He just improved the design and made a lot of money selling them.) The most popular flush toilet in North America is the siphoning toilet. Its most important components are a tank, a bowl, and a trapway. The trapway is usually S- or U-shaped and curves up higher than the outlet of the bowl before descending into a drainpipe that eventually feeds the sewer. The tank is initially full of water.

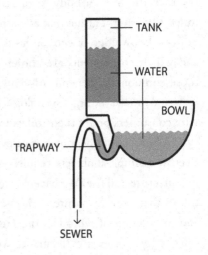

When the toilet is flushed, the water flows from the tank quickly into the bowl, raising the water level above the highest curve of the trapway. This purges the trapway of air, filling it with water. As soon as the trapway fills, the magic occurs: A siphon effect is created that sucks the water out of the bowl and sends it through the trapway down the drain. It is the same siphon action that you can use to steal gasoline out of a car by placing one end in the tank and sucking on the other end. The siphon action stops when the water level in the bowl is lower than the first bend of the trapway, allowing air to interrupt the process. Once the water in the bowl has been siphoned away, water is pumped back up into the tank to wait for next time. It is quite an elegant mechanical process, requiring only minimal effort by the user. Is it simple? Well, it is simple enough to describe in a paragraph but not so simple that everyone understands it. In fact, you are now one of the few people who do.

To fully understand toilets requires more than a short description of its mechanism. It requires knowledge of ceramics, metal, and plastic to know how the toilet is made; of chemistry to understand how the seal works so the toilet doesn't leak onto the bathroom floor; of the human body to understand the size and shape of the toilet. One might argue that a complete understanding of toilets requires a knowledge of economics to appreciate how they are priced and which components are chosen to make them. The quality of those components depends on consumers' demand and willingness to pay. Understanding psychology is important for understanding why consumers prefer their toilets to be one color and not another.

Nobody could be a master of every facet of even a single thing. Even the simplest objects require complex webs of knowledge to manufacture and use. We haven't even mentioned really complicated things that arise in nature such as bacteria, trees, hurricanes, love, and the process of reproduction. How do those work? Most people can't tell you how a coffeemaker works, how glue holds paper together, or how the focus works on a camera, let alone something as complex as love.

Our point is not that people are ignorant. It's that people are more ignorant than they think they are. We all suffer, to a greater or lesser extent, from an illusion of understanding, an illusion that we understand how things work when in fact our understanding is meager.

Some of you might be thinking, "Well, I don't know much about how stuff works, but I don't live in an illusion. I'm not a scientist and I'm not an engineer. It's not important for me to know those things. I know what I have to know to get along and make good decisions." What domain do you know a lot about? History? Politics? Economic policy? Do you really understand things within your area of specialty in great detail?

The Japanese attacked Pearl Harbor on December 7, 1941. The world was at war, Japan was an ally of Germany, and while the United States was not yet a participant, it was clear whose side it was on—the heroic Allies and not the evil Axis. These facts surrounding the attack are familiar and give us a sense that we understand the

event. But how well do you really understand why Japan attacked, and specifically why they attacked a naval base on the Hawaiian Islands? Can you explain what actually happened and why?

It turns out that the United States and Japan were on the verge of war at the time of the attack. Japan was on the march, having invaded Manchuria in 1931, massacred the population of Nanking, China, in 1937, and invaded French Indochina in 1940. The reason that a naval base even existed in Hawaii was to stop perceived Japanese aggression. U.S. president Franklin D. Roosevelt moved the Pacific Fleet to Hawaii from its base in San Diego in 1941. So an attack by Japan was not a huge surprise. According to a Gallup poll, 52 percent of Americans expected war with Japan a week before the attack occurred.

So the attack on Pearl Harbor was more a consequence of a long-standing struggle in Southeast Asia than a result of the European war. It might well have happened even if Hitler had never invented the blitzkrieg and invaded Poland in 1939. The attack on Pearl Harbor certainly influenced the course of events in Europe during World War II, but it was not caused directly by them.

History is full of events like this, events that seem familiar, that elicit a sense of mild to deep understanding, but whose true historical context is different than we imagine. The complex details get lost in the mist of time while myths emerge that simplify and make stories digestible, in part to service one interest group or another.

Of course, if you have carefully studied the attack on Pearl Harbor, then we're wrong; you do have a lot to say. But such cases are the exception. They have to be because nobody has time to study very many events. We wager that, except for a few areas that you've developed expertise in, your level of knowledge about the causal mechanisms that control not only devices, but the mechanisms that determine how events begin, how they unfold, and how one event leads to another is relatively shallow. But before you stopped to consider what you actually know, you may not have appreciated how shallow it is.

We can't possibly understand everything, and the sane among us don't even try. We rely on abstract knowledge, vague and unanalyzed. We've all seen the exceptions—people who cherish detail and love to talk about it at great length, sometimes in fascinating ways. And we all have domains in which we are experts, in which we know a lot in exquisite detail. But on most subjects, we connect only abstract bits of information, and what we know is little more than a feeling of understanding we can't really unpack. In fact, most knowledge is little more than a bunch of associations, high-level links between objects or people that aren't broken down into detailed stories.

So why don't we realize the depth of our ignorance? Why do we think we understand things deeply, that we have systematic webs of knowledge that make sense of everything, when the reality is so different? Why do we live in an illusion of understanding?

What Thinking Is For

To get a better sense of why this illusion is central to how we think, it helps to understand why we think. Thought could have evolved to serve several functions. The function of thought could be to represent the world—to construct a model in our heads that corresponds in critical ways to the way the world is. Or thought could be there to make language possible so we can communicate with others. Or thought could be for problem-solving or decision-making. Or maybe it evolved for a specific purpose such as building tools or showing off to potential mates. All of these ideas may have something to them, but thought surely evolved to serve a larger purpose, a purpose common to all these proposals: Thought is for action. Thinking evolved as an extension of the ability to act effectively; it evolved to make us better at doing what's necessary to achieve our goals. Thought allows us to select from among a set of possible actions by predicting the effects of each action and by imagining how the world would be if we had taken different actions in the past.

One reason to believe that this is why we think is that action came before thought. Even the earliest organisms were capable of action. Single-celled organisms that arose early in the evolutionary cycle ate and moved and reproduced. They did things; they acted on the world and changed it. Evolution selected those organisms whose actions best supported their survival. And the organisms whose actions were most effective were the ones best tuned to the changing conditions of a complex world. If you're an organism that sucks the blood of passing fauna, it's great to be able to latch on to whatever brushes against you. But it's even better to be able to tell whether the object brushing against you is a delicious rodent or bird, not a bloodless leaf blowing in the wind.

The best tools for identifying the appropriate action in a given circumstance are mental faculties that can process information. Visual systems must be able to do a fair amount of sophisticated processing to distinguish a rat from a leaf. Other mental processes are also critical for selecting the appropriate action. Memory can help indicate which actions have been most effective under similar conditions in the past, and reasoning can help predict what will happen under new conditions. The ability to think vastly increases the effectiveness of action. In that sense, thought is an extension of action.

Understanding how thought operates is not so simple. How do people engage in thinking for action? What mental faculties do people need to allow them to pursue their goals using memory and reason? We will see that humans specialize in reasoning about how the world works, about *causality*. Predicting the effects of action requires reasoning about how causes produce effects, and figuring out why something happened requires reasoning about which causes are likely to have produced an effect. This is what the mind is designed to do. Whether we are thinking about physical objects, social systems, other individuals, our pet dog—whatever—our expertise is in determining how actions and other causes produce effects. We know that kicking a ball will send it flying, but kicking a dog will cause pain. Our thought processes, our language, and our emotions are all designed to engage causal reasoning to help us to act in reasonable ways.

This makes human ignorance all the more surprising. If causality is so critical to selecting the best actions, why do individuals have so little detailed knowledge about how the world works? It's because thought is masterful at extracting only what it needs and filtering out everything else. When you hear a sentence uttered, your speech recognition system goes to work extracting the gist, the underlying meaning of the utterance, and forgetting the specific words. When you encounter a complicated causal system, you similarly extract the gist and forget the details. If you're someone who likes figuring out how things work, you might open up an old appliance on occasion, perhaps a coffee machine. If you do, then you don't memorize the shape, color, and location of each individual part. Instead, you look for the major components and try to figure out how they are connected to one another so that you can answer big questions like how the water gets heated. If you're like most people and you're not interested in investigating the insides of a coffee machine, then you know even less detail about how it works. Your causal understanding is limited to only what you need to know: how to make the thing work (with any luck you've mastered that).

The mind is not built to acquire details about every individual object or situation. We learn from experience so that we can generalize to new objects and situations. The ability to act in a new context requires understanding only the deep regularities in the way the world works, not the superficial details.

The Community of Knowledge

We would not be such competent thinkers if we had to rely only on the limited knowledge stored in our heads and our facility for causal reasoning. The secret to our success is that we live in a world in which knowledge is all around us. It is in the things we make, in our bodies and workspaces, and in other people. We live in a community of knowledge.

We have access to huge amounts of knowledge that sit in other people's heads: We have our friends and family who each have their little domains of expertise. We have experts that we can contact to, say, fix our dishwasher when it breaks down for the umpteenth time. We have professors and talking heads on television to inform us about events and how things work. We have books, and we have the richest source of information of all time at our fingertips, the Internet.

On top of that, we have things themselves. Sometimes we can fix an appliance or a bicycle by looking at it to see how it works. On occasion, what's broken is obvious when we take a look (if only this were more common!). You might not know how a guitar works, but a couple of minutes playing with one, seeing what happens when the strings resonate and how their pitch changes when their lengths are changed, might be enough to give you at least a basic understanding of its operation. In that sense, knowledge of a guitar can be found in the guitar itself. There is no better way to discover a city than to travel around it. The city itself holds the knowledge about how it is laid out, where the interesting places to go are, and what you can see from various vantage points.

We have access to more knowledge today than ever before. Not only can we learn how things are made or how the universe came to be by watching TV, we can answer almost any factual question by typing a few characters on a keyboard and enlisting a search engine.

We can frequently find the information we need in Wikipedia or somewhere else on the web. But the ability to access knowledge outside our own heads is not true only of life in the modern world.

There has always been what cognitive scientists like to call a division of cognitive labor. From the beginning of civilization, people have developed distinctive expertise within their group, clan, or society. They have become the local expert on agriculture, medicine, manufacturing, navigating, music, storytelling, cooking, hunting, fighting, or one of many other specialties. One individual may have some expertise in more than one skill, perhaps several, but never all, and never in every aspect of any one thing. No chef can cook all dishes. Though some are mighty impressive, no musician can play every instrument or every type of music. No one has ever been able to do everything.

So we collaborate. That's a major benefit of living in social groups, to make it easy to share our skills and knowledge. It's not surprising that we fail to identify what's in our heads versus what's in others', because we're generally—perhaps always—doing things that involve both. Whenever either of us washes the dishes, we thank heaven that someone knows how to make dish soap and someone else knows how to provide warm water from the faucet. We wouldn't have a clue.

Sharing skills and knowledge is more sophisticated than it sounds. Human beings don't merely make individual contributions to a project, like machines operating in an assembly line. Rather, we are able to work together, aware of others and what they are trying to accomplish. We pay attention together and we share goals. In the language of cognitive science, we share intentionality. This is a form of collaboration that you don't see in other animals. We actually enjoy sharing our mind space with others. In one form, it's called playing.

Our skulls may delimit the frontier of our brains, but they do not delimit the frontier of our knowledge. The mind stretches beyond the brain to include the body, the environment, and people other than oneself, so the study of the mind cannot be reduced to the study of the brain. Cognitive science is not the same as neuroscience.

Representing knowledge is hard, but representing it in a way that respects what you don't know is very hard. To participate in a community of knowledge—that is to say, to engage in a world in which only some of the knowledge you have resides in your head—requires that you know what information is available, even when it is not stored in memory. Knowing what's available is no mean feat. The separation between what's inside your head and what's outside of it must be seamless. Our minds need to be designed to treat information that resides in the external environment as continuous with the information that resides in our brains. Human beings sometimes underestimate how much they don't know, but we do remarkably well overall. That we do is one of evolution's greatest achievements.

You now have the background you need to understand the origin of the knowledge illusion. The nature of thought is to seamlessly draw on knowledge wherever it can be found, inside and outside of our own heads. We live under the knowledge illusion because we fail to draw an accurate line between what is inside and outside our heads. And we fail because there is no sharp line. So we frequently don't know what we don't know.

Why It Matters

Understanding the mind in this way can offer us improved ways of approaching our most complex problems. Recognizing the limits of our understanding should make us more humble, opening our minds to other people's ideas and ways of thinking. It offers lessons about how to avoid things like bad financial decisions. It can enable us to improve our political system and help us assess how much reliance we should have on experts versus how much decision-making power should be given to individual voters.

This book is being written at a time of immense polarization on the American political scene. Liberals and conservatives find each other's views repugnant, and as a result, Democrats and Republicans cannot find common ground or compromise. The U.S. Congress is unable to pass even benign legislation; the Senate is preventing the administration from making important judicial and administrative appointments merely because the appointments are coming from the other side.

One reason for this gridlock is that both politicians and voters don't realize how little they understand. Whenever an issue is important enough for public debate, it is also complicated enough to be difficult to understand. Reading a newspaper article or two just isn't enough. Social issues have complex causes and unpredictable consequences. It takes a lot of expertise to really understand the implications of a position, and even expertise may not be enough. Conflicts between, say, police and minorities cannot be reduced to simple fear or racism or even to both. Along with fear and racism, conflicts arise because of individual experiences and expectations, because of the dynamics of a specific situation, because of misguided training and misunderstandings. Complexity abounds. If everybody understood this, our society would likely be less polarized.

Instead of appreciating complexity, people tend to affiliate with one or another social dogma. Because our knowledge is enmeshed with that of others, the community shapes our beliefs and attitudes. It is so hard to reject an opinion shared by our peers that too often we don't even try to evaluate claims based on their merits. We let our group do our thinking for us. Appreciating the communal nature of knowledge should make us more realistic about what's determining our beliefs and values.

This would improve how we make decisions. We all make decisions that we're not proud of. These include mistakes like failing to save for retirement, as well as regrets like giving in to temptation when we really should know better. We'll see that we can deploy the community of knowledge to help people overcome their natural limitations in ways that increase the well-being of the community at large.

Appreciating the communal nature of knowledge can reveal biases in how we see the world. People love heroes. We glorify individual strength, talent, and good looks. Our movies and books idolize characters who, like Superman, can save the planet all by themselves. TV dramas present brilliant but understated detectives who both solve the crime and make the climactic final arrest after a flash of insight. Individuals are given credit for major breakthroughs. Marie Curie is treated as if she worked alone to discover radioactivity, Newton as if he discovered the laws of motion in a bubble. All the successes of the Mongols in the twelfth and thirteenth century are attributed to Genghis Khan, and all the evils of Rome during the time of Jesus are often identified with a single person, Pontius Pilate.

The truth is that in the real world, nobody operates in a vacuum. Detectives have teams who attend meetings and think and act as a group. Scientists not only have labs with students who contribute critical ideas, but also have colleagues, friends and nemeses who are doing similar work, thinking similar thoughts, and without whom the scientist would get nowhere. And then there are other scientists who are working on different problems, sometimes in different fields, but nevertheless set the stage through their own findings and ideas. Once we start appreciating that knowledge isn't all in the head, that it's shared within a community, our heroes change. Instead of focusing on the individual, we begin to focus on a larger group.

The knowledge illusion also has important implications for the evolution of society and the future of technology. As technological systems become more and more complex, no individual fully understands them. Modern airplanes are a good example. Flying is now a collaborative effort between the pilot and the automated systems in control most of the time. Knowledge about how to operate a plane is distributed across the pilots, the instruments, and the system designers. The knowledge is shared so seamlessly that pilots may not realize the gaps in their understanding. This can make it hard to see catastrophe coming, and we have seen the unfortunate consequences. Understanding ourselves better may help to create better safeguards. The knowledge illusion also affects how we should think about the most transformative technology of our age, the Internet. As the Internet becomes ever more integrated into our lives, the community of knowledge has never been richer, as vast, or as easily accessible.

There are other implications too. Because we think communally, we tend to operate in teams. This means that the contributions we make as individuals depend more on our ability to work with others than on our individual mental horsepower. Individual intelligence is overrated. It also means that we learn best when we're thinking with others. Some of the best teaching techniques at every level of education have students learning as a team. This isn't news to education researchers, but the insight is not implemented in the classroom as widely as it could be.

We hope that this book will leave you with a richer understanding of the mind, one in which you have a greater appreciation for how much of your own knowledge and thought depends on the things and people around you. What goes on between our ears is extraordinary, but it intimately depends on what goes on elsewhere.

ONE

What We Know

Nuclear warfare lends itself to illusion. Alvin Graves was the scientific director of the U.S. military's bomb testing program in the early fifties. He was the person who gave the order to go ahead with the disastrous Castle Bravo detonation discussed in the last chapter. No one in the world should have understood the dangers of radioactivity better than Graves. Eight years before Castle Bravo, in 1946, Graves was one of eight men in a room in Los Alamos, the nuclear laboratory in New Mexico, while another researcher, Louis Slotin, performed a tricky maneuver the great physicist Richard Feynman nicknamed "tickling the dragon's tail." Slotin was experimenting with plutonium, one of the radioactive ingredients used in nuclear bombs, to see how it behaved. The experiment involved closing the gap between two hemispheres of beryllium surrounding a core of plutonium. As the hemispheres got closer together, neutrons released from the plutonium reflected back off the beryllium, causing more neutrons to be released. The experiment was dangerous. If the hemispheres got too close, a chain reaction could release a burst of radiation. Remarkably, Slotin, an experienced and talented physicist, was using a flathead screwdriver to keep the hemispheres separated. When the screwdriver slipped and the hemispheres crashed together, the eight physicists in the room were bombarded with dangerous doses of radiation. Slotin took the worst of it and died in the infirmary nine days later. The rest of the team eventually recovered from the initial radiation sickness, though several died young of cancers and other diseases that may have been related to the accident.

How could such smart people be so dumb?

It's true that accidents happen all the time. We're all guilty of slicing our fingers with a knife or closing the car door on someone's hand by mistake. But you'd hope a group of eminent physicists would know to depend on more than a handheld flathead screwdriver to separate themselves from fatal radiation poisoning. According to one of Slotin's colleagues, there were much safer ways to do the plutonium experiment, and Slotin knew it. For instance, he could have fixed one hemisphere in position and raised the other from below. Then, if anything slipped out of position, gravity would separate the hemispheres harmlessly.

Why was Slotin so reckless? We suspect it's because he experienced the same illusion that we have all experienced: that we understand how things work even when we don't. The physicists' surprise was like the surprise you feel when you try to fix a leaky faucet and end up flooding the bathroom, or when you try to help your daughter with her math homework and end up stumped by quadratic equations. Too often, our confidence that we know what's going on is greater at the beginning of an episode than it is at the end.

Are such cases just random examples, or is there something more systematic going on? Do people have a habit of overestimating their understanding of how things work? Is knowledge more superficial than it seems? These are the questions that obsessed Frank Keil, a cognitive scientist who worked at Cornell for many years and moved to Yale in 1998. At Cornell, Keil had been busy studying the theories people have about how things work. He soon came to realize how shallow and incomplete those theories are, but he ran into a roadblock. He could not find a good method to demonstrate scientifically how much people know relative to how much they think they know. The methods he tried took too long or were too hard to score or led participants to just make stuff up. And then he had an epiphany, coming up with a method to show what he called the illusion of explanatory depth (IoED, for short) that did not suffer from these problems: "I distinctly remember one morning standing in the shower in our home in Guilford, Connecticut, and almost the entire IoED paradigm spilled out in that one long shower. I rushed into work and grabbed Leon Rozenblit, who had been working with me on the division of cognitive labor, and we started to map out all the details."

Thus a method for studying ignorance was born, a method that involved simply asking people to generate an explanation and showing how that explanation affected their rating of their own understanding. If you were one of the many people that Rozenblit and Keil subsequently tested, you would be asked a series of questions like the following:

1. On a scale from 1 to 7, how well do you understand how zippers work?
2. How does a zipper work? Describe in as much detail as you can all the steps involved in a zipper's operation.

If you're like most of Rozenblit and Keil's participants, you don't work in a zipper factory and you have little to say in answer to the second question. You just don't really know how zippers work. So, when asked this question:

3. Now, on the same 1 to 7 scale, rate your knowledge of how a zipper works again.

This time, you show a little more humility by lowering your rating. After trying to explain how a zipper works, most people realize they have little idea and thus lower their knowledge rating by a point or two.

This sort of demonstration shows that people live in an illusion. By their own admission, respondents thought they understood how zippers work better than they did. When people rated their knowledge the second time as lower, they were essentially saying, "I know less than I thought." It's remarkable how easy it is to disabuse people of their illusion; you merely have to ask them for an explanation. And this is true of more than zippers. Rozenblit and Keil obtained the same result with speedometers, piano keys, flush toilets, cylinder locks, helicopters, quartz watches, and sewing machines. And everyone they tested showed the illusion: graduate students at Yale as well as undergraduates at both an elite university and a regional public one. We have found the illusion countless times with undergraduates at a different Ivy League university, at a large public school, and testing random samples of Americans over the Internet. We have also found that people experience the illusion not only with everyday objects but with just about everything: People overestimate their understanding of political issues like tax policy and foreign relations, of hot-button scientific topics like GMOs and climate change, and even of their own finances. We have been studying psychological phenomena for a long time and it is rare to come across one as robust as the illusion of understanding.

One interpretation of what occurs in these experiments is that the effort people make to explain something changes how they interpret what "knowledge" means. Maybe when asked to rate their knowledge, they are answering a different question the first time they are asked than they are the second time. They may interpret the first question as "How effective am I at thinking about zippers?" After attempting to explain how the object works, they instead assess how much knowledge they are actually able to articulate. If so, their second answer might have been to a question that they understood more as "How much knowledge about zippers am I able to put into words?" This seems unlikely, because Rozenblit and Keil used such careful and explicit instructions when they asked the knowledge questions. They told participants precisely what they meant by each scale value (1 to 7). But even if respondents were answering different questions before and after they tried to explain how the object worked, it remains true that their attempts to generate an explanation taught them about themselves: They realized that they have less knowledge that they can articulate than they thought. *This* is the essence of the illusion of explanatory depth. Before trying to explain something, people feel they have a reasonable level of understanding; after explaining, they don't. Even if they lower their score because they're defining the term "knowledge" differently, it remains a revelation to them that they know relatively little. According to Rozenblit and Keil, "many participants reported genuine surprise and new humility at how much less they knew than they originally thought."

A telling example of the illusion of explanatory depth can be found in what people know about bicycles. Rebecca Lawson, a psychologist at the University of Liverpool, showed a group of psychology undergraduates a schematic drawing of a bicycle that was missing several parts of the frame as well as the chain and the pedals.

She asked the students to fill in the missing parts. Try it. What parts of the frame are missing? Where do the chain and pedals go?

It's surprisingly difficult to answer these questions. In Lawson's study, about half the students were unable to complete the drawings correctly (you can see some examples on the next page). They didn't do any better when they were shown the correct drawings as well as three incorrect ones and were asked to pick out the correct one. Many chose pictures showing the chain around the front

wheel as well as the back wheel, a configuration that would make it impossible to turn. Even expert cyclists were far less than perfect on this apparently easy task. It is striking how sketchy and shallow our understanding of familiar objects is, even objects that we encounter all the time that operate via mechanisms that are easily perceived.

How Much Do We Know?

So we overestimate how much we know, suggesting that we're more ignorant than we think we are. But how ignorant are we? Is it possible to estimate how much we know? Thomas Landauer tried to answer this question.

Landauer was a pioneer of cognitive science, holding academic appointments at Harvard, Dartmouth, Stanford, and Princeton and also spending twenty-five years trying to apply his insights at Bell Labs. He started his career in the 1960s, a time when cognitive scientists took seriously the idea that the mind is a kind of computer.

Cognitive science emerged as a field in sync with the modern computer. As great mathematical minds like John von Neumann and Alan Turing developed the foundations of computing as we know it, the question arose whether the human mind works in the same way. Computers have an operating system that is run by a central processor that reads and writes to a digital memory using a small set of rules. Early cognitive scientists ran with the idea that the mind does too. The computer served as a metaphor that governed how the business of cognitive science was done. Thinking was assumed to be a kind of computer program that runs in people's brains. One of Alan Turing's claims to fame is that he took this idea to its logical extreme. If people work like computers, then it should be possible to program a computer to do what a human being can. Motivated by this idea, his classic paper "Computing Machinery and Intelligence" in 1950 addressed the question *Can machines think?*

In the 1980s, Landauer decided to estimate the size of human memory on the same scale that is used to measure the size of computer memories. As we write this book, a laptop computer comes with around 250 or 500 gigabytes of memory as long-term storage. Landauer used several clever techniques to measure how much knowledge people have. For instance, he estimated the size of an average adult's vocabulary and calculated how many bytes would be required to store that much information. He then used the result of that to estimate the size of the average adult's entire knowledge base. The answer he got was half of a gigabyte.

He also made the estimate in a completely different way. Many experiments have been run by psychologists that ask people to read text, look at pictures, or hear words (real or nonsensical), sentences, or short passages of music. After a delay of between a few minutes and a few weeks, the psychologists test the memory of their subjects. One way to do this is to ask people to reproduce the material originally presented to them. This is a test of recall and can be quite punishing. Do you think you could recall a passage right now that you had heard only once before, a few weeks ago? Landauer analyzed a number of experiments that weren't so hard on people. The experiments tended to test recognition—whether participants could identify a newly presented item (often a picture, word, or passage of music) as one that had been presented before or not. In some of these experiments, people were shown several items and had to pick the one they had seen before. This is a very sensitive way of testing memory; people would be able to do well even if their memories were weak. To estimate how much people remembered, Landauer relied on the difference in recognition performance between a group that had been exposed to the items and a group that had not. This difference is as pure a measure of memory as one can get.

Landauer's brilliant move was to divide the measure of memory (the difference in recognition performance between the two groups) by the amount of time people spent learning the material in the first place. This told him the rate at which people are able to acquire information that they later remember. He also found a way to take into account the fact that people forget. The remarkable result of his analysis is that people acquire information at roughly the same rate regardless of the details of the procedure used in the experiment or the type of material being learned. They learned at approximately the same rate whether the items were visual, verbal, or musical.

Landauer next calculated how much information people have on hand—what the size of their knowledge base is—by assuming they learn at this same rate over the course of a seventy-year lifetime. Every technique he tried led to roughly the same answer: 1 gigabyte. He didn't claim that this answer is precisely correct. But even if it's off by a factor of 10, even if people store 10 times more or 10 less than 1 gigabyte, it remains a puny amount. It's just a tiny fraction of what a modern laptop can retain. Human beings are not warehouses of knowledge.

From one perspective, this is shocking. There is so much to know and, as functioning adults, we know a lot. We watch the news and don't get hopelessly confused. We engage in conversations about a wide range of topics. We get at least a few answers right when we watch *Jeopardy!* We all speak at least one language. Surely we know much more than a fraction of what can be retained by a small machine that can be carried around in a backpack.

But this is only shocking if you believe the human mind works like a computer. The model of the mind as a machine designed to encode and retain memories breaks down when you consider the complexity of the world we interact with. It would be futile for memory to be designed to hold tons of information because there's just too much out there.

Cognitive scientists don't take the computer metaphor so seriously anymore. There is a place for it; some models of how people think when they're thinking slowly and carefully—when they are deliberating step-by-step as opposed to being intuitive and less careful—look like computer programs. But for the most part these days, cognitive scientists point to how we differ from computers. Deliberation is only a tiny part of what goes on when we think. Most of cognition consists of intuitive thought that occurs below the surface of consciousness. It involves processing huge quantities of information in parallel. When people search for a word, for example, we don't consider one word at a time sequentially. Instead, we search our entire lexicon—our mental dictionary—simultaneously, and the word we're looking for usually rises to the top. That's not the kind of computation that von Neumann and Turing had in mind in the early days of computer science and cognitive science.

More to the point, people are not computers in that we don't just rely on a central processor that reads and writes to a memory to think. As we'll discuss in some detail later in the book, people rely on their bodies, on the world around them, and on other minds. There's just no way we could store in our heads all there is to know about our environment.

To get a sense of just how complex the world is, let's consider the different sources of complexity. Some things that humans make are complicated by design. According to Toyota, modern cars have about 30,000 parts. But their real complexity isn't in the number of parts but rather in the number of ways the parts can be designed and connected to one another. Think about everything a car designer has to worry about: appearance, power, efficiency, handling, reliability, size, safety, and more. Beyond the familiar, an important part of engineering a modern car is to predict and measure its vibration, as this determines both how much noise a car generates and how much it shakes. Often parts are substituted for one another to change these vibration characteristics. Cars are now so complicated that teenagers can't open the hood and start messing around with a wrench. Too much training and too many electrical gadgets are required to repair or tune up a modern car. Teenagers today have to get greasy by working on old cars whose engines are simple enough for an amateur tinkerer to understand. Even professional mechanics have been heard to complain that they don't fix cars anymore; they just replace the modules that their computer tells them to replace.

You could say the same about anything that makes use of modern technology, from airliners to clock radios. Modern airplanes are so complicated that no one person completely understands them. Rather, different people understand different aspects of them. Some are experts on flight dynamics, others on navigation systems; several are required to understand jet engines; and some understand the ergonomics of seating well enough that companies are able to pack people into economy class with the same efficiency that Pringles are packed into a can. And modern consumer appliances like clock radios and coffee machines are so sophisticated that they are not even worth fixing when they break. We just throw them out and replace them.

The complexity of human invention pales in comparison to the complexity of the natural world. Rocks and minerals are more complicated than they seem once you take a close look. Scientists still don't fully understand natural phenomena such as how black holes work or even why ice is slippery. But if you want to experience serious complexity, pick up a biology textbook. Even microscopic organisms like cancer cells have required a concerted effort by thousands of scientists and physicians to understand what they are, the varieties they come in, what causes them to multiply and die, and how they can be distinguished from noncancerous cells. If science and medicine could answer these questions, humanity would be rid of the plague of diseases that are lumped together as "cancer." Science and medicine are making progress, but there's still a lot that escapes them.

Complexity multiplies with multicellular organisms. To take an extreme example, consider nervous systems. Even a sea slug has about 18,000 neurons. By evolutionary standards, fruit flies and lobsters are both quite intelligent; they have more like 100,000 neurons to process information. Honeybees have almost a million neurons to work with. Not surprisingly, mammals are in a different category of complexity. Rats have about 200 million neurons, cats have almost a billion, and humans have in the vicinity of 100 billion. The cerebral cortex, the newest part of the brain whose complexity is what sets humans apart from other animals, has around 20 billion neurons. Brains really do have a lot going on in them.

Despite the number of cells we have in our brains, there aren't enough to retain everything we encounter at every level of detail. There's too much complexity out there. Ironically, the brain is a perfect example of a system too complex to fully understand. When you're studying a system as big as the brain, you can't expect to comprehend it in great detail. Despite this, neuroscientists have made tremendous strides in the last couple of decades describing how single neurons operate and also in describing the large-scale functional units of the brain, areas generally consisting of millions of neurons. They have described many of the systems in the brain, and cognitive neuroscientists have made deep inroads into discovering how those systems connect to different functions. Perhaps the best-understood function is vision. Scientists know how light enters the eye, how it gets converted to brain activation, and where that activation gets analyzed into meaningful properties of the world (like motion, orientation, and color) in the occipital lobe. We even know where the activation goes from there to allow us to identify objects (the temporal lobe) and locate them in space (the parietal lobe).

But neuroscientists know very little about what aspects of complex entities the brain responds to and how it actually computes. Scientists are still trying to figure out what is innate and what is learned, what we forget and how quickly we do so, what the nature of consciousness is and what it is for, what an emotion is and to what degree it can be controlled, and how people (including babies) identify the intentions of other people. Evolution created a brain so complex that it's hard to appreciate its full complexity.

Another complex system that scientists try to understand is the weather. Weather scientists have made vast strides in weather forecasting. Many extreme weather events can now be predicted days in advance, a feat that could not be performed even a decade or two ago. This is known as short-range forecasting, and its improvement is due to the greater availability of vast quantities of data, better weather models, and much faster computing. This is an enormous advance. The weather is a hugely complicated system—like the brain—with an inordinate number of moving parts and results determined by complex interactions among those parts. The weather in your location today depends on how much sunshine there has been lately, how far you are above sea level, whether or not you're close to mountains, whether or not there are large bodies of water near you conserving or sucking up heat, whether there have been serious weather events (like hurricanes and thunderstorms) nearby, and what the distribution of air pressure is around you.

Integrating these forces into a weather prediction is no easy matter. And in fact meteorologists still can't make specific predictions such as where the next tornado is going to touch down. Moreover, long-range weather forecasting is still a long way off (and may never be possible). You can trust your daily weather forecast for the next few days (if you're willing to risk some surprises), but don't expect your local meteorologist to tell you what the weather will be like in a few weeks. We do have some sense of how the climate is changing over a long period of time, but work on climate change does not help to predict specific short-term weather events. We know that we should expect more extreme events because of climate change, but we don't know exactly what will happen and where they will occur.

Some of the things we try to understand are infinitely complex—they aren't understandable even in principle. Let's say you're going to a class reunion and you're trying to predict whether your former boyfriend or girlfriend will be there. Assume you have lost track of this person and it's been years since you have heard anything about him or her. You can still make a prediction based on very general facts like the proportion of people who attend reunions in general. Friends might be able to give you an inkling of how likely any random individual is to come. You might even generate a prediction based on how well your ex got along with others or how nostalgic you remember this person to be. What you can't do is make an estimate based on specific facts like whether or not the person lives close enough to come or can afford the trip or, God forbid, is no longer alive. The person might be married or divorced. He or she might have one, two, or eight children to care for, might have entered any number of careers, or might be stuck in prison. In fact, there are an infinite number of trajectories the person's life might have taken. There's just no way to know.

Military strategists are familiar with this problem. No matter how many directions you prepare for an enemy attack, the strike might come from somewhere else. There are the likely directions (by land or by sea), but then there are the many unlikely directions (from tunnels dug underground or from wooden horses found outside the gates of your city). And because your enemy doesn't want you to know where they're attacking from, the unlikely directions may actually be the more likely ones.

Sometimes we have to predict not only events that are unlikely but also events that we can't even formulate clearly enough to know that we should be worried about them. Donald Rumsfeld was the U.S. secretary of defense under both presidents Gerald Ford and George W. Bush. One of his claims to fame was to distinguish different kinds of not knowing:

> There are known knowns. These are things we know that we
> know. There are known unknowns. That is to say, there are
> things that we know we don't know. But there are also unknown
> unknowns. There are things we don't know we don't know.

Known unknowns can be handled. It might be hard, but at least it is clear what to prepare for. If the military knows an attack is coming but doesn't know where or when, then they can put their reserves on notice, prepare their weaponry, and make everything as mobile as they can. In early 2001, law enforcement knew that the World Trade Center in New York was a target of Middle Eastern terrorists. After all, it had already been bombed in 1993, an attack that killed six people and injured a thousand more. Knowing it was a target, law enforcement improved security in a number of ways, for instance by adding security guards and putting car barriers in place.

But it is the unknown unknowns that present real problems. How can you prepare for something when you don't know what you're preparing for? Who could have predicted that major airliners would be used as missiles on September 11, 2001, to bring down the World Trade Center? That attack changed the way Americans view security and started a chain of events in the Middle East that has been nothing less than catastrophic, from major wars in Afghanistan, Iraq, and Syria to new methods of warfare and new terrorist organizations.

Unknown unknowns bedevil more than just military strategists; we must all deal with them. They make all stock trading inherently risky because one never knows when some catastrophic event is going to cause a sudden downturn in the market. In 2011, the Japanese Nikkei index, an indicator of the state of the Japanese stock market, declined by 1.7 percent after a massive earthquake and subsequent tsunami devastated parts of Japan. Unknown unknowns can turn families inside out when they are struck by tragedy or by good fortune (like finding treasure in the backyard). No amount of understanding can predict unknown unknowns, and yet they occur all the time.

Many of the things that people must know about exhibit enormous complexity no matter how closely you look at them. In mathematics, phenomena that possess this property are called *fractals*. Just as a forest is composed of a large number of trees, trees are composed of a large number of branches, branches are composed of leaves, and leaves themselves are ingrained with complex patterns of branching capillaries that look like veins. If you looked at a capillary under a powerful microscope, you would see just as much complex structure at the cellular level. A fractal retains complexity at every level you look. Much of the natural world follows a fractal pattern. The standard example is a coastline. Looking at the coast of England from an airliner 30,000 feet aboveground, you see a jagged edge that divides the land from water. No matter how close you get, you still see a jagged edge. Even if you're on the beach, peering at a rock that is at the water's edge with a magnifying glass, you still see a similar jagged edge. Looking closer at things just raises more questions. There is always more to understand.

Even simple everyday objects have multiple facets that can each introduce fractal-like complexity. To fully understand a hairpin would entail understanding all the uses and potential uses of a hairpin: the various materials it is made of, where each material comes from, how each material is used to manufacture hairpins, where hairpins are sold, and who buys them. And to fully appreciate the answer to each of these questions would require understanding the answer to a number of other questions. Fully understanding who buys hairpins would require an analysis of hairstyles, which in turn would require understanding fashion and its underlying social structure. Computer scientists refer to this problem of ever-growing information needs as combinatorial explosion. To achieve complete understanding necessitates understanding increasingly more and more, and the combination of everything you need to understand to achieve complete understanding quickly becomes more than you can bear without, well, exploding.

Chaos theory is another mathematical tool that shows that the complexity of the world is too much to handle. In a chaotic system, tiny differences at the beginning of a process can lead to massive differences down the road. The famous metaphor is that a butterfly flapping its wings in China can lead to a hurricane in the United States. In a chaotic system, tiny differences can get amplified in the same way that your speed downhill will get amplified if you fall off a cliff. Stephen Jay Gould explained how chaos introduces complexity into the study of history: "little quirks at the outset, occurring for no particular reason, unleash cascades of consequences that make a particular future seem inevitable in retrospect. But the slightest early nudge contacts a different groove, and history veers into another plausible channel, diverging continually from its original pathway.

The end results are so different, the initial perturbation so apparently trivial." Gould's observation that events seem inevitable in retrospect is a deep insight about human ignorance. We just don't appreciate what it takes to make things happen.

The Allure of Illusion

We've seen that people are surprisingly ignorant, more ignorant than they think. We've also seen that the world is complex, even more complex than one might have thought. So why aren't we overwhelmed by this complexity if we're so ignorant? How can we get around, sound knowledgeable, and take ourselves seriously while understanding only a tiny fraction of what there is to know?

The answer is that we do so by living a lie. We ignore complexity by overestimating how much we know about how things work, by living life in the belief that we know how things work even when we don't. We tell ourselves that we understand what's going on, that our opinions are justified by our knowledge, and that our actions are grounded in justified beliefs even though they are not. We tolerate complexity by failing to recognize it. That's the illusion of understanding.

We've all heard young kids ask why again and again until the adult they are talking to resorts to a conversation-ending "because." Kids implicitly understand the complexity of things, that explaining at a deeper level just prompts more questions. One way to think about the illusion of explanatory depth is that adults forget how complex things are and decide to just stop asking questions. Because we are not conscious that we have made this decision to stop probing, we end up thinking we understand how things work more deeply than we do.

Eventually we'll address a deeper question. Rather than asking how we tolerate complexity, we'll ask how we manage it. How can humanity achieve so much when people are so ignorant? It turns out we have been very successful at dividing up our cognitive labor. But to understand how we share our knowledge with our communities, we must first understand how we think as individuals.

TWO

Why We Think

Would you like to have a better memory? What about a perfect memory? Sounds pretty good, doesn't it?

The great Argentine writer Jorge Luis Borges mused on this question in a wonderful short story, "Funes the Memorious" ("Funes el Memorioso" in the original Spanish). Funes is a young man living in a frontier town in Uruguay called Fray Bentos. He has a remarkable capacity for remembering his experiences:

> We, at one glance, can perceive three glasses on a table; Funes, all the leaves and tendrils and fruit that make up a grape vine. He knew by heart the forms of the southern clouds at dawn on the 30th of April, 1882, and he could compare them in his memory with mottled streaks on a book in Spanish binding that he had only seen once and with the outlines of the foam raised by an oar in the Río Negro the night before the Quebracho uprising. These memories were not simple ones; each visual image was linked to muscular sensations, thermal sensations, etc. He could reconstruct all of his dreams, all of his half-dreams. Two or three times he had reconstructed a whole day; he never hesitated, but each reconstruction had required a whole day.

It sounds like a superpower, and as would be true with any worthwhile superhero, Funes's abilities even have an origin story, though it's not quite as fanciful as getting bitten by a radioactive spider or zapped with gamma rays; Funes's feats of memory began when he fell off a horse and banged his head.

Borges is renowned for his ability to weave the fantastical into otherwise mundane circumstances, and until recently the story was considered a fantasy. But in 2006, Elizabeth Parker, Larry Cahill, and James McGaugh of UC Irvine and the University of Southern California published an extraordinary case study of a patient they refer to as AJ. AJ is a lot like Funes. She remembers just about everything she experiences, every tiny detail of every meal she's ever eaten and every social interaction she's ever had.

She explained her experiences in an e-mail to McGaugh:

> I am thirty-four years old and since I was eleven I have had this unbeliev-able ability to recall my past, but not just recollections. My first memo-ries are of being a toddler in the crib (circa 1967) however I can take a date, between 1974 and today, and tell you what day it falls on, what I was doing that day and if anything of great importance . . . occurred on that day I can describe that to you as well. I do not look at calendars before-hand and I do not read twenty-four years of my journals either. When-ever I see a date flash on the television (or anywhere else for that matter) I automatically go back to that day and remember where I was, what I was doing, what day it fell on and on and on and on and on.

This condition is called hyperthymesia, or highly superior auto-biographical memory. It is exceedingly rare, seen in only a handful of people.

Most of us cannot remember where we left our keys, so AJ's abilities seem miraculous. But maybe we shouldn't be so impressed. Computationally speaking, storage is a relatively easy problem to solve. As soon as humans invented computers, we began to learn how to store a lot of information really efficiently, and computer storage has increased exponentially. As we write, Amazon.com sells a 1-terabyte thumb drive for less than $100. It's about the size of a pack of gum and can hold the equivalent of almost two million copies of the text of this book, 200,000 songs, or 310,000 photographs.

If computers can retain so much information, then you might expect human brains to be able to as well. Indeed, the fact that hyperthymesia exists at all indicates that the brain is capable of storing troves of detail. Why don't we all have these abilities?

The answer is that the brain was not designed by computer engineers. It was shaped by the forces of evolution to solve specific kinds of problems, and remembering tons of details doesn't help achieve that. Borges understood this. Consider how he shifts from the language of elevation and wonderment as Funes describes his abilities:

> "I alone have more memories than all mankind has probably had since the world has been the world. . . . My dreams are like you people's waking hours."

To more prosaic language in the next line:

> "My memory, sir, is like a garbage heap."

AJ's experience also suggests that her "superpower" is actually not all that super. She describes her hyperthymesia as a terrible burden:

> It is nonstop, uncontrollable and totally exhausting. Some people call me the human calendar while others run out of the room in complete fear but the one reaction I get from everyone who eventually finds out about this "gift" is total amazement. Then they start throwing dates at me to try to stump me . . . I haven't been stumped yet. Most have called it a gift but I call it

a burden. I run my entire life through my head every day and it drives me crazy!!!

AJ is not alone in struggling with her condition. A story on National Public Radio in 2013 reported that of the fifty-five hyperthymesics that have been identified, most have struggled with depression.

To understand why remembering everything might not be so great, let's begin at the beginning and consider what thinking is for. What problem did it evolve to solve?

What Good Is a Brain?

Almost all animals have brains. The neuron was one of the earliest adaptations when animals branched off from other organisms. Even animals that don't have fully structured brains have nervous systems, networks of neurons that work together to process information. Plants, on the other hand, do not have brains. No plant evolved cells that can organize into networks to process information.

There are many differences between plants and animals, but the most fundamental one is that animals are capable of sophisticated actions. They are capable of responding to their environment in complex ways. Plants can be marvelously complex and fascinating (a plant called *Paris japonica* has a genome fifty times larger than that of humans), but they are not capable of sophisticated action. That's why it's so easy to cut down a tree or pick a flower; they can't do anything about it. Plants have found an evolutionary niche that does not require sophisticated action. Their most important adaptation, of course, is photosynthesis. Animal life would be very different if we could get our nourishment by standing in the sun.

Some plants are capable of rudimentary actions. Many plants can orient leaves toward the sun, some can attach to other objects for support, and some even recoil from touch. Our favorite example of a plant that seems to be capable of "animal-like" action is the carnivorous Venus flytrap. Venus flytraps live in environments where the soil is bereft of certain critical nutrients. To obtain these nutrients, they have evolved the ability to trap and consume insects. The mechanism they use is a marvel of nature: they have two lobe-shaped leaves that secrete nectar to lure in bugs and then snap shut. The shutting motion is initiated when the trigger hairs on the top of the leaf are stimulated. This initiates a series of mechanical and chemical reactions that cause the lobes to close and the plant to secrete digestive enzymes.

The mechanical nature of this predation means that Venus flytraps are not so smart. Evolution has provided them with some controls against making the most egregious errors. For instance, for the leaves to close, their trigger hairs must be stimulated twice within a short time period. This allows the plant to differentiate an insect crawling across its leaf from a raindrop or bit of debris. Still, they are pretty easy to fool.

You can think of the Venus flytrap as a kind of information-processing system. Stimuli from the environment come in and are transformed into a signal to close or not to close. The signal is acted on by a fairly complex set of mechanical processes. Notice that the information processing takes place in the mechanics of the plant itself. It's very hard to rearrange or change these mechanisms to handle information differently. The Venus flytrap has evolved a pretty good rule for when to close. Evolution has not found a way to make it more sophisticated.

Earlier we mentioned that *almost* all animals have brains. The exception is the sea sponge. It's no coincidence that this is also the only animal incapable of action. It sits stationary on the seafloor and has mechanisms for filtering nutrients from seawater and expelling waste. It's not a very exciting life (though we suspect the sea sponge doesn't mind).

As soon as animals developed neurons and nervous systems, the complexity of their actions exploded and developed at a remarkable rate. This happened because the neuron is the building block of a flexible system that evolution can use to program more and more complex information-processing algorithms.

Take the lowly jellyfish. It has one of the simplest nervous systems in the animal kingdom, not even a real brain. Jellyfish have only about 800 neurons, yet their actions are radically more sophisticated than that of Venus flytraps. They can react to salinity levels in the water, engage in a basic kind of hunting by shooting their tentacles at the right kind of prey, and move captured prey from their tentacles to their mouths, and they have tricks for evading predators. Let's not overstate their abilities, though; jellyfish mostly just float around.

Increase brain size a bit more, and magic starts to happen. In animals with thousands of neurons we start to see really complex behavior like flight and locomotion. In the million-neuron range we start to find animals like rats that can navigate mazes and build nests for their young. With billions of neurons, we get humans with the ability to create symphonies and spaceships.

The Discerning Brain

If you've ever been to a New England beach between the full moons in May and June, there's a good chance that you've seen a remarkable sight: the mating of the Atlantic horseshoe crab, *Limulus polyphemus*. The crabs live in the ocean throughout the year but come to the beach by the thousands to find a mate and lay eggs. Volunteers counted 157,016 crabs mating in a single night in 2012 on the beaches of Delaware Bay.

Horseshoe crabs have been doing this dance for over 450 million years. To give some perspective, that is 2,250 times as long as modern humans have been around. What explains the incredible longevity of this species? What are their capabilities, and what is going on in their brains that makes these capabilities possible?

Haldan Hartline was a physiologist whose insights into these questions won him the Nobel Prize in 1967. Sometimes seemingly mundane circumstances conspire to produce the most remarkable scientific findings. Hartline worked at the University of Pennsylvania, not far from the beaches of the eastern seaboard. This made it easy to go to the beach between the full moons of May and June to collect as many specimens as he could carry back to his lab.

The relatively simple nature of the *Limulus* brain makes it possible for scientists to identify almost exactly what it is doing. As we saw in the last chapter, brains are, in general, hard to understand. Much of the functionality of the human brain is still a total mystery due to its complexity. The simplicity of the *Limulus* brain makes it a wonderful tool to study brain physiology. Today it is still one of the best-understood neural systems in nature. The *Limulus* brain has several functions, but one of the most important is visual perception, and this was the focus of Hartline's work.

Limulus has two compound eyes, one on either side of its carapace. Each eye is composed of about 800 light-sensing cells called ommatidia. When stimulated by light, each ommatidium sends a signal to the brain that reflects the intensity of the light. So the Limulus visual system essentially creates a map of the intensity of the light coming into the eye.

Hartline's key discovery was that the map in the *Limulus* brain is not a perfect image of the light coming from the environment. Instead, the light intensity information is changed in a very systematic way. When a strong signal comes from one region of the eye, the signals from other regions close to it are damped down. This is called lateral inhibition. The key effect of lateral inhibition is that it creates contrast in the visual input. The bright areas stick out more from the dark areas. The effect is not too different from that of signal-processing algorithms used to remaster old images or videos that have faded and lost contrast over time. For the *Limulus*, the result of lateral inhibition is that its map of light intensities is amplified in areas of high intensity relative to areas nearby.

Hartline's research prompted many new questions, but perhaps the most pressing was why *Limulus* developed this capability. What good was it to be able to increase the contrast of visual inputs?

In 1982, a team led by Hartline's student Robert Barlow conducted an experiment that began to answer this question. Evolution dictates that there is no more important action than mating. (We know people who feel the same way.) Barlow's findings suggested that lateral inhibition in the *Limulus* visual system is critical to finding a mate. Barlow created cement casings that differed in form and color and placed them on the beach during mating season. Like Venus flytraps, it turns out that male horseshoe crabs are not geniuses. They consistently attempted to mate with the cement casings. But, critically, their romantic overtures were mainly focused on the casings that most resembled actual females in form and in the way they contrasted with the sand. This shows that vision is what allows them to find a mate; it helps them to identify objects that are most likely to be female horseshoe crabs.

Imagine a male horseshoe crab that climbs up onshore. His number one goal is to quickly find an available female. He has probably never seen this particular area of the beach before. The sun could be out or it could be cloudy, and there could be bunches of seaweed or driftwood obscuring the view. A horde of other males all have the same goal, and to make matters worse, males outnumber females by a significant margin. So quickly identifying and navigating to an unattached female is the difference between reproductive success and failure. Now the benefit of lateral inhibition starts to become apparent. Enhanced contrast will make the alluring dark carapaces of the females stick out against the noisy background. The males that do this the best will have the best chance at getting lucky.

The horseshoe crab's eye processes information from the environment to make it a little better at finding a mate. That information-processing ability makes the crab less likely to be fooled by background conditions like whether the sun is out or if there is seaweed on the beach. It helps the male crab to see female crabs no matter what the visual conditions happen to be. It is still easily fooled by painted concrete, though, because it is responding to a very simple property. Anything that kind of looks like a female has that property even if it isn't a female.

As brains get larger and more complex, what goes on inside the brain gets further removed from what is happening in the environment. To see what we mean, consider face recognition. People are tremendously skilled at recognizing faces. This is a really hard information-processing problem. At a coarse level, we all pretty much look the same. We are all about the same size and have two eyes, a nose, and a mouth in roughly the same positions. Yet people are capable of discriminating between thousands of slightly different faces. What makes the problem especially challenging is that we need to be able to recognize the same face under many different conditions. Every time we see a face, it is at a different orientation in our visual field, it might have new makeup or facial hair, and the lighting will come from a slightly different location, casting different shadows. If our brains tried to recognize faces primarily based on the sensory input coming into our eyes, we would fail miserably.

We recently saw a (surprisingly handsome) graduation picture of Danny DeVito from his high school yearbook. What is remarkable about the photo is that it is clearly Danny DeVito. If you put the graduation photo next to a recent photo of Danny DeVito, you would be hard-pressed to find any visual similarity between the two. Yet we are able to discern that these two pictures are of the same person. How do we do that?

The answer is that the face-processing system is finely tuned to pick out deep properties of a face that are present in every view we have of the face, but distinguish one person's face from others'. If Danny DeVito had a scar or some other unusual feature, this would be easy. A scar, if it's big enough, would be visible whatever the lighting conditions, whatever makeup he's wearing, and from all viewing angles in which his face is visible. But he doesn't have a scar, so our facial recognition system has to rely on more abstract properties that somehow make Danny DeVito look like Danny DeVito. For instance, the relative positions of different features are an important ingredient in face perception. Humans can detect tiny variations in the distances between the eyes or the relative vertical positioning of the mouth, nose, and eyes.

What is true of face perception is true of all perception. Being smart is all about having the ability to extract deeper, more abstract information from the flood of data that comes into our senses. Instead of just reacting to the light, sounds, and smells that surround them, animals with sophisticated large brains respond to deep, abstract properties of the world that they are sensing. This allows them to detect extraordinarily subtle and complex similarities and differences in new situations that allow them to act effectively, even in situations they've never encountered before.

The reason that deeper, more abstract information is helpful is that it can be used to pick out what we're interested in from an incredibly complex array of possibilities, regardless of how the focus of our interest presents itself. We make use of abstract information to, for example, recognize familiar melodies. Once you've heard Brahms's Lullaby, you can recognize it no matter what key it's played in or what instrument it's played on, even if it's played with several errors.

Whatever it is that allows us to recognize a familiar tune, it is not a memory of the specific event of hearing that tune in the past. It must be something quite abstract. We rely on this abstract information to recognize stuff all the time, and we're not even aware that we're doing so.

Funes's Curse

Ever the visionary, Borges understood that remembering everything is in conflict with what the mind does best: abstraction. This is why Funes describes his mind as being like a garbage heap. It is so filled with junk that it makes it impossible to generalize or to comprehend, for instance, that all those encounters with four-legged furry creatures were with the same animal:

> He was, let us not forget, almost incapable of ideas of a general, Platonic sort. Not only was it difficult for him to comprehend that the generic symbol *dog* embraces so many unlike individuals of diverse size and form; it bothered him that the dog at three fourteen (seen from the side) should have the same name as the dog at three fifteen (seen from the front).

The reason most of us are not hyperthymesics is because it would make us less successful at what we evolved to do. The mind is busy trying to choose actions by picking out the most useful stuff and leaving the rest behind. Remembering everything gets in the way of focusing on the deeper principles that allow us to recognize how a new situation resembles past situations and what kinds of actions will be effective.

There is no shortage of ideas about what the mind is adapted to do. Edgar Rice Burroughs distinguished Tarzan from the other apes by Tarzan's ability to reason (and to shave). Others have proposed the mind evolved to support language, or that it is adapted for social interaction, hunting, foraging, navigating, or acclimatizing to changing environments. We don't disagree with any of these ideas. In fact, they are probably all right because the mind actually evolved to do something more general than any of them, something that includes them all. Namely, the mind evolved to support our ability to act effectively. Thinking beings were more likely to survive than their competitors because they were more likely to take actions that benefited them in the short run and the long run. This has important implications for how we should understand the shape of thought.

As brains get more complex, they get better at responding to deeper, more abstract cues from the environment, and this makes them ever more adaptive to new situations. This is critical to understanding the knowledge illusion: Storing details is often unnecessary to act effectively; a broad picture is generally all we need. Sometimes storing details is counterproductive, as in the case of hyperthymesics and Funes the Memorious.

If we had evolved in an environment that favored other kinds of capacities rather than the ability to choose effective actions, the human mind would probably follow a different kind of logic than it does. If we evolved in a world that rewarded gambling on games of chance, we would probably be able to reason flawlessly about probability distributions and the laws of statistics. If we evolved in a world that rewarded deductive reasoning, we would probably all be like Spock, masterful at deducing conclusions. But most of us are miserable at both these things. Instead, we evolved in a world ruled by the logic of action, and that is why this kind of thought is so central to what makes us human. In the next chapter we will explain in more detail what the logic of action is and how it differs from other kinds of logic.

THREE

How We Think

One of us, Steve, has a dog named Cassie. Cassie and her master have much in common. One similarity is our attitude toward food. When dinnertime rolls around, we both become obsessed by hunger pangs. Cassie's solution is to stand by her food dish as suppertime approaches. That's not a bad idea. After all, that's where food arrives pretty much every night, and when she gets noticed, she gets fed. The problem with her solution is that if someone is not in the kitchen to see her standing by her dish, she's out of luck until someone remembers it's her mealtime.

Cassie's master is marginally smarter than his dog. Rather than going to the location of the food, he goes to the source of the food. When he sees dinnertime in his future, he hangs around his wife because she is responsible for preparing dinner in the family. Eventually, to get him off her back, she starts getting dinner together. This solution works whether or not someone is in the kitchen. It works whenever his wife is available. His solution is admittedly not perfect. It doesn't work if his wife is out of town or if his dependent behavior annoys her.

Cassie has established a firm connection in her own mind between eating and the location of her food dish, a link that guides her behavior. But the dog's master has done something more sophisticated:

He has figured out what causes food to be available (his wife), and his strategy targets this cause. His dog targets the effect (the dish where her food is delivered) and as a result sometimes goes hungry. Targeting causes rather than effects is a pretty effective strategy for solving a number of problems. If you're suffering from the symptoms of a disease, it's better to cure the disease (the cause) than the symptoms (the effects). And if you don't want an entire community to go hungry, you can make more of a difference by creating conditions that allow people to feed themselves than by simply giving people food.

Maybe we're being too hard on Cassie. Historically, the field of psychology spent decades following the lead of the great Russian physiologist Ivan Pavlov, whose famous experiments in the late nineteenth century were interpreted as showing that animals could learn to associate any arbitrary stimuli, like the ringing of a bell and food. Pavlov found that dogs salivated before food entered their mouths (so do we). He thus measured whether they expected food by measuring the production of their salivary glands (roughly, how much the dogs drooled). He would feed his dogs regularly after he rang a bell. Later, he found that the dogs would salivate merely at the sound of the bell, with no food required. He claimed the dogs had developed an association between the sound and food so that the sound elicited a response similar to that of food. The bell was intended to be an arbitrary stimulus—it could have been anything as long as the dogs could perceive it. The food was not so arbitrary. Pavlov chose it because it was something that the dogs wanted. But he assumed that it had no prior association in the dogs' memories to bells. That connection was arbitrary. The community of scientists believed him: He won the Nobel Prize for this work in 1904, and Pavlov's associationist theories served as a cornerstone of the behaviorist tradition that ruled psychology through the first half of the twentieth century.

In the 1950s, a psychologist named John Garcia began poking holes in the claim that any arbitrary association could be learned. In one of Garcia's studies, rats were presented with trials of different kinds of paired stimuli. The rats either first experienced a noisy, flashing light or an unusual sweet taste in their water. Later they were either given an electric shock or a stomachache (via a compound added to their water). The rats easily learned to associate the noisy flashing light with the electric shock and the sweetened water with an impending stomachache. But they were unable to learn the other associations, between the noisy flashing light and the stomachache or between the sweetened water and the electric shock.

The kinds of mechanisms that cause flashing lights are the same as the mechanisms that cause electric shocks. Relatedly, drinking water with an additive—even a sweet additive—is a potential cause of stomachache. Both of these pairings make causal sense. The opposite pairings don't. It's hard to see how sweetened water could cause electric shock or how a flashing light could cause a stomachache. The rats were able to learn the associations that made causal sense, but they failed to learn the ones that were arbitrary. Garcia's study suggests that rats are predisposed to learn causally meaningful relations, not arbitrary links. Even rats engage in a kind of simple causal reasoning, figuring out the likely causes of their distress.

If rats are causal thinkers and don't rely only on simple associations, the same is presumably true of dogs. Pavlovian associations don't occur between arbitrary pairs of stimuli, they happen only when the association has some possibility of making causal sense. So we apologize for defaming Cassie's cognitive abilities. We have great respect for dogs and their ability to think causally. We have even greater respect for human causal cognition.

Human Reasoning Is Causal

Human beings are the world's master causal thinkers. We can predict what will happen when we rub a match against a rough surface, if we go out in the rain without an umbrella, or if we say the wrong thing to our sensitive colleague. All of this requires causal reasoning. In each case, we imagine the world in some state and then imagine the operation of a mechanism that changes that state. In the first case, we imagine a match and a rough surface, and then imagine the mechanism of rubbing the match against the rough surface. We know enough about that mechanism to know that it will produce sparks and that those sparks will cause the flammable substance in the match to catch fire. In the second case, we imagine that we're inside and dry and that it's raining outside. Then we imagine the mechanism that consists of many droplets of water falling on us. We know enough about that mechanism to know that our clothing and hair will absorb some of the droplets and that others will come to rest on our skin. In short, we'll get wet. Making predictions using causal knowledge—knowledge about how mechanisms work—seems simple enough, but it requires familiarity with a lot of mechanisms: rubbing a match against a rough surface, being covered by droplets of water, covering a cold body with a heavy blanket, shouting at a young child, pressing the power button on an electronic appliance, hitting a window with a baseball, watering a plant, pressing the accelerator of a car—the list goes on and on. We are familiar with a huge number of mechanisms that produce effects.

And we're not just familiar with them; we understand *how* they work. We know that sparks won't be produced if the match or the rubbing surface is wet or if the match is pressed too softly or too hard. We know that we won't get wet in the rain if we're wearing rain gear or if the rain is fine enough that water evaporates off us as quickly as it settles on us. For each mechanism we're familiar with, we understand enough about how it works to know what must be true for the mechanism to have the effect we expect (a child will cry if shouted at only if the child perceives that the shout is angry rather than playful) and what must be false for the mechanism not to have its effect (the child will not cry if you're shouting from so far away the child cannot hear you).

There are other kinds of reasoning that most people do not find so natural. It's hard to reason about the cube root of 8,743; it's hard to reason about quantum mechanics; it's hard to predict the odds of winning the next time you gamble in Reno, Nevada. It's even hard to think about whether Reno is east or west of Los Angeles (look it up; the answer might surprise you). We're not good at everything. What we do excel at is reasoning about how the world works. We're gifted causal reasoners, and rats, as it happens, are too. What could be more useful if you're an animal who has evolved to operate in the world?

In the last chapter we saw that the purpose of thinking is to choose the most effective action given the current situation. That requires discerning the deep properties that are constant across situations. What sets humans apart is our skill at figuring out what those deep, invariant properties are. It takes human genius to identify the key properties that indicate if someone has suffered a concussion or has a communicable disease, or that it's time to pump up a car's tires.

All of the examples we have discussed so far are quite simple. We have not claimed that people are any good at predicting the outcome of war or the effect of a new health plan on an organization or even how a toilet works. We may be better at causal reasoning than other kinds of reasoning, but the illusion of explanatory depth shows that we are still quite limited as individuals in how much of it we can do.

Causal reasoning is our attempt to use our knowledge of causal mechanisms to understand change. It helps us guess what will happen in the future by reasoning about how mechanisms will transform causes into effects. Here's some evidence that people naturally engage in causal reasoning. Consider the following story problem:

A lobbyist was overheard saying to a senator, "If you support my bill, you won't have to raise money for a year." Over the next few months, as the Senate battled over the bill, the senator was a staunch supporter. How much time do you think the senator spent raising money that year?

This is not a hard question; the senator is clearly more likely to be sitting back drinking fancy scotch and smoking cigars at the lobbyist's expense than traveling around raising money. The reason that the question is so easy is that people are inference machines. We infer all kinds of things that we're not told and we don't observe directly. The lobbyist example is a simple case of a logical schema called *modus ponens*. In the abstract, it takes this form:

If A, then B.
A.
Therefore B.

Who could argue with that? If A implies B, then once you have A, you also have B. It almost sounds as if we're saying the same thing twice. But in fact, it is not obvious at all that this is true. Maybe the senator supported the bill but rejected the lobbyist's funding. Maybe the lobbyist was lying. Effects can be disabled. Logical schema like *modus ponens* seem natural in the abstract, but once we give them substance, they can seem less natural because causal considerations naturally come into play.

Many logical schema don't seem natural at all, and some arguments that aren't logical seem like they are. Here's an example:

If my underwear is blue, then my socks are guaranteed to be green.

My socks are in fact green.

Therefore, my underwear is blue.

Is that a valid inference? Most people think it is, but from the perspective of the most basic kind of textbook logic (known as propositional logic), the answer is: no way. This is a logical fallacy called affirmation of the consequent.

Now consider an argument that isn't just about what facts are true, but about causes and effects:

If I fall into the sewer, then I'll need to take a shower.

I took a shower.

Therefore, I fell into the sewer.

Most people are not fooled in this case. The fact that I took a shower does not imply that I fell into the sewer because there are many other reasons for me to take a shower. In this case, the first statement is causal: falling into the sewer is a cause of my taking a shower. When we are reasoning causally, we are much more aware of all of the considerations that allow us to make correct inferences. And it requires some pretty heavy-duty mental machinery to do so. We have to understand that falling into the sewer could be a cause of taking a shower and not the other way around. We have to bring to mind the possibility that I took a shower for some other reason. We have to evaluate the plausibility of those reasons. And we have to translate these insights into an answer to the question. We do all this in seconds. We are naturals when it comes to causal reasoning.

People are not logic machines in the same way that computers are. We may make inferences all the time, but those inferences are not based on textbook logic; they are based on the logic of causality.

Just as people don't think only associatively (as Pavlov thought we do), people do not reason via logical deduction. We reason by causal analysis. People make inferences by reasoning about the way the world works. We think about how causes produce effects, what kinds of things disable or prevent effects, and what factors must be in place for causes to have their influence. Rather than thinking in terms of *propositional* logic, the logic that tells us whether a statement is true or false, people think in terms of *causal* logic, the logic of causation that incorporates knowledge about how events actually come about in order to reach conclusions.

The ability to reason causally allows us to solve a lot of real-world problems. Fashioning a bridge to cross a chasm or a body of water is the result of causal reasoning. Bridge designers must reason about the weight-supporting mechanisms that can carry loads as heavy as cars and trucks to build a safe bridge. Attaching a wheel to a vehicle to enable the vehicle to move by rolling requires reasoning about a different kind of causal mechanism. The ability to conceive of a bridge or a wheel was necessary to actually construct bridges and wheels, which in turn allowed humanity to expand its territory, escape predators, and in general win in the evolutionary competition for scarce resources.

Our ability to project our thoughts into the distant future is also a kind of causal reasoning. It involves thinking about the mechanisms that influence the state of the world over the long term. Such long-term planning is necessary to motivate us to spend years of our lives learning. Learning is the mechanism by which we develop skills whose value may become apparent only many years later. It takes years to learn the fine art of kayak building. But nobody in a community that uses kayaks would invest the time if they didn't understand that the art would be required way down the road, after the current generation of kayak builders had taken their last paddle, so that the community could continue fishing and traveling in its customary ways. Taking the time to learn a useful technique or art makes sense only if you can see far enough into the future by reasoning about the causal mechanisms that govern social change, like death.

We excel at causal analysis not just when dealing with physical objects and social change, but also when confronted by problems in the psychological realm. Imagine that someone—let's say your spouse—refuses to talk to you. Now you have a problem to solve. You need to engage in causal reasoning to identify the problem and to figure out what to do about it.

To identify the problem, you need to reason causally about human reactions and emotions. What would cause someone to react negatively to you? Did you insult the person? Did you remind him or her of some past misdeed? Did you offend the person's moral sensibilities? Just as with physical objects, this requires sophisticated causal analysis. It requires understanding human thought and motivation and how those lead to action. To identify what's pissing someone off, you have to know a little about the person's beliefs. For example, what does the person know about your past? What moral values does he or she hold dear? You also have to know something about the person's desires. What is the individual sensitive about? What does he or she want to achieve by giving you the silent treatment? In other words, your job is to single out the intention driving the person's action and identify the consequences he or she is hoping will come of it. This is a kind of causal analysis we engage in with every social encounter, and it's one that most people are exceedingly good at.

Figuring out what to do to solve the problem also requires causal reasoning: What would be the consequences of the various actions available? If you try to console the person, he or she might feel better but it may be understood as an admission of guilt that would give the person the upper hand. If you start a fight, you might not give up the upper hand, but you might end the relationship or at least make it untenable for a while. Predicting the effects of our actions on other people is sometimes hard, but again, we do it all the time, mostly successfully. Making a simple request politely usually elicits happy compliance and making a joke usually elicits a tolerant semi-smile (in our experience). People are very good at causal reasoning, not only about physical things, but about human behavior as well.

Reasoning Forward and Backward

Causal reasoning is the basis of human cognition; it's in large part what the mind does. Yet not all aspects of it are equally easy. We reason both forward and backward. Forward reasoning is thinking about how causes produce effects. We use it to predict the future, how events today will cause events tomorrow. We also use it to figure out how things work: how, for example, pushing a sequence of buttons will finally set the alarm on our new clock. The example of the *modus ponens* logical schema above used forward reasoning. We asked you to reason forward from the senator's actions to whether the senator would have to spend time fundraising.

Reasoning backward is reasoning from effects to causes. Doctors do it to diagnose the cause of symptoms and mechanics do it to diagnose what's wrong with your car. Backward causal reasoning generally involves explanation, figuring out how something that happened came about. It's easier for us to reason forward—from cause to effect—than diagnostically from effect to cause. For instance, it's easier for a doctor to predict that someone with a peptic ulcer will have abdominal pain than it is to reach the conclusion that someone with abdominal pain has a peptic ulcer. Backward reasoning also takes longer than forward reasoning. Backward reasoning from effect to cause may be hard, but it's also what makes humans special; it's not clear that any other organism has the capacity or interest to figure out the causes of what has happened.

To reason forward, we often run little mental simulations. If I ask you to predict how long it will take you to make an omelet, you can imagine running through the various steps required, estimate how long each will take, and add them up. To predict the effects of starting a war with Russia, you might imagine intercontinental ballistic missiles flying through the air, radar picking them up, and other intercontinental ballistic missiles being fired in response. Diagnostic inferences from effect to cause aren't so easy. If there is war with Russia and we want to know what caused it, we need some other means of picking out possible causes and then evaluating the ability of each cause to predict what actually happened.

Ironically, the fact that we're better at predictive than diagnostic reasoning leads to a certain kind of error we make with predictive reasoning that we don't make when reasoning diagnostically. Pretend you're a mental health care worker presented with the following case:

Ms. Y is a thirty-two-year-old female who has been diagnosed with depression. Please indicate the likelihood that she presents with lethargy.

In other words, if you don't know anything except that someone is a thirty-two-year-old female and that she's depressed, what's the likelihood that she'd be lethargic? If you don't know the relevant statistics (and not many people do), this is a tough question to answer. But there are certain things you do know. You know, for instance, that the probability that she is lethargic should be at least a little lower if there's no other reason for her to be lethargic. So if we ask you:

> Ms. Y is a thirty-two-year-old female who has been diagnosed with depression. **A complete diagnostic workup reveals that she has not been diagnosed with any other medical or psychiatric disorder that would cause lethargy.** Please indicate the likelihood that she presents with lethargy.

You should give a lower number, maybe not much lower, but there is at least a little less reason to think that she'll be lethargic.

That's not what people do. What people do is ignore what is in bold in the second question. We presented the questions to groups of mental health professionals attending a Harvard University–sponsored workshop. When different groups were asked to answer each question, they gave exactly the same answer to both questions. The reason they ignored what is in bold is that people don't worry about alternative causes when thinking about the likelihood of an effect given a cause. They imagine a young, depressed woman and investigate their mental picture to see if she's lethargic. This mental picture has no place in it to indicate whether she's dehydrated or tired or lethargic for some other reason.

Surprisingly, diagnostic reasoning does not suffer from this limitation. We made the following request to different groups at the same workshop:

> Ms. Y is a thirty-two-year-old female who presented with lethargy. Please indicate the likelihood that she has been diagnosed with depression.

We've turned the question around here. Instead of asking about the probability of an effect given a cause, we're asking about the probability of a cause given an effect. This time we compared judgments to what people say in response to:

Ms. Y is a thirty-two-year-old female who presented with lethargy. **Please indicate the likelihood that she has been diagnosed with depression given that a complete diagnostic workup revealed that she has not been diagnosed with any other medical or psychiatric disorder that would cause lethargy.**

The text in bold again indicates that Ms. Y suffers from no alternative causes of lethargy. In this case, the absence of an alternative cause should increase people's judgments. If I ask you what the probability is that A is true when A is the cause of B and you know that B happened, then once you know that nothing else caused B, A must be very likely. In fact, if you believe that every event has a cause (and most people do), then A is guaranteed to be true, as it is the only cause of B available.

And this is exactly what the mental health professionals told us. In the absence of an alternative cause, they judged Ms. Y more likely to be depressed than when nothing was said about an alternative cause. When reasoning diagnostically, from effect to cause, our respondents didn't neglect alternative causes.

People ignore alternative causes when reasoning from cause to effect because their mental simulations have no room for them, and because we're unable to run mental simulations backward in time from effect to cause.

Even though we're not great at diagnostic reasoning, our ability to do it may be what makes us human. There's hardly any evidence that any other animal can do it. Animals may be able to respond to their environments in very sophisticated ways, and we saw earlier that rats are sensitive to causal considerations, but no animals have been shown to exhibit diagnostic reasoning from effect to cause.

The strongest evidence that we're wrong, that animals can reason diagnostically, doesn't come from studies testing the animals that you might expect, chimpanzees or bonobos (which are even closer genetic cousins of humans than chimps) or dolphins (who are well known to have an intelligence far beyond that of humans and who are patiently waiting for their moment to take over the earth). No, the animal whose reasoning abilities have most impressed scientists is the crow.

In one study, six New Caledonian crows were presented with a transparent tube with a tasty morsel of meat inside it. The tricky experimenters outfitted the tube with a hole so that the only way to get the food was to use a tool to push or pull the meat out while avoiding the hole. Three of the six crows not only figured out how to get the food out of the original tube, but they seemed to diagnose the causal structure of the problem. They were able to extract food from other tubes that had holes in different positions. This feat is quite remarkable given what nonhumans are usually capable (and not capable) of in the lab; even chimps are not able to do it. But it still pales in comparison to the refined and abstract reasoning capabilities of humans. No crow has ever diagnosed a chromosomal abnormality in a sick child (or in a sick crow, for that matter). So the hypothesis that only humans are capable of true diagnostic reasoning—causal reasoning from effect to cause—can still be defended. But crows are highly impressive animals nonetheless.

Storytelling

Causal analysis comes in many forms. Figuring out how a new coffee machine works requires causal analysis, as does figuring out how to mend a sweater with a hole in it or how to care for your arthritic knee. As a society, we trade information about causal analysis in a variety of ways. We include assembly instructions when we sell a new appliance that requires assembly, we share videos about how to fix a dishwasher on YouTube, and we read books by professionals about how to treat sick people, how to impress people, and how to run a business effectively.

Perhaps the most common way that people pass causal information to one another is by storytelling. Consider the old Yiddish story about the shopkeeper who arrived at his shop only to find abusive and derogatory graffiti spray-painted all over his store window. He cleaned the window, but the same thing happened again the next day. So he hatched a plan: On the third day, he waited until the local ruffians showed up and did their dirty work and then paid them $10 to thank them for their effort. The next day, he thanked them again but only paid them $5. He continued to pay them to deface his property but the amount kept decreasing so that soon they were only getting $1. They stopped coming. Why bother doing all that work to abuse the shopkeeper for so little money?

This apocryphal tale is really a causal lesson. It's about what causes people to act and how you can modify their motivations, to make them think they're doing something for a different reason than they initially thought.

Stories about human motivation are common, but stories carry other sorts of revelations about the way the world works and how we should behave. One tale from the Bible discusses the root cause of everything, how the world was created. Many biblical stories tell us about the consequences of our actions and why, therefore, certain actions are right and others wrong. The story of Adam and Eve teaches us to do what God dictates, and the story of Cain and Abel tells us that we should love our brother. Fairy tales and urban legends tend to teach us about what we should avoid, what's dangerous, and how we determine whom to trust. Stories about heroic acts tell us about the surprising extent of our own potential.

Storytelling is our natural way of making causal sense of sequences of events. That's why we find stories everywhere. In one of the classic demonstrations in social psychology from the 1940s, Fritz Heider and Marianne Simmel showed people a simple animated film starring a circle and two triangles moving around a screen. That's it: no sound, no text. Sometimes two of the geometric figures would get close to each other; sometimes one would appear to chase another; sometimes they would appear to fight. People inevitably saw more than circles and triangles; they saw a romantic drama play out. People see stories everywhere.

A good story goes beyond just describing what actually happened. It tells us about how the world works more broadly, in ways that pertain to things that didn't actually happen or at least haven't happened yet. When Shakespeare's Lady Macbeth can't stop washing her hands after killing King Duncan and cries, "Out, damned spot! out, I say!—One: two: why, then 'tis time to do't.—Hell is murky!" we learn not only about the remorse of a single fictional character, but also about the emotional consequences of murder. We learn a causal rule: Killing someone causes one to suffer a guilt that does not go away.

A good story has a moral that applies not just to this world but also to other worlds that we might find ourselves in. The reason we recount Abraham sacrificing his son Isaac on Mount Moriah is not just to add to our inventory of facts about Abraham and his family; it is surely to learn a lesson about loyalty to God in whatever situation we find ourselves.

In that sense, storytelling requires that we do something that is way beyond the capabilities of any nonhuman animal. It requires that we use our understanding of our world's causal mechanisms to build whole alternative worlds to think about. Storytelling helps us to imagine how the world would be if something were different. This is clearest in science fiction: Authors help readers imagine alternative worlds with life on other planets or drugs that guarantee happiness or robots that take over the world. But many other kinds of stories also involve alternative worlds, especially stories we tell ourselves. You might imagine, for instance, that you're a rock star. What would the consequences be? To find out, you can consult your understanding of how the world works and draw out the effects that being a rock star would cause. For one, you'd probably stay in fancier hotels, drive around in limousines, and spend a lot of time signing autographs. Feel free to fantasize about any others. Thinking about alternative possible worlds is an important part of being human. It is called counterfactual thought, and you can see that it depends on our capacity to reason causally.

Why do we do this? Why do we so naturally tell stories that require reasoning about counterfactual worlds? Perhaps the main motivation is that it allows us to consider alternative courses of action. We are very comfortable thinking about what the world would be like if we did something differently—if we changed our hairstyle, bought a new lawn mower, or sold our house and bought a yacht. And because we can think about such hypothetical actions, occasionally we actually pursue them. A thinker who can't conceive of a new hairstyle is not going to go out and get one (at least not intentionally). And a thinker who can't conceive of a bill of rights or a new kind of vacuum cleaner is not going to get one of those, either. The ability to think counterfactually makes it possible to take both extraordinary and ordinary action.

Some of humankind's greatest discoveries are due to counterfactual thought experiments. It is well known that Galileo dropped weights from the Leaning Tower of Pisa to prove that different masses fall at the same rate. Historians disagree about whether this event actually took place, but what we do know is that long before the alleged experiment, Galileo knew how it would come out based on an experiment that occurred in his head. As he describes in his sixteenth-century book *On Motion,* he imagined two objects of different weights joined by a string falling. Using his understanding of the physical laws that guided his thinking, he was able to accurately infer that objects fall at the same rate regardless of their weight.

Our private imaginings aren't usually as insightful as Galileo's, but each of us does some version of this on a regular basis. Many decisions are made by running little mental simulations to figure out the likely outcomes of different courses of action, based on our understanding of the causal laws governing the situation. When traffic is heavy, we imagine different routes and choose the one that should have the least traffic without taking too long. When choosing what to have for lunch, some of us imagine how each item will taste and consider whether that taste is an experience we crave at the moment. These mental simulations are micro-stories that we tell ourselves and others. Their purpose is to identify and consider a causal pathway alternative to the one that we are on.

Psychologists have proposed that stories make up our identities, both our individual identities and the identities of the groups we are a part of. We tell stories about the past—we reminisce and romanticize. We tell stories about the future—we predict and fantasize. And we tell stories about the present—we construct who we are and daydream. All of this is about identifying causes and foreseeing effects. How did we come to be? Where are we going? What actions should I take right now?

Stories are used to transmit causal information and lessons among people, as well as to share experiences, to organize a community's collective memory, and to illustrate and announce an attitude. When a community agrees to buy into a particular story, they are accepting the attitude implied by the story. Americans who tell the story of the Sons of Liberty tossing chests of British tea overboard in Boston

Harbor in 1773 are telling a story of proud defiance against coercion. When the British traders of the era whose tea was spoiled told the story, they were describing a bunch of thieving hooligans who needed to be taught a lesson. Thus stories generally belong to a community, not to an individual, and they are intimately tied to a community's belief system.

Stories may be communal entities, but telling them requires that individuals possess a cognitive system that's up to the task. We have seen that the cognitive system's ability to represent and reason about causal systems is limited, that we can't as individuals deal with the actual complexity of the world. This is surely why stories tend to simplify and sometimes oversimplify events. Most people know little more about Henry VIII than that his appetites were huge, that this is one reason he had six wives, and that most of his wives didn't survive. We just can't remember and disseminate stories whose complexity approaches that of real life.

Nevertheless, stories are about the causal relations in the world, however much we simplify them. So individuals need a cognitive system that can understand the causality inherent in whatever the story they are telling is about. We need a cognitive system that can understand what protagonists and antagonists want to achieve, how obstacles prevent achievement of those goals, and how those obstacles are overcome (or not, as the case may be). These are all causal notions involving agents trying to cause the world to be a certain way. It is no coincidence that storytelling, the most natural mode of human discourse, depends on the very same resource—causal knowledge—that allows thinking to produce more effective action.

FOUR

Why We Think What Isn't So

The Angelina Jolie movie *Wanted* grossed $135 million at the U.S. box office in 2008. In the movie, would-be superspies are trained to curve bullets around obstructions by twisting their arms in just the right way before pulling the trigger. The scenes may make sense to most viewers, but they drive physicists in the audience nuts.

The problem is that our naive understanding of physics doesn't correspond to actual physics. People's expectations of physical events can be inconsistent with Newton's laws of motion, which accurately predict the movements of objects in most situations we encounter. To see the impossibility of curving bullets, imagine you're spinning a rock tied to a string around your head. Then your evil big brother comes along and cuts the string. The situation looks like this:

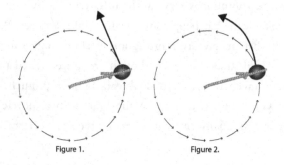

Figure 1.   Figure 2.

What path is the rock going to take as it flies away from you? Most people think it's going to take a curved path (the right side of the figure). In fact, Newton's laws dictate that it will fly off in a straight path (toward your brother if you're lucky). We don't always expect objects to behave according to Newton's laws because everyday observations often don't appear to follow them. (This is one reason it took such insight for Isaac Newton to discover them in the first place.) For example, Newton's first law states that a body in motion tends to remain in motion at the same speed and in the same direction. But usually we don't observe this. If you push a brick across the floor it will stop pretty quickly. Physicists correctly attribute this phenomenon to friction. Nonphysicists tend to understand this in a very non-Newtonian way, thinking, for instance, that when you push on the brick you impart an "impetus" that dissipates over time. When the impetus is completely used up, the brick stops.

Newton's first law similarly implies that when the string is cut and no force is acting to keep the rock moving in a circle, the rock will move in a straight line. But people believe instead that the spinning imparts a circular impetus to the rock that will dissipate after some time, and they therefore expect it to move along a circular path. The producers of *Wanted* made the same mistake with curving bullets, or at least they assumed their audience would. You don't make money in Hollywood by being accurate. You make money by appealing to people's intuitions.

Causal reasoning may serve as the infrastructure of thought, but that doesn't mean that people are ideal causal reasoners. We've already seen that people are more ignorant about how things work than they think they are. Even though we are designed to reason about causal mechanisms, individuals can do only so much.

Have you ever tried to adjust the brakes on a bicycle? It can be done, but for many of us it seems to require years of training and practice. Thinking through the entire mechanism and deciding which of the many possible adjustments to make, and how much to adjust each one, has made many an otherwise reasonable person question their sanity. Similarly, you're not alone if you've never figured out how to set the clock on your stove and have decided to live with a blinking 12:00. Normal human thought is just not engineered to figure out some things.

That's one reason there's no universal agreement about the best diet, how we should run our economy, or whether and how our governments should engage in the Middle East. Life and social systems are complicated and there's no one correct path to understanding them. Thought is full of guesswork and approximation.

Another striking example of the difficulty of reasoning about physical properties comes from research by Andrea diSessa, an education researcher at the University of California, Berkeley. Consider the two coins in the figure below. If the top coin is rolled around the edge of the bottom coin such that it comes to rest directly beneath, which way will the arrow be facing?

Most people think that the arrow will face down. In fact, it faces up. Try it with a set of quarters. In daily life we see objects rolling all

the time, but it's very uncommon to see objects rolling along curved surfaces, so we have terrible intuitions about how the coin will behave. In an ordinary case of an object rolling along a flat surface, the rolling object rotates in proportion to the distance it covers on the surface. A coin that rolls along a distance that is half its circumference in length will turn half a revolution; if the coin rolls along a flat surface for half its circumference, the arrow would point down. When rolling along a curved surface, this rule no longer applies, yet people tend to incorrectly use the causal model that they have learned for the flat surface. This is the source of the faulty intuition.

Causal models are not just confined to understanding how objects move. People understand electricity via analogy to things they have observed too, often to flowing water or flowing crowds of people. Causal models also determine how people interact with the machinery of their daily lives. For instance, many people who are cold jack their thermostat up high in a futile effort to achieve the temperature they want more quickly. This is because they are employing a causal model of heating systems in which the speed of reaching a final temperature depends on a target temperature. People seem to believe, incorrectly, that they are making the thermostat work harder by giving it a more ambitious goal. Here's one experimental participant explaining his faulty understanding:

> I think it's pretty simple really. Um, I assume, um, that there is some kind of linear relationship between where the lever is and the way some kind of heat generating system functions. And, um, that is like stepping on the gas pedal; that there I have a notion of hydraulics, you know, the harder you push there is, the more fluid gets pushed into the engine, and the more explosions there are, and the faster it goes. And so here, the harder or the more you push the lever or twist the lever . . . the more power the system puts out to generate heat.

Later he refers to a bunch of other objects that operate according to the same principle:

> I just flashed to electric mixers. The higher you turn them, the faster they go . . . the harder you push on the gas, the faster the car moves . . . turning on the faucet . . . you can see the water

squirting out in greater volume at a greater rate, you know, as
the lever is increased to turn it up.

Evidently, this causal model is intuitive because we experience it
so frequently. It is rare for us to directly perceive the mechanisms
that create outcomes. We experience our actions and we experience
the outcomes of those actions; only by peering inside the machine
do we see the mechanism that makes it tick. We can peer inside
when the components are visible. For instance, we can see how mechanical clocks with transparent faces work or how leaves get raked
up. But most mechanisms are too small (like the molecular changes
that cause water to boil) or too abstract (like the economic drivers of
poverty) or inaccessible (like how hearts pump blood around your
body). We can't see what vaccines are doing or how food is genetically modified, so we fill in the missing pieces with what we've experienced, and this can lead to false beliefs.

Good Enough

It would be a mistake to berate ourselves for not being ideal causal
reasoners. Think about what it would take to make correct causal
inferences in every situation. You would need to know everything
about what the universe is like and you would need complete knowledge about how things change. Because the world is complex and
because there are so many ways that things change, both kinds of
knowledge are guaranteed to be far from perfect: incomplete, uncertain, and imprecise. In the real world, your knowledge is necessarily
mostly about the part of the world that you've experienced. You also
know more about things that are important to you than things you
don't care about. You know more about how to get ahead in your
chosen career path than about how to become a professional hockey

player (assuming your career goal is not to play in the National Hockey League).

You're also unlikely to know a lot about the position, direction, and motion of molecules. That's just not the level of granularity at which we live our lives. Our perceptual and motor systems are designed to operate at a higher level—a level at which we actually interact with the material world, with flora, fauna (especially other people), and human-made artifacts. So our knowledge is especially well suited to objects at this level of granularity—the level at which we live—and perhaps a little higher (communities and other social organizations). That's the level at which knowledge is organized.

So people know less than everything (surprise, surprise). In fact, we know a lot less. We know just enough to get by. Because our knowledge is limited, our understanding of how things change is correspondingly limited. Most of us don't have to worry about the causal laws that apply to molecules and atoms because we're not chemists or physicists. That's why Newtonian physics is good enough to describe human experience even though it fails to be precisely correct both at microscopic levels (how atomic particles behave) and macroscopic levels (how the universe behaves at the largest scales). We just don't experience the quantum effects physicists worry about that describe the world at levels outside our experience. Most people—in fact, even chemists and physicists when they take off their lab coats and become ordinary people—only have to worry about causal laws that govern motion of the kinds of objects we can see with the naked eye, temperatures within the small range that we experience between summer and winter, the interactions we have with people, and more generally, the mechanisms that govern the everyday events that occur in our experience. For the small range of conditions we encounter, shallow causal reasoning is all we need to get by. That's lucky because we would quickly get swamped if we had to know everything.

Reasoning about social situations is like reasoning about physical objects: pretty shallow. Everyday casual encounters do require that we understand the intentions of the people we come across, but these intentions are pretty close to the surface. Are they trying to get by us on the sidewalk or do they want to ask us a question or do they want our money? These are simple and straightforward inferences that we make all the time. What's impressive about people is not the depth of the inferences we make in situations like this, but the fact that we make them at all.

There are situations when deeper inferences are called for. If a con man is trying to fool you by pulling a bait and switch, then figuring out the person's intentions can be tricky. Or if a loved one is depressed or is behaving erratically, then figuring out why and what to do about it can require a tremendous amount of sensitivity and depth of understanding. Most people are actually pretty bad at making appropriate inferences in these situations. Con men are around because they are successful; people get tricked all the time. And the sad truth is that the people who can really understand and help when someone is in pain are few and far between. Most of us who want to provide assistance end up looking for others to help us: friends and family to help figure out what's really going on or experts to assist in an intervention. Again, the point is that people excel at causal reasoning; we just tend to do it superficially outside our area of expertise.

The Two Causal Reasoners Inside Us

We're engaged in some type of causal reasoning all the time, but not all causal reasoning is the same. Some is fast. When a rat attributes feeling sick to food and not a flash of light, we assume that inference is made without a lot of thought and reflection. It's quick and automatic in the same way that a man might conclude that the reason his hand hurts is because he bashed it against a wall or a student might conclude that the cause of her joy is that she aced the math test. Such conclusions hardly deserve the label "reasoning" because they are so obvious and arrived at so quickly.

Other kinds of causal reasoning require a lot more thought and analysis. What were the causes of World War I? Why won't your car start? Why does your boss still fail to appreciate your contribution after all your hard work? Answering questions such as these requires time and effort. We have to engage in slow, thoughtful deliberation to draw conclusions. They demand reasoning in the normal sense of the word.

This distinction between two different kinds of thought can be found throughout classical and modern philosophy, psychology, and cognitive science. Daniel Kahneman celebrated the distinction in his book *Thinking, Fast and Slow*. This is a distinction thousands of years old; it goes by a variety of names in cognitive science. For example, the two systems of reasoning have been referred to as associative versus rule-based thinking or simply as System 1 versus System 2. We'll refer to it as the distinction between intuition and deliberation.

What's an animal whose name starts with the letter *e*?

Did "elephant" come to mind? It does for almost everyone. Some items come to mind quickly, spontaneously, and effortlessly. These are provided by intuition.

It's worthwhile thinking about what the roles of consciousness are in intuition versus deliberation. When we intuit a thought, it comes to mind by itself. There's no effort required to solve the following anagram:

inituitve

The answer immediately pops into your mind. You are not conscious of the process that produces the response, though you are conscious of the end result. The word "intuitive" appears magically on a mental stage that you can visualize.

But when you deliberate, you're conscious not only of the response but also how you got there. Consider a harder anagram:

vaeertidebli

If you were able to solve it (the answer appears at the bottom of this page[1]), you were conscious not only of the final result but also of the thinking process by which you got there. You were able to watch the thought process in which you moved letters around on your mental stage looking for something that worked. Similarly, when solving a hard arithmetic problem, you are conscious of each step along the way just as you are when debating the merits of a political candidate.

The distinction between intuition and deliberation has a venerable place in intellectual history. The ancient Greek philosopher Aristotle, for one, pointed out how hard it is to overcome ingrained intuitions and habits via deliberation:

> Now if arguments were in themselves enough to make men
> good, they would justly . . . have won very great rewards . . .
> But as things are . . . they are not able to encourage the many to
> nobility and goodness . . . What argument would remold such
> people? It is hard, if not impossible, to remove by argument the
> traits that have long since been incorporated in the character.
>
> ARISTOTLE, *Nicomachean Ethics,* 1179

---

[1] deliberative

Plato was more metaphorical in pointing out the link between intuition and desire. Here is an abbreviated version:

> Let us, then, liken the soul to the natural union of a team of winged horses and their charioteer. One of the horses is a lover of honor and is guided by verbal commands alone; the other is companion to wild boasts and indecency, and barely yields to the goad.
>
> PLATO, *Phaedrus,* 246 and 253

Plato is distinguishing between passion and reason, the two horses that pull in opposite directions when we're faced with temptation. We can all agree that Plato's "reason" is a lot like Aristotle's "argument" and the same as what cognitive scientists call deliberation. It's the careful conscious thinking that we engage in to help us solve problems and to prevent our cravings from taking control of our actions. It's the little voice that whispers inside our head to remind us what is important and how to achieve our long-term goals. It's the thought process that prevents us from eating a second piece of chocolate cake or that makes us feel guilty when we do anyway.

But is intuition the same as passion? Our intuitions are thoughts that come to mind automatically, through deeply ingrained knowledge, thoughts like "that person is Canadian" if I hear the person say "about" in a certain way. Such thoughts are not themselves desires. The mere thought that someone is a Canadian does not make that person an object of desire—though it doesn't hurt. Some intuitions do make things more desirable. A bakery box might elicit the intuition that there is cake inside, and that might stir up one's passion for sugar and fat. On the flip side, desires can elicit intuitive responses. If we see a desirable car, we imagine driving it. If we're in a desirable house, we imagine living in it. A desirable dessert makes us imagine eating it. A desirable person makes us imagine . . . well, you get the point. Our passions are associated with certain intuitions, even if it is not the case that all intuitions are associated with passions. So intuitions and passions are not the same, but there is a close link between them. Both intuition and desire can cooperate and both can compete with deliberation.

With regard to causal reasoning, the conclusions we come to quickly and intuitively are not always the same as the conclusions we come to through careful deliberation. Our intuitive response might be that dropping bombs on the enemy will cause them to capitulate, but more reasoned deliberation might lead to the conclusion that dropping bombs might just serve our enemy's purpose by terrorizing the population. Sometimes deliberation helps calm us when our responses to an event are governed by fear and dread. A little careful thought and we realize there's nothing to be scared of. In other words, sometimes the conclusions we come to intuitively—quickly and effortlessly—are overruled by conclusions that we come to more slowly and effortfully, via deliberation. Intuition leads to one conclusion, but deliberation makes us hesitate.

The distinction between intuition and deliberation is not found only in Western thought. According to certain Hindu and yoga traditions, there are seven wheels of energy, or *chakras,* that are "breath centers," spiritual elements associated with different aspects of a person's being and wellness. They are sometimes referred to as life force energy centers. The chakras are each associated with a part of the body. The first chakra is lowest down and has to do with rooting to the earth. The sacral chakra is located slightly below the navel and is associated with sexuality and related entities and drives. The third is slightly above the navel and relates to fire; the fourth is in the center of the chest—near the heart—and has to do with love. The fifth chakra is in the throat and is related to communication. The sixth and seventh chakra are closely related to what cognitive scientists think about as thought. The sixth chakra, also called the Ajna chakra, is located between the eyebrows. You might have encountered it in Hindu art as a third eye. It is often associated with such things as visual imagery. We think of it as the Eastern way of describing what we call intuition, the thoughts that come automatically, shaped by unconscious processes.

The seventh, or Sahaswara chakra, is located at the crown of the head. It is associated with intelligence and with consciousness. This chakra connects us to our higher selves and to other beings. It doesn't seem a huge stretch to see an analogy between the seventh chakra and what we're calling deliberation.

The implication is that intuition is of your own making. It is a property of your individual thought process. Deliberation is different. One way to deliberate is to talk to yourself, much as you would talk to another person. Deliberation connects you to people. A team of people cannot intuit something together, but they can deliberate together. This notion of thinking as a community will play a central role in the following chapters. We will see that we manage to overcome the weakness and error inherent in our intuitive causal models by deliberating in step with our community. By doing so, we create an exceptionally powerful social mind.

Intuition, Deliberation, and the Illusion of Explanatory Depth

Recall the illusion of explanatory depth, the finding that people think they understand causal systems better than they in fact do. The illusion is a product of the intuitive mind; we think about how things work automatically and effortlessly. But when we deliberate about our knowledge, our illusion is shattered. This helps to explain why not everybody falls for the illusion. Yale marketing professor Shane Frederick has introduced a simple test to determine whether a person is more intuitive or more deliberative. He calls the test the CRT (for Cognitive Reflection Test). It consists of three simple problems. Shane found one of them in a book of riddles:

> A bat and a ball cost $1.10. The bat costs one dollar more than the ball. How much does the ball cost?

Do you think the answer is 10¢? You're in good company. Most people report that as the answer (including the majority of students at Ivy League colleges). More to the point, "10¢" pops into almost everyone's mind. The real question is whether you just accept this intuitive response or check it. If you check it, you'll see that if the ball costs 10¢ and the bat costs $1.00 more than the ball, then the bat costs $1.10 and together they cost $1.20. So the answer is not 10¢.

A small proportion of people do check their intuitive answer and realize 10¢ is wrong. Most of them are able to calculate the right answer.[2] Frederick refers to such people as reflective. What he means is that they tend to suppress their intuitive response and deliberate before responding.

The bat-and-ball problem shares a characteristic with the other two problems on the CRT. Here's one of them:

> In a lake, there is a patch of lily pads. Every day, the patch doubles in size. If it takes 48 days for the patch to cover the entire lake, how long would it take for the patch to cover half of the lake?

Did the answer "24" come to mind? It does for just about everybody, and most people report it to be the correct answer. Is it? Well, if the patch doubles in size every day, then if the lake is half covered

---

[2] The correct answer is 5¢.

on day 24, it would be fully covered on day 25. But the problem states that the lake is fully covered only on day 48. So 24 can't be correct. The right answer must be one day before it's fully covered, day 47.

Here's the remaining problem:

If it takes 5 machines 5 minutes to make 5 widgets, how long would it take 100 machines to make 100 widgets?

Here's a hint: The answer is *not* 100.[3]

What the three problems of the CRT have in common is that an incorrect answer pops to mind. To get the right answer, the intuitive answer must be suppressed and you must do a little calculation. Most people don't bother. Rather than suppressing the incorrect intuitive answer and engaging in the little bit of deliberation to figure out the right answer, people just blurt out the intuitive answer, the first answer to pop to mind. Less than 20 percent of the U.S. population gets the three problems of the CRT right. Mathematicians and engineers do better than poets and painters, but not that much better. About 48 percent of students at the Massachusetts Institute of Technology got all three correct when Frederick tested them; only 26 percent of Princeton students did.

The CRT distinguishes people who like to reflect before they answer from those who just answer with the first thing that comes to mind. People who are more reflective depend more on their deliberative powers of thought and expression; those who are less reflective depend more on their intuitions. These people differ in a number of ways. People who are more reflective tend to be more careful when given problems that involve reasoning. They make fewer errors and are less likely to fall for tricks than less reflective people fall

---

[3] The correct answer is 5 minutes (each machine takes 5 minutes to make one widget).

for. For instance, they are better at detecting when a statement was intended to be profound or whether it's essentially a random collection of words (like "Hidden meaning transforms unparalleled abstract beauty"). They are also more willing to take risks and they are less impulsive. In general, they are more likely to take a chance or to wait longer if it means getting a bigger reward. Their preferences differ in other ways as well. More reflective people are more likely than less reflective people to prefer dark chocolate to milk chocolate. They are also less likely to believe in God.

What's more relevant to our discussion is that more reflective people—people who score better on the CRT—show less of an illusion of explanatory depth than less reflective people. In a study we asked participants to judge their understanding of the mechanisms of various obscure consumer items (such as Aqua Globes, which automatically water your plants for two weeks) both before and after they provided an explanation of their understanding. Participants who did well on the CRT showed no illusion. In stark contrast, participants who scored zero or answered only one question correctly on the CRT showed a big illusion. In other words, the more reflective participants judged their understanding to be identical before and after an explanation, whereas the less reflective participants were less confident in their initial judgments after providing an explanation.

Intuition gives us a simplified, coarse, and usually good enough analysis, and this gives us the illusion that we know a fair amount. But when we deliberate, we come to appreciate how complex things actually are, and this reveals to us how little we actually know.

Why didn't those who scored well on the CRT exhibit the illusion of explanatory depth? Another study we did suggests one possible answer. We created a bunch of advertisements for products that differed in the amount of detailed description for each product. We showed consumers the ads and asked them how much they liked each product. Participants who were more reflective—who did well on the CRT—preferred the products with more detail in the description. This contrasts with less reflective people—that is, most of us. Those who scored lower on the CRT preferred products with only a tiny bit of explanation; too much detail turned them off. Unlike most people, highly reflective people crave detail. They like to explain things, so it is not far-fetched to assume that they explain things even before they are asked to. And anyone who does that will not suffer the illusion of explanatory depth.

Intuitions are personal; they reside in our own heads. Deliberation involves reflecting on what we know personally as well as on facts that we're only dimly aware of or that we know only superficially, facts in other people's heads. For instance, if I'm deliberating about which candidate to vote for, I may well ask for the advice of someone I greatly respect. In that sense, deliberation depends on a community of knowledge. So one way to conceive of the illusion of explanatory depth is that our intuitive system overestimates what it can deliberate about. When I ask you how a toilet works, your intuitive system reports, "No problem, I'm very comfortable with toilets. They are part of my daily experience." But when your deliberative system is probed by a request to explain how they work, it is at a loss because your intuitions are only superficial. The real knowledge lies elsewhere. The next two chapters of this book will reveal where it's hiding.

FIVE

Thinking with Our Bodies
and the World

Cognitive science is the study of human intelligence—the search for the magic ingredients that allow people to perceive, think, and act in the astonishing ways that they do. Artificial intelligence (AI) is the study of machine intelligence—how to build a machine that can behave in intelligent ways. The two fields grew up together alongside the development of modern computers, so it isn't surprising the histories of the two fields took a similar turn.

Early work in AI, from the 1940s up to the 1980s, focused on individual computers. The goal was to build a great mind out of silicon, like Hal, the brilliant computer in the classic Arthur C. Clarke books and subsequent film *2001: A Space Odyssey*. Hal played a great game of chess and acted as the crew's right-hand machine before having a sort of mental breakdown. Like the fictional inventors of Hal, early AI researchers tried to put large amounts of knowledge and sophisticated reasoning abilities inside a computer. Smart computers were designed to have huge memory stores that were packed full of all kinds of knowledge and fast processors that could use that knowledge to figure out the answer to just about any question (as long as it didn't concern categories that remained the province of human beings, like love or fear). Artificial intelligence researchers were busy trying to produce a super-robot that had all the resources at its disposal to conquer all the problems and perform all the functions that human users would prefer to pawn off on a machine.

But this superintelligent agent has not come to be, as some AI researchers have lamented. In 2003, Marvin Minsky, one of the cofounders of MIT's Artificial Intelligence Lab and an early proponent of AI, said in an interview, "There is no computer that has common sense. We're only getting the kinds of things that are capable of making an airline reservation. No computer can look around a room and tell you about it." Minsky was mostly referring to an old way of doing AI (the only way of doing it prior to the 1980s), an approach that saw intelligent machinery as operating in ways not that different from a sophisticated cash register. Cash registers take in information (like keystrokes indicating what you want to purchase), do some computation while you sit there and wait (adding up your purchases), and then spit out an output (the total you owe). This kind of traditional step-by-step computation is time consuming and inefficient. It requires a computer to apply a long series of simple rules to transform one set of symbols to another set of symbols (just as a cash register transforms a set of prices into a total price). It might apply the rules really fast, but it's always transforming symbols one rule at a time. Even doing simple arithmetic on a computer demands hundreds, if not thousands, of simple operations in sequence.

Symbol-processing AI of this type had some minor successes, such as programs that could play a good game of chess or advise doctors on diagnoses, but nothing like the superintelligent computing machines that early researchers had dreamed about. The beginning of the end came when philosopher John Haugeland, a pioneer in the philosophy of artificial intelligence, dismissively dubbed this project Good Old-Fashioned Artificial Intelligence (GOFAI).

GOFAI assumes that the realms of software and hardware are distinct. Algorithms (recipes for computation) are software, and they can be designed independently of the hardware used to implement them. In principle, they can run on any computer that is sufficiently powerful. In that sense, the hardware (the physical computer) doesn't matter. The hardware may determine things like the speed of a computation, but it'll perform the same computation as any other computer.

This way of understanding machine intelligence is a direct descendant of the dualist approach to human intelligence espoused by the French philosopher René Descartes in the seventeenth century. Descartes argued that the human mind is not a material substance, that it is a completely different sort of thing than the material body. Descartes's famous line *Cogito ergo sum*, I think therefore I am, reflects his view that his identity—his knowledge that he exists—derives from his ability to think, not from his physical body. He draws from this the conclusion that thinking belongs in a spiritual realm distinct from the material realm of the physical body. But the two must interact. After all, thought knows about the world only through the body; the information we think about comes in through the eyes, ears, nose, and other sensory organs. And they interact in the other direction too: Thought makes decisions that tell the body what to do. Descartes even pinpointed the locus of their interaction. The spiritual and the physical realms talk to each other, Descartes claimed, in the pineal gland in the brain. GOFAI also divides thought and action into two separate realms: immaterial software and material hardware (though there's no analogue to the pineal gland).

GOFAI has some major failings as a model of human intelligence. To understand one of them, let's consider the famous poem "Casey at the Bat" by Ernest Lawrence Thayer. It starts like this:

> *The outlook wasn't brilliant for the Mudville nine that day:*
> *The score stood four to two, with but one inning more to play,*

Those of you familiar with the poem know the state of the Mud-ville fans:

> *A straggling few got up to go in deep despair. The rest*
> *Clung to that hope which springs eternal in the human breast;*
> *They thought, "If only Casey could but get a whack at that—*
> *We'd put up even money now, with Casey at the bat."*

You also know they finally got their wish:

> *And now the pitcher holds the ball, and now he lets it go,*
> *And now the air is shattered by the force of Casey's blow.*

No spoiler alert required; we won't tell you what happens next. Instead, we'd like you to consider the possibilities. If you know base-ball, you know that Casey either hit the ball or swung and missed. If he hit it, he likely hit it hard, though he could have miffed and dinked the ball. Let's say he hit it hard; in fact, let's say he hit it out of the park. What consequences would arise from that action? For one, he would go running around the bases and his team would get at least one run. The crowd would also react. Presumably the Mudville spec-tators would jump with excitement and joy, hailing all of Casey's virtues. Not everybody would be so excited: not fans of the other team, not the vendors selling peanuts at the game who don't give a damn about baseball, not the woman giving birth a block away who has other things on her mind. But those within earshot of the game might or might not depending on who they support, which team they bet on, and whether they know enough about baseball to make sense of the crowd noise at the ballpark. In other words, it's compli-cated. Determining what an action changes and what it doesn't is hard. If you're a computer operating on the principles of GOFAI, all of these possible consequences must be programmed into your software using algorithms you can understand. You need a long list of all the changes you need to make to your representation of the world for each possible action, and an even longer list of all the changes you must not make. In fact, those lists might have to be infinitely long.

This problem of programming what to change and what not to is known to computer scientists and philosophers as the frame problem. Despite the existence of a number of ideas, it is far from being solved. To see why the problem is so hard, think about what you have to know to solve it. You have to know the rules of baseball, but you also have to know something about human emotions to understand why some people would react positively and others negatively. You also have to know quite a lot about human culture to understand why some people would care and others wouldn't. You even have to know a little physics to understand that people far away from the ballpark are probably not reacting. And all of this knowledge must come into play from just a few lines of a poem. Somehow you have to identify the key features of the event from the poem and then you have to use those key features to elicit all the relevant knowledge.

Here's another problem faced by GOFAI. Imagine walking through a forest. Every step you take is an adventure. Your feet pass over sticks and bramble and rocks at different heights; sometimes you'll even have to distribute your weight on loose rock or on a boulder. At every scale, your foot has to conform to its environment. At the highest level, it has to move in the direction you have decided to go. On a shorter time scale, it must avoid getting tangled or wet by sidestepping obstacles and icky places. On an even shorter time scale, it must conform to whatever it lands on. If there's a pebble in its way, it might just have to drape itself over that pebble. If each of these actions by your foot were planned, if your nervous system calculated the precise trajectory of your foot and the movement of every one of the many muscles that control your foot, if it planned out a route that took you where you wanted to go while avoiding obstacles and conforming to the ground, that would be a lot of computation. That would be enough computation to keep a supercomputer busy for a long time.

If you calculated the precise trajectory that your foot takes at every step, it would take you hours, if not days, to walk around the block. You'd spend most of your time immobile, paralyzed in thought, doing engineering calculations. But this is what GOFAI systems do: They optimize and plan everything they do before they act. A GOFAI system that makes coffee spends most of its time thinking and only a little time actually making coffee. GOFAI robots are souped-up armchair philosophers, spending lots of time in thought and little in action.

If a robot's computer is fast enough, then it might not look like it's spending much time thinking and planning. And there are really fast computers today that compute extraordinarily quickly. But even today's fastest computers are not fast enough for GOFAI. Robots today are impressive because they've incorporated a different style of computation into their decision-making and action, a style inspired by how animals compute.

Embodied Intelligence

Rodney Brooks was a computer science professor at MIT for over twenty years starting in the mid-1980s. He was at the center of the revolution in robotics. His attitude toward machines was foreshadowed when, as a twelve-year-old growing up in Australia, he built an electronic tic-tac-toe game. Rather than doing it the old-fashioned way, by programming the logic of tic-tac-toe into the software of an existing computer, he built the game from scratch, out of scrap metal, switches, wires, and lightbulbs. Despite his unconventional approach, the game was hard to beat.

What Brooks didn't like about traditional GOFAI robots is that they need explicit descriptions of the tasks they are asked to perform. Somebody—a programmer—has to carefully figure out what needs to be computed (how to do arithmetic, how to get across a room, or how to play a good game of tic-tac-toe), write it all down as a very well-defined recipe—an algorithm—and then program the robot to follow the recipe by giving it a set of explicit rules to follow. Brooks didn't think that a truly intelligent robot should need such explicit instructions.

Brooks championed an alternative approach to robotics called embodied intelligence, inspired by the design of biological creatures. Evolution doesn't design an animal in one fell swoop. Rather, new species emerge slowly, over many years, through a gradual accumulation of biological functions inherited from their ancestors. The first human was not delivered to the world fully formed; rather, humans evolved from simpler life-forms, life-forms that couldn't think but that could do things like swim or crawl around, find food, and reproduce. They had dedicated systems for doing these things, systems that survived natural selection and still operate in fish, insects, and other animals, including humans. When animals walk, they use neural pathways that were carved out millions of years ago by ancestors that first swam and then slithered and then walked on more and more sophisticated limbs. Those ancient animals also had perceptual systems that evolved into modern mammalian eyes, noses, and ears.

So when Brooks's team built a robot, they would start with a simple machine that could do nothing but, say, walk. But it walked very well. Instead of planning every step in great detail, it would respond to its environment in real time. Limbs would generally not be governed by a know-it-all central processing unit, but each limb would have springs and shock absorbers and its own power to make tiny decisions that would allow it to respond to simple problems intelligently all by itself. The limbs of Brooks's robots would avoid and adjust to obstacles individually, without a central authority telling them what to do. Such a robot wouldn't be able to navigate through a complex maze all by itself, but it was very stable when it walked. It wouldn't stumble on pebbles or ruts in the road, it could handle rocks or sand, and it could go uphill or downhill with relative ease. Brooks's idea was that more sophisticated robots would make use of this walking architecture by subsuming it into a more sophisticated task. A new module might talk to the basic walking modules and allow them to interact with, say, modules that sense light and interpret visual signals.

An example of a robot of this kind that you might have encountered is iRobot's Roomba vacuum cleaner. You may even own one yourself. They are the disklike things that travel around people's homes vacuuming the floor while avoiding obstacles and staying away from dangerous staircases. A Roomba has two wheels that operate independently and a bunch of sensors that tell it if it's going to bump into something. If a Roomba is about to encounter a wall or an object, it turns away from it and goes elsewhere. But it doesn't have a master plan; it just spins its wheels in a different direction. Its sensors and its controllers each do their thing without knowing what else is going on. Each part does something simple but effective, with the result that the larger whole does something quite impressive: It vacuums your floor.

This method of designing a robot that has embodied intelligence is called a subsumption architecture because the higher level modules are designed to subsume the lower level functions. It conceives of intelligence as a grand hierarchy: High-level sophisticated tasks are performed by combining simpler skills that are in turn just organizations of even simpler skills. Sophisticated tasks get done not through exhaustive computation and planning but by engaging a hierarchy of actors in an organized way that, at the lowest level, are just responding directly to the environment. Brooks never managed to build a robot that could do anything really sophisticated, but his ideas have been incorporated into the minimalist design of mainstream modern robotics. Rather than having all their sophisticated abilities built into them, today's cutting-edge robots are equipped to react effectively to the world they are operating in. That way, they don't have to compute every little movement by planning ahead. The world does a lot of the computation for them.

How Humans Are Designed

A corresponding revolution has occurred in the study of how people think. Just as there was an old-fashioned AI conception of robots, there was an old-fashioned cognitive science conception of people that shared all the key features of GOFAI and held sway during a similar time period. According to this conception, people process symbols like a computer does but using human software, drawing reasoned conclusions and filing the results away in a memory store. The idea was that people engage in reams of computation to construct a model of the world. We navigate and make decisions by doing calculations to figure out the best course of action, to store information, and to constantly update what we know. If this is really how we think, we should all be exhausted all the time. But we're not actually busy most of the time building a model to describe the world.

In one series of experiments, participants were asked to read text displayed on a computer screen. Each participant wore an eye-tracking device that told the computer where the person was looking. The studies used a clever trick: Most of what the computer displayed was actually junk, sequences of random letters. The only meaningful text was in a small window right where the person was looking. Because the computer knew where the person was looking, it was able to show the small window of real text in just the spot where the eye was focused. So as readers moved their gaze along the line of text, the window moved too. Real text always appeared in the small window right where the person was looking, while all the surrounding text was a jumble of random letters. The researchers conducting the study found that, as long as the window wasn't too small, the participants had no idea there was any nonsense on the screen just outside their gaze. The document appeared to be completely normal, full of nothing but meaningful text. Typically, the window can have a width as small as 17 or 18 characters, about 2 to 3 characters to the left of where the eyes are fixated and about 15 characters to the right (because in English, we read left to right). That's just a few words, less than 6. Even if everything outside just a few words is random letters, participants believe they are reading normal text. For anyone standing behind the reader looking at the screen, most of what they would see is nonsense, and yet the reader has no idea. Because what the reader is seeing at any given moment is meaningful, the reader assumes everything is meaningful.

What the readers experienced in this study was not the actual world—the actual world was full of nonsense and they were experiencing a world full of sensible text. Wherever they looked, the text they saw made sense, so they assumed what they weren't looking at also made sense. They were perceiving the world with a sort of tunnel vision, oblivious to how confused things were outside their little perceptual window. This study suggests that we draw conclusions about the world based on small glimpses. But are we constructing a model of the world and presenting it to ourselves like a play on a stage? This seems unlikely because there's a simpler explanation: Participants thought everything else made sense because the world usually does make sense (ordinarily, psychologists, magicians, and artists are not trying to trick us). Participants experienced normality in this experiment because the little bit they could see conformed to their customary experience of the world.

This assumption that the world is behaving normally gives people a giant crutch. It means that we don't have to remember everything because the information is stored in the world. If I need to know something, all I have to do is look at it. If I need to know what the sentence was at the top of the page, I don't have to remember it. I just have to look at the top of the page. As one of the researchers doing these experiments said, "the visual environment functions as a sort of outside memory store."

Consider what this work implies about our everyday experience of the world. What do you understand about the space you're in right now? Think about the objects nearby and where they are relative to you. Doesn't it seem like you know the space? If a machine could come and read your mind, wouldn't it get a pretty detailed picture of the environment you're in right now? You might have to move your eyes and head a bit, or maybe you even have to move your entire body to get the full picture, but the sense you have is that you're directly perceiving your environment. The moving window paradigm just described suggests this sense of understanding is only apparent. Your feeling that you have a spatial model of your environment is illusory. All you can see is a small spotlight around where your eyes are focused.

Why does it feel like you know the entire space? It's because you see that space no matter where you look. Your sense of knowing the entire environment emerges from the fact that everything makes sense regardless of what your gaze falls on. Everything makes sense because the world behaves in ways you understand (furniture isn't floating up to the ceiling; trees aren't fluctuating in and out of existence). You're seeing only a tiny bit of the world at a time, but you know the rest is there, just not in your head. Wherever you look, you'll see something that is reassuringly normal and consistent with the other things you see. The world is acting as your memory. You know the lamp is to the left of you because when you look to the left, there it is. Here's one way to convince yourself: Close your eyes and try to reconstruct what's around you. Be specific. What's above your normal line of vision? If you're like most people, you'll be surprised by how poorly you answer that question. We feel like we have a model of our environment in our heads, a detailed representation of everything that is there. But we don't.

In chapter 2, we discussed hyperthymesics, individuals who remember a vast number of autobiographical life experiences to an astounding degree of detail. We wondered whether hyperthymesics differ from the rest of us in how they encode their environments in memory. Perhaps their extreme memory capacities make them more able to do computation in their heads; perhaps they can build models of their environments more faithfully than the average person can. If so, then they wouldn't depend as much as others on external information. But the data suggest that hyperthymesics are pretty much like everyone else in this respect. For instance, the hyperthymesic AJ has trouble keeping track of which of her keys opens which door. At one point, experimenters asked her to close her eyes and tell them what they were wearing. She couldn't. After all, what's impressive about hyperthymesics is what they can remember about their own life experience, not what they understand about the world.

The World Is Your Computer

As we've already focused on baseball in this chapter, let's stick with the theme to further illustrate the point that we are not engaged in intensive computation inside our heads. Imagine a fly ball has been hit straight toward you. How do you go about deciding where you should be to catch it? The traditional cognitive science answer is that the little Isaac Newton inside you takes over. You start calculating trajectories and predicting where the ball is going to fall using everything you know about physics. You may have forgotten much of the calculus that you learned in high school, but it's possible that your motor system knows what it needs to: that, when hit, the path a ball takes has the shape of a parabola (neglecting wind and friction). All you have to do is estimate a few parameters, remember that parabolas can be described using quadratic equations, quickly solve the resulting math problem, and you're done. The equation will tell you where you have to be. This is just what a robot following the rules of GOFAI would do. It would sit and think for a while—hopefully not too long—and then move to the correct position (if it got it right).

Making it to the major leagues doesn't actually require memorizing and internalizing quadratic equations. It turns out there's an easier way to catch a ball that hardly involves thinking at all. Instead of calculating trajectories, there's a trick that will take you to where the ball is going to land. If a fly ball is coming in your direction, a natural thing to do is stare at the ball as it rises into the air, raising your head to elevate your gaze as the ball comes toward you. The direction of your gaze specifies an angle relative to the ground. Here's the trick: To end up where the ball is going to land, all you have to do is move forward or backward so that this angle is always increasing at a constant rate. In order to keep your eye on the ball after it's hit, you'll have to continuously tilt your head (or your eyeballs) upward to track the ball's motion. What may surprise you is that you'll have to continue to lift your gaze even after the ball starts to descend. If you watch an outfielder running to catch a ball, you'll see him adjust his body's direction and speed so that his gaze is always moving upward at the same constant rate. These adjustments lead him to the right spot to intercept the ball. Then all he has to do is catch it.

Experiments carefully measuring the movement of experienced baseball and softball players catching real balls and chasing virtual balls that follow impossible trajectories yielded consistent results: Ballplayers don't calculate where the ball is going. They watch the ball and let their steadily lifting gaze direct them to the right spot.

This gaze-direction strategy has some other advantages in addition to being much simpler than calculating a trajectory. First, all the information you need is immediately available; hardly any memory is required. To know your direction of gaze, all you need to do is to know where the ground is and where you're looking. To know the speed at which your direction of gaze is changing, all you need to know is how fast your head is moving, something your sensory system already knows. In contrast, doing the computation-heavy GOFAI thing requires constructing a parabolic trajectory, which means identifying at least three points on the ball's path and interpolating a mathematical function. Not so easy.

The second advantage of the gaze-direction strategy is that it allows the player to move right away. Rather than doing a bunch of computation before moving, the player can—indeed, must—start moving to begin increasing gaze angles immediately. This gives the player more time to get to the ball. No wonder that's how professional ballplayers do it.

An even simpler and more powerful example of using the world to do computation for us involves navigating through tight spaces. Imagine running through a field of wheat (or try it out if you're lucky enough to have a field close by). The blades of wheat close to you seem like they're moving faster than the blades far away. This has to do with the way light is traveling from the surface of the field to your eye. The geometry of the situation creates systematic patterns that reflect how you are traversing the field. If you make a sharp turn, then the wheat traces out concentric arcs that follow your path because of how the light reflects off them and into your eyes. What you are experiencing is optic flow, the patterns that light makes as it reflects off surfaces and hits your eye while you're moving. Optic flow obeys definite rules. For instance, if you take the same path through an apple orchard that you take through the field of wheat, you'll experience the same optic flow. What you see will of course be different (apple trees versus wheat), but the patterns will be the same: Just as the wheat farther from you seems to be moving more slowly, the trees farther from you will seem to be moving more slowly than the ones close by.

Another place you experience optic flow is on the highway. The lines on the road painted by the Department of Transportation are there to keep you on the straight and narrow. As long as the flow of lines on one side of you appears to be moving by you at the same rate as the flow on the other side, you'll stay in your lane. We know this from experiments done in driving simulators. If you put someone in a simulator with a computer display and make the lines go faster on one side than the other, the person will drift toward the side with the slower lines. The Department of Transportation takes advantage of people's sensitivity to optic flow when it wants drivers to slow down by painting lines in such a way that they seem like they're going faster than they are. This trick is particularly useful on highway exit ramps.

People also use optic flow to enter doorways. Say you want to go through the middle of a doorway so that you don't bump into the doorjamb on either side. One way is to estimate your distance from the door, estimate the width of the door, and calculate what angle you would have to take to intersect the middle of the doorway. That's what a GOFAI robot would do. This takes a lot of calculation and requires a lot of estimation. Such estimations could be difficult if you're a robot in a hurry. Here's a faster, simpler way: Walk through the door making sure that both sides of the door frame are approaching you at the same speed (more technically: make sure the optic flow on either side of you is symmetrical). That's it. If you can do that, you'll enter every room without sore shoulders. And that is how people do it. We know that because if you artificially speed up the optic flow on one side using virtual reality, people no longer travel corridors in the middle; they move away from the side with the faster flow.

Bees and other insects make similar use of optic flow. Bees use it to enter their nests and guide themselves through tunnels. This has been shown by experiments that make bees fly through special tunnels in which the optic flow on each side can be varied. Bees fly closer to whichever wall has slower optic flow. If bees and other insects can do it, it can't require too much computation; doing it must be pretty simple.

All these studies show that people (and bugs) aren't old-fashioned model builders that engage in loads of computation punctuated by action. Instead, people use facts about the world—like the optics of balls and surfaces—to simplify what they do. In so many cases, the information we respond to isn't in our heads; it's in the world. This isn't just true of catching balls and entering doorways. When we wash the dishes, the pile of dirty dishes tells us what needs to be done, the shininess of each dish tells us if it's clean, and the absence of dripping water tells us we can put the dishes away. There's hardly anything to remember. Similarly, when we're reading a page, all we need to know is the string of words that our eyes are focused on. The page will take care of the rest.

The examples we've discussed of how people read and catch balls demonstrate that not everything we retain is in our heads. At the most basic levels of functioning, we use the world as our memory store. At higher levels, this is obvious. The piles of paper work on our desk remind us of things we have to do. More and more, our e-mail queue serves as a reminder of our to-do list. Calendars—

paper or electronic—are also designed to do that. Next we'll discuss how we use our bodies as an especially useful and flexible repository of memories.

The Brain Is in the Mind

Where do you think the mind is located? Most people respond that it's in the brain. Most people assume that the locus of thought—the most impressive of human capacities—is in the most sophisticated of human organs, the brain. If this view of the mind is correct, it has implications for how you perform simple tasks. Consider deciding whether a photograph of a common everyday object like a watering can is upright or inverted. Your job is to just look at the picture and consult your brain to see what the normal orientation of the object is. You can then respond yes if the object in the photograph has the normal orientation, and otherwise respond no.

In an experiment that asked people to do this, participants sometimes pushed a button with their left hand to indicate yes, and sometimes they used their right hand. So far, so good. People had no problem with the task and responded in not much more than half a second. But the experimenters were tricky, and they varied one little detail, a detail that shouldn't have mattered. The objects were oriented either to the left or to the right. For instance, the handle of the watering can was on the right-hand side in half the pictures and on the left-hand side in the other half. If all you're doing to decide whether the object is upright or upside down is consulting the knowledge stored in your brain about the object's orientation, then whether the handle is on the left or right should make no difference. But it did. When responding yes with their right hand, people were faster when the handle was on the right than when the handle was on the left. And when they were asked to say yes by pressing a button with their left hand, people were faster when the handle was on the left.

What this shows is that a photograph of a utensil with a handle on the right makes it easier to use your right hand. You see the photograph and you immediately and unconsciously start organizing your body to interact with the pictured object. The handle is calling for your right hand, not your left, even though the handle is not real. It's just a photograph. And the fact that your right hand is primed for action makes you faster to respond with it, even to a question about the orientation of the object, which has nothing to do with action. By priming your hand to interact with the object, your body is directly affecting how long it takes you to answer the question. You don't just pull the answer out of your brain. Rather, your body and brain respond in synchrony to the photograph to retrieve an answer.

Examples abound of how we use our bodies to think and remember. One study showed, for instance, that acting out a scene is more effective than other memorization techniques for recalling the scene. Results of this kind provide evidence for what is often called *embodiment,* a cluster of ideas about the important role that the body plays in cognitive processing. Rather than doing calculations on a mental blackboard, thinking takes place through actions that engage the objects of thought.

Arithmetic is made much easier by the presence of an external aid like a piece of paper or a blackboard (a calculator can help too). In some cultures, number systems are designed around the body. The Oksapmin people of New Guinea count along an ordered sequence of twenty-seven body parts. The sequence starts at the thumb of one hand, goes up to the nose, then down the other side of the body to the pinkie of the other hand. Thus, their system for counting is base 27. Several other cultures have related body-based counting systems. Western culture may be one of them. We probably rely so heavily on base 10 because we have ten fingers. Note that children often use their fingers to help them do arithmetic.

Our cognition is unified with the objects that we're thinking about and with. When we make music, our thought about music and the music we make with our mouth or an instrument are part of the same process and highly interdependent. It's much easier to move your fingers as if you're playing a guitar if you actually have a guitar, and it's much easier to spell a word or do arithmetic if you write down what you're thinking. In general, the fact that thought is more effective when it is done in conjunction with the physical world suggests that thought is not a disembodied process that takes place on a stage inside the head. Mental activities do not simply occur in the brain. Rather, the brain is only one part of a processing system that also includes the body and other aspects of the world.

We even use our emotional reactions as a kind of memory. When we react with pleasure, pain, or fear to an event, we discover what to pay attention to and what to avoid. Antonio Damasio, a neuroscientist at the University of Southern California, called these reactions *somatic markers* from the Greek *soma*, meaning body. Our bodies produce feelings to make us aware and warn us. When an option is pleasing, we have a positive affective reaction—a good feeling. That's our body telling us that we should pay attention and investigate. That's why we feel good in a French pâtisserie. Our bodies are trying to draw our attention to all the delectables within sight. When an option is displeasing, we have a negative affective reaction like disgust or fear. The reaction tells us to avoid the option because it might be infectious, dangerous in some other way, or just annoying. A well-placed disgust response tells us to get away from whatever caused it. That's adaptive when encountering a pool of brown liquid in the middle of the street, but it can be problematic if it's something that we have to clean up. A similar lesson applies to a response of fear: It can be useful when we encounter a snake or enemy, but it can be problematic when we respond to a stranger that way.

These emotional reactions influence our decision-making. They determine what we think about and what options we consider. We're more likely to think carefully about something that doesn't scare us than something that does, and we're more likely to ponder French pastries than disgusting pools of liquid. In that sense, emotional reactions not only influence thought but can substitute for it.

Where do these reactions come from? It's enticing to think that some of them are built in, that our fear of snakes is knowledge built into our genes over millennia of being surrounded by dangerous snakes. And it could be true. Phobias occur when our fears are out of control, and the common phobias tend to concern things that were in fact dangerous in our prehistoric past: arachnophobia (fear of spiders), acrophobia (fear of heights), agoraphobia (fear of open or crowded spaces). These fears are all of things that presented some danger to our evolutionary ancestors. There may be cases of, say, mp3ophobia or BMWaphobia, but we're not aware of any. Natural selection would have little incentive to build them in. But there are fears that can't be easily grounded in our evolutionary history. Some people have an extreme fear of flying (aviophobia) or a fear of ventriloquist's dummies (automatophobia). Fears like these develop over time through exposure and presumably require some conceptual or cultural support. For instance, fear of flying might have to do with how hard flying is to conceptualize. It violates our causal beliefs about physics. How can such large and heavy hunks of metal ever get off the ground?

A reaction of disgust is a kind of somatic or bodily signal that tells us something is unhealthy and should be avoided. We react with disgust to things that are unhealthy to be near, and the reaction helpfully drives us away from them. We don't react only to bodily fluids and other germ-carrying agents with disgust. We also react to certain behaviors with disgust. Some psychologists have proposed that disgust drives some of our moral reactions. Some people find the thought of homosexual sex disgusting; more people find the thought of sex with a sibling disgusting. This reaction of horror and distaste at the thought of certain actions could be a case of a somatic marker operating at an abstract level. Our body is telling us whether it considers an action appropriate or not. Fortunately, we (our deliberating homunculi) retain the option of agreeing or not with our bodies' opinions.

These are just a couple of examples of how we use our bodies to think and remember. The main lesson is that we should not think of the mind as an information processor that spends its time doing abstract computation in the brain. The brain and the body and the external environment all work together to remember, reason, and make decisions. The knowledge is spread through the system, beyond just the brain. Thought does not take place on a stage inside the brain. Thought uses knowledge in the brain, the body, and the world more generally to support intelligent action. In other words, the mind is not in the brain. Rather, the brain is in the mind. The mind uses the brain and other things to process information.

We've now provided part of the answer to the question of how humanity masters its environment when individuals are relatively ignorant. Individuals are much less ignorant when they can use external aids. The world itself, including our own bodies, serves as a memory device and external aid that makes us much less ignorant than we otherwise would be. In the next chapter, we'll see that we make use of an even bigger memory store and processing aid: other people.

SIX

Thinking with Other People

We have seen that thinking evolved to support complex action. The mind processes information so that individuals can act, so that they they can transform the environment to their liking. We have also seen that thought uses the environment to do its processing. The world serves as a memory and is part of the thought process. But a single thinker can do only so much. In nature we often see complex behavior arise through the coordination of multiple individuals. When multiple cognitive systems work together, group intelligence can emerge that goes beyond what each individual is capable of.

Bees are a great example of this. A beehive is wonderfully complex, far more than the sum of its parts. The trick that beehives take advantage of is the same as that used by corporations: Different individuals play different roles in the colony. There are workers: females who protect the hive, collect nectar and pollen, make honey to provide food for the winter, build the wax comb where food is stored, and feed the larvae. There is the queen, who starts a new colony, then mates and lays eggs. And there are drones, males who leave the colony and mate with a queen from another colony. The hive itself is carefully organized. Honey and pollen are stored in cells toward the top of the hive. Developing larvae live in cells toward the bottom, where one can also find separate areas for developing workers, drones, and queens.

The beehive solves many tricky problems through cooperation. Workers collect and store food that supports the hive during the winter when pollen and nectar are unavailable. Workers also protect the hive from intruders, safeguarding the food and the young. Genetic diversity is introduced by the queen mating with drones from other colonies.

No individual bee could fend for itself. Workers can't mate. Drones can't feed themselves. Queens can't protect their brood. Each individual has a job to do and is an expert at that job. Workers don't know they are workers. Drones don't know they are drones. They do the job evolution has programmed them to do, and the whole thing works because each individual carries out a relatively simple part of this wildly complex action system.

Individual people are much smarter than individual bees. But at another level, people and bees have an important property in common: We both harness the power of multiple entities working together to generate massive intelligence. Humans are the most complex and powerful species ever, not just because of what happens in individual brains, but because of how communities of brains work together.

The Community Hunt

Survival of a species depends on a few things. Procuring food is one of them. Since the late nineteenth century, the anthropological record has been filled with discoveries suggesting that prehistoric humans were the most prodigious hunters in the history of the world. Great caches of bones have been found all around the world, from Africa to the Middle East to Europe and the Americas, bones that bear the telltale marks of slaughter and butchery. Ancient humans killed everything, including the biggest animals that populated their worlds: mammoths, elephants, rhinoceroses, aurochs, and bison. They were so successful that hunting by humans was likely one of the main drivers of the extinction of many species of large mammals. Our scrawny ancestors did a remarkable job of killing animals many times their size. Before humans, success at hunting mandated superior physical abilities: strength, size, or speed. Then humans appeared with their ability to think and, quite suddenly, being as big as a bus provided scant protection.

Archaeologists and ethnographic researchers have reconstructed some of the techniques and strategies that ancient humans used to accomplish these great feats. What is clear is that hunting was a communal enterprise requiring a level of cooperation and division of labor unique to humans. Communal hunts were highly sophisticated and coordinated, involving dozens of participants. But the payoff was huge; the hunters were often able to dispatch large numbers of gigantic animals in a single expedition, providing for months of subsistence.

Anthropologist John Speth describes communal bison hunts in western North America during the end of the last Ice Age, the late Pleistocene. Human hunters led bison herds—sometimes for miles—to locations where they'd set traps. These traps could be natural arroyos that penned the animals in or corrals specially built to do so. Sometimes the hunters purposely led a herd off the edge of a cliff, making the animals fall to their deaths.

These hunts required great expertise, careful planning, and close coordination. Hunts were led by a shaman who was an expert on bison behavior. To control the herd's behavior, the shaman needed specialized knowledge honed over years of practice. He used clever tricks, like wearing a bison pelt to fool the animals into thinking he was one of them, a lead animal. Other community members were stationed strategically along the drive route to keep the animals moving in the right direction. Hunters waited at the trap location to kill the animals at the opportune moment. The whole thing was carefully orchestrated. The hunt could be ruined if the animals detected the smell of humans and became suspicious, or if they stampeded before arriving at the trap.

Killing the animals was only one of the goals of the hunt. Once the animals were slaughtered, the meat had to be butchered and preserved. This too was a major undertaking. Imagine the effort required to butcher and preserve a dozen bison, each weighing 3,500 pounds. It required a coordinated effort by the entire community.

Clearly, individual intelligence is useful for hunting. It takes an impressive intelligence to build an effective weapon, to predict how an animal will react when threatened, to butcher and preserve meat, and so on. But none of this is even close to sufficient to take out multiple bison in a single hunt, not to mention even larger animals like mammoths. No individual could do this alone. What made all this possible was the division of cognitive labor. Each community member mastered a skill that contributed to achieving the community's goals. The shaman devoted time and energy to mastering bison herding. But this was possible only because others in the community filled the other roles—spear wielding, butchery, making fire. There's an explosive gain in efficiency and power when cognitive labor is divided.

This explosive gain resulting from the division of cognitive labor can be seen directly in the construction of a building. Individuals working alone can put up a tent or even build a log cabin. Modern homes, with indoor plumbing, insulation, temperature control, full-service kitchens, and home entertainment systems, require a group effort. Consider the variety of trades that participate in building a modern home: surveyors, excavators, framers, bricklayers, roofers, plumbers, drywall and window installers, carpenters, painters, plasterers, electricians, cabinetmakers, landscapers, and carpet installers. Some people can do more than one job, but nobody can do all of them in a way that meets legal codes and satisfies the modern consumer.

Significant building construction has always required a division of cognitive labor, from ancient Egyptian pyramids to modern skyscrapers. Medieval cathedrals were made possible by the availability of traveling stonecutters and many other skilled trades: quarrymen, plasterers, mortar makers, and masons. And of course patrons, architects, and other designers were required to get the process started. Building these cathedrals was seen as a community project taking decades and sometimes centuries. Most workers did not expect to see them finished during their lifetimes. That communal effort and ownership explains the startling grandeur, beauty, and longevity of so many cathedrals around the world today.

These examples illustrate one of the key properties of the mind: It did not evolve in the context of individuals sitting alone solving problems. It evolved in the context of group collaboration, and our thinking evolved interdependently, to operate in conjunction with the thinking of others. Much like a beehive, when each individual is master of a domain, the group intelligence that emerges is more than the sum of its parts.

Braininess

The evolution of modern humans from other species of hominids—primate species related to people—was extremely rapid on an evolutionary time scale. It began with the emergence of the genus Homo on the African savannah 2 to 3 million years ago, with modern humans emerging about 200,000 years ago. The great leap that humanity made during that period was cognitive. Modern humans weren't stronger or faster than their predecessors; their advantage was brain size. The brain mass of modern humans is about three times that of our early hominid ancestors. Anthropologists call this rapid increase in brain mass encephalization ("encephalic" means relating to the brain). Such rapid growth has produced a puzzle for evolutionary theory. Large brains are costly, using a huge amount of energy. Because there are only a finite number of calories available, our bodies have to be physically weaker to compensate. Large brains also mean large skulls and, consequently, painful and dangerous childbirth. How did we get so smart so fast, despite these costs?

The explosion of brain size and intelligence marking the emergence of modern humans can be explained in a couple of ways. The ecological theory posits that it was driven by individuals' increasing abilities to deal with the environment. For instance, better foraging skills such as the ability to extract fruit from shells or skins that are hard to penetrate may have provided an adaptive advantage for smarter hominids. They could get more calories that way. Similarly, the ability to maintain a mental map of a larger roaming area would have made more food resources available, thus increasing fitness.

While the ecological hypothesis focuses on individual capabilities, a rival idea suggests that the driving force of the evolution of human intelligence was the coordination of multiple cognitive systems to pursue complex, shared goals. This is called the social brain hypothesis. It attributes the increase in intelligence to the increasing size and complexity of hominid social groups. Living in a group confers advantages, as we have seen with hunting, but it also demands certain cognitive abilities. It requires the ability to communicate in sophisticated ways, to understand and incorporate the perspectives of others, and to share common goals. The social brain hypothesis posits that the cognitive demands and adaptive advantages associated with living in a group created a snowball effect: As groups got larger and developed more complex joint behaviors, individuals developed new capabilities to support those behaviors. These new capabilities in turn allowed groups to get even larger and allowed group behavior to become even more complex.

Hunting is an example of a coordinated activity that became increasingly complex over time. Early hominid hunters were surely clever enough to surround individual prey to block their escape routes (dogs do this too). It took millennia before communities were sophisticated enough to engage in the coordinated activities required to capture, slaughter, and butcher dozens of bison. Such hunting ability may be what sets anatomically modern humans apart from any species that preceded us. Hunting may have been instrumental to human evolution.

Anthropologist Robin Dunbar set out to test the rival theories—the ecological hypothesis and the social brain hypothesis—by collecting data on many species of primates. He collected data on brain sizes as well as facts about the environments they lived in like the extent of their roaming territory and dietary habits, and facts about their societies such as their average group size. It turns out that brain size and group size are closely related. Primate species that live in larger groups have bigger brains. In contrast, environmental measures such as territory size and diet were unrelated to brain sizes. This finding suggests that large brains are specifically suited to support the skills necessary to live in a community.

Language is the most obvious example of a function dependent on sophisticated mental processes that evolved in coordination with other people. Many species are capable of simple communication. Bees communicate the location of flowers with high nectar yields to other individuals through a kind of dance and by emitting pheromones. The success of the hive depends on communication. Large numbers of workers can search for promising locations and let the other members of the hive know if they've discovered treasure. By

communicating what they've found, the swarm can focus its foraging efforts on the most bountiful areas. Communication allows the
hive to do its work.

But only so much information can be passed by dancing and
emitting pheromones; humans clearly win the gold medal for communication. What sets people apart is the ability to seamlessly
communicate ideas of arbitrary complexity through language. All
animals that hunt in packs may be able to communicate well enough
to coordinate their behavior. But the type of hunting that early humans mastered required the seamless communication of much more
complex ideas: spatial ideas indicating the location of prey and where
they were going to be shepherded to as well as complex causal ideas
about how the herding, slaughtering, and butchering were going to
be done, never mind the language necessary to discuss how the prize
was going to be divvied up.

If we're hunting together, then it's useful for me to know what
you're up to. I learn your intentions not just from communication,
but also by reasoning about your actions. If I see you raise your bow
and arrow and point it at a bison, then it's natural for me to infer that
your plan is to shoot the bison. Making this inference requires a surprising amount of mental machinery. I have to reason backward
from your action (raising and pointing the bow and arrow) to figure
out your intention (shooting the bison). This requires knowing or
figuring out something about your desires (that you want to kill a
bison) and something about your beliefs (that you know you can kill
a bison by shooting an arrow). It also requires knowing something
about your character (that you're not morally opposed to killing
bison). If I go on my way and allow you to shoot the bison on your
own, that suggests I trust that you're cooperative and you're not
going to disappear with the bison meat. People engage in this kind
of reasoning about the mental states of others automatically without
any effort all the time. People certainly differ in how well they can

decipher others' intentions and mental states, but everyone can do it to some extent. Dogs are pretty good at it too, though not as good. No dog is going to infer your goal of killing a bison from your pointing a bow and arrow. The ability to reason about other people's mental states is a critical talent for working together in large groups.

Shared Intentionality

Humans can do even more than read what others are trying to do. Humans have an ability that no other machine or animal cognitive system does: Humans can share their attention with someone else. When humans interact with one another, they do not merely experience the same event; they also *know* they are experiencing the same event. And this knowledge that they are sharing their attention changes more than the nature of the experience; it also changes what they do and what they're able to accomplish in conjunction with others.

Sharing attention is a crucial step on the road to being a full collaborator in a group sharing cognitive labor, in a community of knowledge. Once we can share attention, we can do something even more impressive—we can share common ground. We know some things that we know others know, and we know that they know that we know (and of course we know that they know that we know that they know, etc.). The knowledge is not just distributed; it is shared. Once knowledge is shared in this way, we can share *intentionality*; we can jointly pursue a common goal. A basic human talent is to share intentions with others so that we accomplish things collaboratively.

These ideas are due, in large part, to the great Russian psychologist Lev Vygotsky, who in the early twentieth century developed the idea that the mind is a social entity. Vygotsky argued that it is not individual brainpower that distinguishes human beings. It is that humans can learn through other people and culture and that people collaborate: they engage with others in collective activities. Vygotsky's insights are one of the roots of the idea of a community of knowledge.

Michael Tomasello and his colleagues at the Max Planck Institute for Evolutionary Anthropology in Leipzig, Germany, have been working with both children and chimpanzees for years developing a deeper understanding of how shared intentionality works. Why do children develop into adults who participate in a culture with art and literature, higher education and sophisticated machinery, as well as legalized marijuana, bourbon, and country and western music, while chimps today live pretty much the same social lives that they did when they first arrived on the evolutionary scene?

Consider one of their observations. An adult and infant are together in a room with an opaque bucket. The infant sees the adult point at the bucket. If the adult points out of the blue, the infant is confused. What is the adult's intention? What exactly is the adult pointing at? Is the adult trying to direct the infant's attention to the container's shape, color, material, or something else? Now imagine the two are playing a game: The adult hides something for the infant to find. When the adult points to the bucket while playing the game, the infant should understand the adult's goal: to let the infant know where to find the hidden object. The researchers found that infants as young as fourteen months old were able to perform this task; they understood the adult's intention in this situation. Chimpanzees and other apes did not at any age.

Apes are sophisticated, but they cannot share a human's intention. An ape can follow a human's gaze to see what they are looking at but cannot understand that the human is pointing to an object that they were playing with together. They cannot attend to the object and understand that the human is attending to the same object. The ape can't think, "Hmm, that human is trying to get me to think about what the human is thinking about, that object that we were just playing with." Apes can understand that a human is trying to achieve something, but they cannot collaborate by sharing attention and thus engage in joint pursuit of a goal.

Consider gesture. Gestures are an important part of human communication. We use gestures to convey information (by pointing or mimicking a movement), to empathize (by opening or closing our arms), or to make a request (beckoning someone over). Human babies as young as nine months old use gesture to attract other people's attention so they can jointly attend to objects. In contrast, chimps and other apes gesture only as a way of manipulating others—telling others how to do things or to respond to requests. Humans gesture to get on the same wavelength as someone else; apes gesture to get things done.

In another study, Tomasello and his colleagues had an adult experimenter work on a task with a child but then give up. Children would encourage the experimenter to re-engage. When he did the same thing with chimps, they never attempted to get the experimenter to re-engage. "[C]hildren," Tomasello and his team write, "but not chimpanzees, often seemed to collaborate just for the sake of collaborating. For example, they collaborated in social games as well as instrumental tasks, and also, after obtaining a toy in the instrumental tasks, they often replaced it in the apparatus to start the activity again." Children wanted to engage for the sake of engagement; chimps failed to grasp the concept of engagement.

In each of these cases, what distinguishes people is their ability—even their need—to jointly attend with other people to what they are doing. People are built to collaborate.

The ability to share intentionality supports perhaps the most important human capability of all: the ability to store and transmit knowledge from one generation to the next. This leads to what anthropologists call cumulative culture. The transmission of knowledge enabled by our social brains via language, cooperation, and the division of labor accumulates to create a culture. It is one of the most important ingredients in the human success story. Human capabilities are constantly increasing, but not because individuals are getting smarter. Unlike beehives, which have operated pretty much the same way for millions of years, our shared pursuits are always growing more complex and our shared intelligence more powerful.

We often think of social skills and intelligence as being negatively correlated. Turn on almost any eighties movie and you'll find a stereotypical nerd character who is great at math or physics, but can't carry on a simple conversation with a member of the opposite sex. These depictions belie the deep connection between individual and group intelligence. As we'll soon see, the smartest among us—in the sense of being most successful—may well be those who are best able to understand others.

Modern-Day Teamwork

The marks of our shared cognitive evolution are all around us. Watch young children interact. Most of them actively engage in group thinking with adults and children alike. They make up games, role-play, solve problems together, and argue.

Adults are no different. If you're sitting around a table telling jokes with friends, people tend to feed off one another. Occasionally there's a storyteller in the group who dominates the floor while everyone else just listens. But most conversations involve groups working together. Jokes emerge as different individuals contribute ideas and free-associate to one another's comments.

And this isn't just what hanging out with friends is like. Scientific laboratory meetings have the same quality. Researchers sit around a table, usually with some kind of visual aid like slides or a whiteboard, and each contributes bits of knowledge and ideas. Questions are asked and sometimes answered, hypotheses are thrown into the mix, disagreements are registered, and a consensus might build, all in a fairly chaotic series of turns and responses.

This is the best way to successfully get things done in many environments. These days, hospitals typically use a team approach for patient care. Medical professionals with various types of expertise—physicians, nurses, students, technicians, pharmacists, and care managers—work collaboratively. There's no clear leader, but rather a collection of expertise that, in the best case, provides a group intelligence greater than the sum of its parts. Airliners are flown by committees including the pilot, the copilot, air traffic controllers, and the sophisticated automated flight systems that play a huge part in managing modern aircraft. So many important decisions are made by committees today—from political policy and jury verdicts to strategy in the military and in sports—that it's fair to say that it's the norm.

Knowledge is so sophisticated at the cutting edge of science that huge teams are required to make progress. If you're a fundamental physicist, the discovery of the Higgs boson in 2012 was a big deal, even earthshaking. The discovery helped physicists settle on the most fundamental theory yet of how the physical world works. Who made the discovery? It is tempting to give credit to Peter Higgs and François Englert, who won the Nobel Prize in Physics in 2013 for their contributions to the effort. But the truth is that the Higgs boson would never have been discovered without the efforts of thousands of physicists, engineers, and students from almost forty countries. Nearly 3,000 people are authors on the key physics papers that led up to the discovery, not to mention all the workers who built and ran the $6.4 billion CERN supercollider in which the observations of the Higgs boson were made. No single individual was capable of even a fraction of the complex, specialized tasks required to do the work. The know-how was distributed among thousands of people.

Psychological research has shown that people naturally divide up cognitive labor, often without thinking about it. Imagine you're cooking up a special dinner with a friend. You're a great cook, but your friend is the wine expert, an amateur sommelier. A neighbor drops by and starts telling you both about the terrific new wines being sold at the liquor store just down the street. There are many new wines, so there's a lot to remember. How hard are you going to try to remember what the neighbor has to say about which wines to buy? Why bother when the information would be better retained by the wine expert sitting next to you? If your friend wasn't around, you might try harder. After all, it would be good to know what a good wine would be for the evening's festivities. But your friend the wine expert is likely to remember the information without even trying.

This effect has been demonstrated in the laboratory by Toni Giuliano and Daniel Wegner. They asked couples that had been seeing each other exclusively for at least three months to remember a series of items like a particular computer brand. They also asked the couples to rate, for each item, which partner had greater expertise for that item (for example, if one partner was a computer programmer and the other a chef, then the first had more expertise for the computer). What they found was that couples distributed the demands on memory, giving each partner more items to remember within their area of expertise. Items for which only one member of the couple was an expert were more likely to be remembered by the expert and forgotten by the nonexpert. Individuals made less of an effort to remember items when their partners' area of expertise included that item. In other words, each partner deferred to the other's expertise to store and recall the items relevant to that expertise. People tend to remember what they have to within a particular community to best make their contribution to the division of cognitive labor. We rely on experts to remember everything else.

Language, memory, attention—indeed, all mental functions—can be thought of as operating in a way that is distributed across a community according to a division of cognitive labor.

Confusion at the Frontier

One implication of the naturalness with which we divide cognitive labor is that there is no sharp boundary between one person's ideas and knowledge and those of other members of the team. How many person-hours have been wasted arguing whether the Beatles were great because of the depth of John Lennon or the brilliance of Paul McCartney? We think the answer is obvious: What made the Beatles great is that John was introduced to Paul on July 6, 1957, in St. Peter's Church in Liverpool, England, just before John was about to go onstage with his band the Quarrymen. It was because of this meeting that they started to work together, and it was their working together alongside George and Ringo that made the Beatles legendary. That great creative spirit that changed popular culture emerged from their interaction, not from their individual contributions.

When developing the ideas for this book, we were working with others, most intensively with our colleagues Craig Fox and Todd Rogers, psychologists from UCLA and Harvard, respectively. Together we had some insights about ignorance and illusions and about how to test those insights scientifically. Which one of us came up with the critical ideas? We think that's the wrong question. We all did. Even if we could reconstruct who said what at the multiple meetings we had to discuss these issues, we still couldn't give credit to individuals. The ideas emerged from conversations to which we all contributed.

When new ideas emerge, it's generally hard to attribute them to any one person because many people in a meeting supply a little crucial piece of the puzzle or some inspiration. The whole group deserves credit (or blame, as the case may be), not any individual. The process involves lots of thinking, but each individual's cognitive processes are so intertwined with everyone else's that the thought process that generated the ideas belongs to the group.

A common occurrence in collaborative work is that participants get confused about who deserves credit for an idea. Several times during the course of writing this book we had conversations that went something like this:

PHIL: I've got a great idea. What if we did X?

STEVE: Wait a second, you hated X when I suggested it three months ago.

PHIL: (ten-second pause). Hmm. I guess it's actually a pretty good idea.

Why does this happen? Because individual thinking and group thinking are so intertwined, it's hard to keep track of the boundaries. If you ask people to estimate the percentage of their contribution to a group project, they take advantage of the uncertainty by giving themselves more credit than they deserve. The total estimate reliably exceeds 100 percent! For instance, each member of a married couple was asked to estimate the percentage of household chores that he or she was responsible for. The average estimate was greater than 50 percent. This tendency to overestimate our individual contributions can lead to conflict, especially when it results in devaluing the contributions of other group members. We work so interdependently in groups that it would be wise to recognize the extreme difficulty of teasing out each person's contribution.

Just as people fail to know where their activities end and those of others begin, people fail to clearly distinguish their knowledge from others. Merely knowing that knowledge is available in the community makes people feel knowledgeable. Imagine coming across the following newspaper clipping:

> A May 19, 2014, study in the journal *Geology* reported the discovery of a new rock that scientists have thoroughly explained. The rock is similar to calcite, yet it glows in the absence of a light source. The authors of the study, Rittenour, Clark, and Xu, fully understand how it works; they provided a description of the remarkable appearance of the mineral and outlined future experiments.

How well would you say you understand how this type of glowing rock works? Presumably not very well; after all, you couldn't have heard of such rocks before because we made them up, and there's not enough in the clipping to let you figure it out for yourself. Would it make a difference to your sense of understanding if the scientists mentioned—Rittenour, Clark, and Xu—had not explained it? Would *you* understand it less well if the scientists didn't understand it? Again, presumably not. What does your understanding of a new phenomenon have to do with the fact that others understand it?

Your intuition may have led you astray in this case. We gave one group of people the scenario above and another group a similar scenario that instead said scientists had not yet explained how the rocks glow. We asked each group of respondents to rate their own understanding of glowing rocks. When the scientists didn't understand it, the participants themselves professed to understand it less well. Part of the participants' sense of understanding derived from the knowledge that others understand it. Merely telling people that scientists understood a phenomenon increased their sense of understanding that phenomenon. We had explicitly told people we were interested in their own personal sense of understanding. It's as if people just cannot distinguish their own understanding from what others know.

At one level, this is perfectly reasonable. Why should it matter that I personally have information in my head? If you ask me whether I know a phone number, does it matter if I've memorized the number, whether it's on a slip of paper in my pocket, or whether it's in the head of the person next to me? My ability to act doesn't depend on the knowledge that happens to be in my head at a given moment; it depends on what knowledge I can access when I need it.

Consider this hypothetical newspaper clipping:

> DARPA has classified as secret a May 2014 study about a newly discovered rock that the agency's scientists have thoroughly explained. The rock is similar to calcite, yet it glows in the absence of a light source. The authors of the study fully understand how it works; they provided a description of the remarkable appearance of the mineral and outlined future experiments. The future experiments are also being kept secret, so no people outside of DARPA have access to information about the new rock.

In case you're wondering, DARPA is the Defense Advanced Research Projects Agency, a research arm of the U.S. military. In this case, someone else understands the glowing rocks, but you have no access to the explanation because it's a secret. Now the knowledge is in someone else's head, but this time it is outside your grasp and thus not a part of your knowledge community. And lo and behold, people rated their understanding as very low in this case. The fact that others understood did not increase their sense of understanding.

In a community of knowledge, what matters more than having knowledge is having access to knowledge. A scientist studying rocks can't store in memory everything that is known about geology and related disciplines, but the scientist can keep track of the reference books, websites, and other experts that will furnish necessary information as needed. A more familiar example is medicine: There has been such an explosion of medical research that primary care physicians can no longer know everything they need to know about all the various maladies and concerns that patients present. Fortunately, they now have access to electronic databases that allow them to look up what they need to know when they need to know it.

Designing an Individual
for a Community of Mind

We've already seen one key ingredient for a community of knowledge in the work of Lev Vygotsky and Michael Tomasello. Individuals must be capable of sharing intentionality. They must be capable of sharing attention and goals with others and they must be able to establish common ground.

Another requirement has to do with how we store information. Communal knowledge is distributed across a group of people. No one person has it all. So what I as an individual know has to connect to the knowledge that other people have. My knowledge has to be full of pointers and placeholders rather than just facts. Let's say I know that the Sphinx is in Egypt but I don't actually know what the Sphinx is. That is, I think and reason about Egypt in a way that makes use of a belief that there is some object there that people call the Sphinx. But I've never seen it, so my beliefs about it depend on what others know about it. I would like to see it someday because others say it's cool. And I believe that it can be visited because I personally know people who have seen it, or at least I know there are people who have seen it. When I say "the Sphinx" to other English speakers, I assume we are talking about the same thing even though they may know as little about it as I do. So my knowledge of the Sphinx is really just a placeholder for others to fill in. The same holds for my knowledge of Egypt. It contains a placeholder that says this is where the Sphinx resides. My knowledge about Egypt is chock-full of pointers like this that tell me that the details are elsewhere.

What's amazing about people is that, at least when we agree, we're gesturing toward the same little piece of the world even though we have different scraps of information about it. And this leads to the second property of communal knowledge: The different bits of knowledge that different members of the community have must be compatible. We may not all always agree entirely, and in many cases we don't, but we have to at least be thinking about related things or the division of cognitive labor would fall apart. If we're building a house, the carpenter and the plumber better be on the same page about the location and shape of the bathroom, who gets to make which decision, and how big the appliances will be. Even if the carpenter knows nothing about plumbing, the bathroom has to be built to allow water pipes in and sewage pipes out. Similarly, our knowledge of things has to be structured so that the knowledge we expect others to fill in has an appropriate place to go.

The Benefits and Perils of the Hive Mind

In the preface to *Saint Joan*, his play about Joan of Arc, the teenager whose visions of saints and archangels stirred soldiers into battle early in the fifteenth century, George Bernard Shaw makes a surprisingly compelling argument that following Joan of Arc's mystical visions was at least as rational as following a modern-day general into today's battlefield full of highly technological and incomprehensible weapons of war. His argument is that the warrior of the twentieth century was driven as much by faith as the warrior of the fifteenth century:

> In the Middle Ages people believed that the earth was flat, for which they had at least the evidence of their senses: we believe it to be round, not because as many as one per cent of us could give the physical reasons for so quaint a belief, but because modern science has convinced us that nothing that is obvious is true, and that everything that is magical, improbable, extraordinary, gigantic, microscopic, heartless, or outrageous is scientific.

Hyperbole, for sure, but it is remarkable how much we depend on what we're told to get by in the modern world. So little of what happens to us is understood through direct sensory experience. From the alarm that wakes us up, to the toilet that we wander to, to the smartphone that we turn on (before or after our visit to the bathroom), to the coffee machine that welcomes us into the kitchen, to the tap that we use to fill the coffee machine, nothing is completely within our conceptual grasp. But we use these tools; we even rely on them, because they work (except when they don't and our life goes a little out of balance). We can thank the experts who created them, for we are dependent on their know-how. We have faith in the masters of modern technology after years of successfully using their devices. But when those devices fail, when the cable service goes out or the drain emits brown sludge, we're rudely reminded of just how little we know about the conveniences of modern life.

The knowledge illusion occurs because we live in a community of knowledge and we fail to distinguish the knowledge that is in our heads from the knowledge outside of it. We think the knowledge we have about how things work sits inside our skulls when in fact we're drawing a lot of it from the environment and from other people. This is as much a feature of cognition as it is a bug. The world and our community house most of our knowledge base. A lot of human understanding consists simply of awareness that the knowledge is out there. Sophisticated understanding usually consists of knowing where to find it. Only the truly erudite actually have the knowledge available in their own memories.

The knowledge illusion is the flip side of what economists call the curse of knowledge. When we know about something, we find it hard to imagine that someone else doesn't know it. If we tap out a tune, we're sometimes shocked that others don't recognize it. It seems so obvious; after all, we can hear it in our heads. If we know the answer to a general knowledge question (who starred in *The Sound of Music*?), we have a tendency to expect others to know the answer too. The curse of knowledge sometimes comes in the form of a hindsight bias. If our team just won a big game or our candidate just won an election, then we feel like we knew it all along and others should have expected that outcome too. The curse of knowledge is that we tend to think what is in our heads is in the heads of others. In the knowledge illusion, we tend to think what is in others' heads is in our heads. In both cases, we fail to discern who knows what.

Because we live inside a hive mind, relying heavily on others and the environment to store our knowledge, most of what is in our heads is quite superficial. We can get away with that superficiality most of the time because other people don't expect us to know more; after all, their knowledge is superficial too. We get by because a division of cognitive labor exists that divides responsibility for different aspects of knowledge across a community.

The division of cognitive labor is fundamental to the way cognition evolved and the way it works today. The ability to share knowledge across a community is what has allowed us go to the moon, to build cars and freeways, to make milk shakes and movies, to veg out in front of the TV, to do everything that we can do by virtue of living in society. The division of cognitive labor makes the difference between the comfort and safety of living in society and of being alone in the wild.

But there are also downsides when we rely on others to hold knowledge for us. Most of you reading this book are probably familiar with Alice (of Wonderland fame), but few people today actually read the Lewis Carroll novels that introduced her to the world. Many know Alice indirectly, through movies, cartoons, and TV shows, not through the unique and mind-bending experience of reading Carroll's marvelous books. If we don't know calculus, we can't understand the beauty of imagining time disappearing by letting it shrink into a moment and how that relates to the tangent of a curve. We can't see what Newton saw that made him so important that the authorities buried him in Westminster Abbey. That's one cost of living in a community of knowledge: We miss out on those things that we know only through the knowledge and experience of others.

There are also more dangerous consequences. Because we confuse the knowledge in our heads with the knowledge we have access to, we are largely unaware of how little we understand. We live with the belief that we understand more than we do. As we will explore in the rest of the book, many of society's most pressing problems stem from this illusion.

SEVEN

Thinking with Technology

Like it or not, the Internet has become a major player in all of our lives. It is our main source of information, a centerpiece in our community of knowledge. It delivers up an endless supply of facts, and we don't have to deal with any of those nasty human interactions to get them. This has led to a lot of great things. Our lives are made easier when we can answer just about any general knowledge question in seconds, purchase online and avoid the mall and its adolescent denizens, use apps to help us avoid traffic jams, and watch movies from the comfort of our homes.

Technology is transforming our lives, and it is happening quickly. Huge numbers of jobs may soon be outsourced to algorithms that can drive long-haul trucks or robots that can make perfect hamburgers. Commerce has moved online, radically transforming the economy and upending entire industries like publishing, music, and movies. Many of the things we used to do at the office can now be done at home. As a result, we're interacting less with colleagues at work. We're also commuting a little less. And we have immediate access to untold numbers of books, images, movies, and magazines, and a seemingly infinite selection of music and information sources.

All of this change brings with it concerns that we are losing touch with what really matters. The new normal may have brought us high-definition TV and sound systems that make you feel like the music you are hearing is live, but it has also led to a decline in direct human contact. Many segments of the population just don't go out to see live music anymore, and attendance at movie theaters is the lowest it's been since 1995. And, while less commuting does mean less stress, it is harder to establish relationships in a workplace if nobody is there.

The old joke about relationships now applies to smartphones: We can't live with 'em and we can't live without 'em. Just as we are reaching into our pocket to check our e-mail or Facebook feed for the ten thousandth time, part of us fantasizes about going somewhere remote and unplugging from the constant stream of information (at least for a few days).

The technological revolution has improved our lives in some ways, but it has also given rise to worry, despair, and even dread. Technological change is leading to all kinds of effects, and some may not be quite what we bargained for.

Some of our greatest entrepreneurs and scientific minds see even darker clouds on the horizon. People like Elon Musk, Stephen Hawking, and Bill Gates have cautioned that technology could become so sophisticated that it decides to pursue its own goals rather than the goals of the humans who created it. The reason to worry has been articulated by Vernor Vinge in a 1993 essay entitled "The Coming Technological Singularity," as well as by Ray Kurzweil in his 2005 book *The Singularity Is Near: When Humans Transcend Biology*, and most recently by Swedish philosopher Nick Bostrom, who works at the University of Oxford. In Bostrom's language, the fear is that technology is advancing so fast that the development of a superintelligence is imminent.

A superintelligence is a machine or collection of machines whose mental powers are far beyond that of human beings. The concern is that the existence of successful artificial intelligence (AI) will feed on itself. AI robots will be able to design smarter AI agents faster than humans can. Once they do, we'll have even smarter machines that can do an even better job of designing even smarter agents, which will in turn produce even smarter agents. . . . You see where this is leading. These futurists predict an explosion in the pace of development of AI akin to the explosion in the productivity of economies that we have witnessed since the industrial revolution. Machines will become more intelligent at an ever-increasing rate so that we will soon have a superintelligence that far surpasses the human capability to think and get things done. According to the doomsayers, once we have that superintelligence, all bets are off. A superintelligent agent will be better than people are at achieving goals, so if the agent has goals that don't align with humanity's, tough luck for humanity.

Technology as an Extension of Thought

The mastery of new technology has gone hand in hand with the evolution of our species. According to Ian Tattersall, curator emeritus with the American Museum of Natural History in New York, "cognitive capacity and technology reinforced each other" as civilization developed. Genetic evolution and technological change have run in tandem throughout our evolutionary history. As brains increased in size from one hominid species to its descendants, tools became more sophisticated and more common. Our predecessors started using rocks with sharp edges. Later generations discovered fire, stone axes, and knives, followed by harpoons and spears, then nets, hooks, traps, snares, and bows and arrows, and eventually farming. Each of these technological changes was accompanied by all the other changes that led to the modern human being: cultural, behavioral, and genetic changes. At each step, tools, culture, cognition, and genes changed together to create a new balance that gave our ancestors more power to alter the environment to their liking. New technologies, like irrigation channels, made civilization possible. Civilization led to the many and varied tools of antiquity, and eventually, to the current era of explosive growth in information technology that started in the middle of the twentieth century. For better or for worse, society and technology have always fed each other's transformations.

Humans are made for technological change. Our bodies and brains are designed to incorporate new tools into our activities as if they were extensions of our bodies. We very quickly learn to move a cursor on a screen with a mouse or a trackpad as if we were moving our finger around the screen. When you write with a pen or pencil (if you still do), you sense the surface of the paper, not what your fingers are actually feeling: the pressure of the writing instrument. This is what allows surgeons to do microsurgery using robots. Similarly, we very quickly adapt to the length of a broom when we sweep the floor. We can almost immediately reach behind a couch with a broom as if the broom were a direct extension of our arm. Sushi chefs train for many years to master their craft. One of the hallmarks of an expert chef is the ability to manipulate the knife as naturally as a hand.

In each of these examples, our brain treats the tool we're using as if it were part of our body. So there is nothing unnatural about technology. On the contrary, using technology is one of the key things that make us human.

What's changed over the last few years and may explain some of the discomfort people are feeling is that technology is no longer just a tool that the user controls. Our technology now outpaces us in many ways. In fact, technology is becoming so advanced that it can seem like a living organism. An article of faith we grew up with is that a computer would always do the same thing if prompted under the same conditions because, after all, it's just a machine. That's no longer true. Now, as if we were dealing with a living creature, we don't always know how our computer is going to respond. The same command issued in apparently the same environment can lead to quite different behaviors.

There are a couple of reasons that machines have become unpredictable. One is complexity. Systems are so complex that we don't always know what state they're in. You think you've turned your phone off, but actually the screen has just gone dark, so when you put it in your pocket and a piece of lint touches the screen, it cold-calls your ex-girlfriend.

Another reason is that external events can affect a machine unexpectedly. Like living organisms, the Internet is constantly changing in ways that we can't foresee or control. These days, machines automatically update their operating systems and their applications. So when you turn on your machine, you can no longer be sure it is the same machine that you were using yesterday. The word processor or e-mail program that you spend twelve hours a day with may have changed just like your sixteen-year-old kid might be unrecognizable after a visit to his friend, the self-proclaimed hairstylist. Our machines can also be hard to predict because their operation depends on the amount of traffic on the network and we usually have no idea how much there is. Once in a while, network traffic simply shuts down our Internet connection. Like a child blossoming into a teenager, our favorite machines are becoming more and more unreliable. We're never quite sure what they're going to do.

One way the Internet has become humanlike is that it can try to trick us and even succeed. We think a web link is going to take us to a quirky video, but in fact it takes us to a warning that we'd better hire a company to clean our hard drives or there will be a disaster. Or we visit a website and mistakenly download malware. These effects are due to malicious people, not technology per se, but the complexity of the technology is what makes such evil possible.

On the positive side, technology is more and more like a living entity in the sense that it sometimes solves its own problems. It can be imbued with curative properties. When you cut yourself, you put on a Band-Aid and wait for the wound to heal. Nowadays, software bugs sometimes disappear on their own as well. An automatic update can actually be helpful. Or the next generation of hardware or software is just so different that the problem you've been having no longer exists. This is the beauty of ignorance. We don't know what's going on and yet good things happen when we're lucky. We rely on the community to make improvements without our help, even without our awareness.

One consequence of these developments is that we are starting to treat our technology more and more like people, like full participants in the community of knowledge. The Internet is a great example. Just as we store understanding in other people, we store understanding in the Internet. We have seen that having knowledge available in other people's heads leads us to overrate our own understanding. Because we live in a community that shares knowledge, each of us individually can fail to distinguish whether knowledge is stored in our own head or in someone else's. This leads to the illusion of explanatory depth: I think I understand things better than I do because I incorporate other people's understanding into my assessment of my own understanding.

Two independent research groups have discovered that we have the same kind of "confusion at the frontier" when we search the Internet. Adrian Ward, a psychologist at the University of Texas, found that engaging in Internet searches increased people's cognitive self-esteem, their sense of their own ability to remember and process information. Moreover, people who searched the Internet for facts they didn't know and were later asked where they found the information often misremembered and reported that they had known it all along. Many of them completely forgot ever having conducted the search. They gave themselves the credit instead of Google.

In a different set of studies by Matt Fisher, then a Ph.D. student at Yale with Frank Keil (one of the original discoverers of the illusion of explanatory depth), participants were asked to answer a series of general causal knowledge questions like "How does a zipper work?" They divided respondents into two groups. One group was asked to search the Internet to confirm the details of their explanation. The other group was asked to answer the questions without using any outside sources. Next, participants were asked to rate how well they could answer questions in domains that had nothing to do with the questions they were asked about in the first phase. For instance, they might be asked to rate their ability to answer questions like "Why are there more Atlantic hurricanes in August and September?"—a question not related to how zippers work. The finding was that those who had searched the Internet rated their ability to answer unrelated questions as higher than those who had not. The act of searching the Internet and finding answers to one set of questions caused the participants to increase their sense that they knew the answers to all questions, including those whose answers they had not researched.

Confusing how much you know and how much the Internet knows does make sense in a perverse way. The Internet is a multipurpose tool that has become indispensable. If we conceive of the human-machine system as a single entity that is performing a task as a unit, then the responsibility for performance isn't in the human or in the machine; it's in the combination. If I've consulted multiple websites to plan a trip—some to get information, others to suggest itineraries, others to make reservations—then who's responsible for the final plan? We've all made a contribution. If I hadn't been there, nothing would have happened. But each website that I consulted might have made a difference too. So we all share in the responsibility.

If you have used the Internet recently to work on a task, you'd find it hard to assess your ability as an individual to perform the task since it is so intertwined with the contribution of the Internet. All the evidence concerns the team, you and the computer operating together. And that team is naturally better at the task than an individual would be, so the evidence suggests that you're better at the task than someone who didn't have the advantage of the Internet at hand. Because thought extends beyond the skull and encompasses all the tools that are available to pursue goals, it's well-nigh impossible to gauge exactly what your individual contribution is. Just like if we're on a team and the team wins, then we win whether our role was large or small.

This has some worrying consequences. The Internet's knowledge is so accessible and so vast that we may be fashioning a society where everyone with a smartphone and a Wi-Fi connection becomes a self-appointed expert in multiple domains. In one study in collaboration with Adrian Ward, we asked doctors and nurses on the website Reddit about their experiences with patients who search for diagnoses on sites like WebMD before visiting their office. The medical professionals told us that such patients don't actually know appreciably more than patients who haven't consulted the Internet. Nonetheless, they tend to be highly confident about their medical knowledge. This can lead them to deny the professional's diagnosis or seek alternative treatments. In another study we asked people to search the Internet for the answers to simple questions about finance, like "What is a stock share?" Next we asked them to play an investment game that was unrelated (the information they looked up was no help in performing better in the game). We also gave them the opportunity to bet on their performance. People who searched the Internet first bet a lot more on their performance than those who did not. But they didn't do any better in the game and ended up earning less money.

The problem is that spending a few minutes (or even hours) perusing WebMD is just not a substitute for the years of study needed to develop enough expertise to make a credible medical diagnosis. Spending a few minutes looking up facts on financial websites is not enough to understand the nuances of investing. Yet when we have the whole world's knowledge at our fingertips, it feels like a lot of it is in our heads.

Technology Does Not (Yet) Share Intentionality

At the time of this writing, an example of the most advanced AI for helping with everyday tasks is GPS (Global Positioning System) mapping software. GPS devices were becoming common in the 1990s and early 2000s; once the smartphone was introduced in 2007 with its built-in GPS, they were omnipresent. As you're driving along, these formidable little systems map out optimal routes, display them visually, update their recommendations according to current traffic conditions and whether or not you've missed your turn, and will even speak to you. Their capacities and power are remarkable, so remarkable that they've completely changed the way most of us navigate. They have even changed many relationships, mostly for the better: No longer do couples have to bicker about whether to stop to ask for directions.

But notice what these amazing machines don't do: They don't decide to go the long route because you're on your way to your parents' house and you'd prefer to be late. They don't take the route that goes by the lake because there's a particularly beautiful sunset this evening. They don't suggest that traffic is really bad today and that you'd be better off staying home. They could do any one of these things, but doing so would have to be programmed in. What they can't do is read your mind to figure out your intentions—your goals and desires and your understanding about how to satisfy them— and then make those intentions their own in order to arrive at novel suggestions. They cannot share your intentions in order to pursue joint goals.

We do not share common ground with our technology in the sense that there is no mutual agreement between a machine and a user about what we know and what we're doing except in the most primitive sense. The machine can ask you if your goal is A, B, or C and respond appropriately to your answer. But it cannot share that goal with you in a way that would justify its taking the initiative to pursue a novel objective at the last second. You have an implicit contract with your machine that says the machine will do what it can do in order to help you pursue your goal. But you have to make sure you've told it what your goal is. The machine is not a collaborator; it's a tool. In that sense, the tools of AI are more like a microwave oven than another human being. Technology may be a big part of the community of knowledge by providing information and useful instruments, but it is not a member of the community in the same way that humans are. We don't collaborate with machines just as we don't collaborate with sheep; we use them.

The ability to share an intention is a critical part of what matters in an intelligent agent. Central human functions like language and conceptualization depend on it because, as we've seen, they are both collaborative activities. We suspect it's been hard to program a computer to share your intentionality because doing so would require the computer to be able to coordinate with others—to be aware of what you know and what others know; it would require an ability to reflect on one's own cognitive processes and those of others. No one knows how to program a computer to be aware. If someone could, we would understand what it means to be conscious. But we don't.

We are at an awkward moment in the history of technology. Almost everything we do is enabled by intelligent machines. Machines are intelligent enough that we rely on them as a central part of our community of knowledge. Yet no machine has that singular ability so central to human activity: No machine can share intentionality. This has consequences for how humans and machines work together.

One critical function of today's human-machine systems is to save lives, and they do it very well, especially when they're not killing us. There's no pretense anymore that people are alone at the helm of airplanes, trains, and industrial machinery. They are surrounded by sophisticated technology that makes what they are doing possible. People even have less control of cars than they used to. Cars today have on the order of fifty microprocessors each. Some are there to keep you comfortable and entertained via satellite radio. Many of them are there to help you control the car: power steering setups can use computers to adjust the force you need to apply at different speeds and antilock brakes use computers to prevent skidding. And the automation revolution is just beginning: Completely automated cars are no longer science fiction. In late 2015, Elon Musk, CEO of Tesla Motors, stated that the technology for full automation will be perfected in about two years, though it may take government regulators longer to work out the legal issues before driverless cars start taking over the roads.

With larger vehicles, technology has already changed the playing field. Modern airplanes simply cannot be flown without the help of automation. The most advanced military jets are fly-by-wire: They are so unstable that they require an automated system that can sense and act many times more quickly than a human operator to maintain control. Our dependence on smart technology has led to a paradox. As the technology improves, it becomes more reliable and more efficient. And because it's reliable and efficient, human operators start to depend on it even more. Eventually they lose focus, become distracted, and check out, leaving the system to run on its own. In the most extreme case, piloting a massive airliner could become a passive occupation, like watching TV. This is fine until something unexpected happens. The unexpected reveals the value of human beings; what we bring to the table is the flexibility to handle new situations. Machines aren't collaborating in pursuit of a joint goal; they are merely serving as tools. So when the human operator gives up oversight, the system is more likely to have a serious accident.

The automation paradox is that the very effectiveness of automated safety systems leads to a dependence on them, and that this dependence undermines the contribution of the human operator, leading to greater danger. Modern technology is extremely sophisticated and getting more so. Automated safety systems are improving. As they get more complex and include additional bells and whistles and backup systems, they get exploited to do more and more. When they fail, the resulting catastrophe is that much bigger. The irony is that automated systems on airplanes, trains, and industrial equipment can compromise overall safety. Because the technology doesn't understand what the system is trying to accomplish—because it doesn't share the humans' intentionality—there's always the danger that something will go wrong. And when the human part of the system isn't ready for the technology to fail, disaster can ensue.

Here's a case in point: An airplane stall occurs when the craft's airspeed is not sufficient to generate enough lift to keep the plane in flight. If it stalls, the airplane essentially falls from the sky. A good way to recover from a stall is to point the nose of the plane down and increase engine power until the plane's airspeed generates sufficient lift to keep the plane aloft. Stall recovery is one of most basic skills that prospective pilots master in flight school. This is why investigators were shocked when they recovered the black box from Air France Flight 447, which crashed into the ocean in 2009, killing 228 people. The Airbus A330 had entered a stall and was falling from the sky. The copilot inexplicably tried to push the nose of the plane up rather than down. How could this happen? A report commissioned by the Federal Aviation Administration in 2013 concluded that pilots have become too reliant on automation and lack basic manual flying skills, leaving them unable to cope in unusual circumstances. In this case, the flight crew may have been unaware that it was even possible for this plane to stall and did not properly interpret the warning signals provided by their equipment. This is a perfect example of the automation paradox: The plane's automation technology was so powerful that when it failed, the pilots as a group didn't know what to do.

You may have already experienced the automation paradox, thanks to the proliferation of GPS devices. Some people have such a close relationship with them that they do whatever their GPS tells them to do. It is easy to forget that your GPS device doesn't really understand what you're trying to accomplish. There are many stories of people driving into bodies of water and off cliffs because they were so busy obeying their GPS master.

In 1995 the cruise ship *Royal Majesty* was sailing along near Nantucket, an island off the coast of Massachusetts. The cable connecting the ship's GPS to its antenna became disconnected after being jostled by the wind. The crew unfortunately did not realize what had happened. The GPS did deliver an error message, a small chirp that emanated from the GPS display, but this was not enough to attract the crew's attention. In the absence of satellite data, the GPS system soon did what it was designed to do: It switched to dead reckoning (estimating the current position from a previous position using estimated speeds, times, and directions). It also stopped chirping. The crew failed to notice the small acronyms on the display indicating both this change ("DR") and the loss of input ("SOL," short for "solution," a rather confusing way of abbreviating "no longer computing accurate position solution"). Dead reckoning is only an educated guess; it cannot correct for winds and tides. So the ship's autopilot was operating on a reasonable but increasingly inaccurate estimate. The crew did monitor the radar map, but it displayed route information from the GPS's guesstimate, and this no longer reflected the ship's actual location. The crew also did not check the GPS against a second available source, a navigational system that triangulates radio signals from shore. An unfortunate coincidence finally sealed the ship's fate: A buoy meant to warn of the treacherous Nantucket waters was in the approximate location where the GPS system *expected* a buoy indicating the appropriate Boston harbor lane. The radar detected it, but the crew continued to think all was running exactly as planned. They didn't notice anything amiss until they observed the change in ocean color indicative of shallow waters. By then it was too late to stop. The 32,000-ton ship hit ground on the shoals ten miles from Nantucket Island.

Fortunately, the story has a happy ending. The *Royal Majesty* was freed by five tugboats twenty-four hours after hitting ground. Thanks to a double bottom hull, it remained operational and was able to deliver its passengers to Boston. It did, however, cost about $2 million to make it seaworthy again.

What can we learn from this near tragedy? The machines did what they were supposed to do. All the backup systems worked as intended. It's true that the machines didn't inform the operators in detail about what was going on. But that's asking too much of a machine. That would require that the machine understands what the humans need to know, and that requires understanding what the humans are trying to do. As we've already seen, that's just not something machines are capable of. Machines are tools, not true collaborators pursuing a common goal.

The only real mistake that occurred on board the ship is that the people in charge trusted their GPS. And they weren't being unreasonable. The machines had always been paragons of accuracy before. The officers were led on by their illusion of understanding. They thought they understood what their devices were telling them but they did not appreciate the importance of unobtrusive symbols that appeared on their monitor (a little "DR" and "SOL") because they didn't really know how the GPS device worked. They didn't know that those symbols meant that it was guessing and could be very wrong. And they didn't double-check because they were unaware of their ignorance. Their many years of successful navigation gave them a deep sense of self-confidence that masked their illusion of understanding.

One of the skills that comes along with being aware of oneself is the ability to reflect on what's going on. People can always observe and evaluate their own behavior. They can step back and make themselves aware of what they're doing and what's happening in their immediate environment. They can even observe some of their own thought processes (the deliberative, conscious parts). If they don't like what they see, they can exert some influence to change it. That influence is limited, to be sure. If you're sliding down a sheet of ice without an ice pick, then there's little you can do to stop. Similarly, if you're obsessed by some fear or desire, you may not be able to control that, either. But at least we have the capacity—when we're awake and conscious—to be aware of what's happening. To the degree that we have control over our actions (if, for instance, we're not being drawn uncontrollably to a big slice of chocolate cake in front of us), we can modify our actions. By contrast, machines always have to obey their programs. Their programs may be sophisticated and there are ways of programming them to adapt to changing environments. But in the end, if the designer of the program has not thought of a situation that the machine does not know how to respond to, and that situation in fact occurs, the machine is going to do the wrong thing. So a critical role for human beings is oversight—

just being there in case something goes terribly wrong. The big danger today is that no one has access to all the knowledge necessary to understand and control modern sophisticated technology. And technology is getting more sophisticated at an even faster rate than ever. There is something to worry about.

Real Superintelligence

Because computers don't have the ability to share intentionality and we see no evidence that they are on the road to getting it, we're not too worried about an evil superintelligence that will pursue its own goals at the expense of humankind. Indeed, we don't see any kind of superintelligence on the horizon. Machines without the basic human ability to share attention and goals will never be able to read our minds and outsmart us because they won't even be able to understand us.

But there is a sense in which technology is enabling superintelligence. The web has provided smart new tools for us to use, like GPS devices and operating systems that talk to us. But one of the most useful forms of web applications turns people themselves into tools. Crowdsourcing applications have created broader and more dynamic communities of knowledge than ever before by aggregating the knowledge and skills of large numbers of people. Crowdsourcing is the critical provider of information to sites and apps that integrate knowledge from different experiences, locations, and knowledge bases. Yelp and Amazon crowdsource reviews for services and products. Waze crowdsources maps of traffic conditions from the input of individual drivers on the road. Then there are sites like Reddit that allow users to ask questions and encourage anyone to provide an answer.

When done right, crowdsourcing is the best way available to

take advantage of expertise in the community. It gets as many people as possible involved in pursuing a goal. This means experts are more likely to offer their input. In the end, that's the best way to achieve an objective: to make use of expertise. Yelp integrates knowledge from restaurant goers who purport to know how good a restaurant is, and Reddit tries to identify who has the most expertise to answer someone's question. So crowdsourcing works best when those with the most expertise have sufficient incentive to participate in the community.

Crowdsourcing creates intelligent machines, but not through AI wizardry. Their intelligence doesn't come from a deep understanding of the best way to reason or through immense computing power. Their intelligence derives from making use of the community. Waze guides you through traffic by integrating the reports of thousands of individuals who know a lot about the traffic conditions where they happen to be located. The advance here is not in intelligence in the conventional sense. It is in the power of connecting people.

One of the big problems facing entrepreneurs using crowdsourcing is how to incentivize experts to contribute. Money is only one incentive. Experts also thrive on being right, often more than on financial incentives. Witness the explosive growth of Wikipedia. It doesn't pay contributors a cent. Nor did the *Oxford English Dictionary* when it first started gathering quotations to identify the meanings of words in 1857. The OED appealed to volunteers to read through countless English texts, and it is still doing so. Most experts love the opportunity to demonstrate their expertise, especially when their contribution is acknowledged. Contributing to the community of knowledge is in our collaborative nature.

Each of us has our little window on the world, a little bit of knowledge that we have access to. Crowdsourcing is a way of looking through tens, hundreds, and sometimes thousands of windows simultaneously. But crowdsourcing works only when it provides access to expertise. Without expertise, it can be useless and even detrimental. Pallokerho-35 (PK-35) is a Finnish soccer club. A few years ago, the team invited fans to participate in decisions regarding recruiting, training, and even game tactics. They voted using cell phones. The outcome was disastrous. The team did poorly, the coach was fired, and the experiment came to an abrupt end. For a crowdsourcing scheme to work, it's not enough just to have a big community; the community needs to have the necessary expertise.

Sometimes expertise is only apparent. Average user ratings on Amazon.com are not all they're cracked up to be. Their ratings do not correlate very well with the evaluations of true experts and are too high for beloved brands and high-priced items. Many consumers just do not have the expertise to accurately assess the quality of technical products like digital cameras and kitchen appliances.

But crowdsourcing can be effective. This was first revealed by Francis Galton in 1907 in a paper entitled *Vox Populi (The Wisdom of Crowds)*. He reports on a contest held at a farmers' fair in Plymouth, England, to guess the weight of a fat ox. The contest was open to everyone willing to pay a small fee with the hope of making a guess close enough to the ox's true weight to win a prize. Guesses came from experts like butchers and farmers as well as the general public. As Galton says, "The average competitor was probably as well fitted for making a just estimate of the dressed weight of the ox, as an average voter is of judging the merits of most political issues on which he votes, and the variety among the voters to judge justly was probably much the same in either case." Galton managed to obtain the tickets with the estimates and counted 787 legible ones. He found that the average guess was within 1 percent of the ox's true weight of 1,198 pounds. When it comes to judging weight, the crowd shows some wisdom. In Galton's understated prose, "This result is, I think, more creditable to the trust-worthiness of a democratic judgment than might have been expected." We may individually suffer from the knowledge illusion, but the expertise that's present in a crowd can overcome individual biases.

Crowdsourcing has been much ballyhooed in the business world. It is typically invoked to explain the success of sites like Wikipedia. A group of economists has sung the praises of a type of crowdsourcing called a prediction market. In a prediction market, people make bets about what will happen in the future. The amount that the crowd is willing to bet on a particular outcome is used to estimate the probability of that outcome. People are motivated to bet because the best predictor wins a prize like money or prestige. Experts are especially motivated because they are more likely to know what will happen than novices, and so experts tend to have an outsize influence on the market. Many government agencies and private companies have used prediction markets to make guesses about what will happen in domestic elections, international affairs, and business environments. They often enjoy more success than traditional forecasting methods.

Crowdsourcing is actually a primitive method of employing the community of knowledge compared to what's on the horizon. Web developers are just beginning to develop applications that allow communities to form dynamically to solve specific problems. The idea of these applications is to make collaboration simple by allowing teams of experts from around the world to come together temporarily to work on specific projects. A number of problems must be solved before these applications go mainstream: Experts must be induced to participate; methods must be designed to choose the right set of experts for any particular problem; cognitive labor needs to be divided up effectively; and methods need to be developed to fairly distribute both the risk and the rewards associated with each project. The success of these applications for collaboration depends on how well these problems are solved.

Platforms to support this kind of decentralized collaborative activity are just coming into being with futuristic names like Ethereum, Sensorica, and Colony. Ethereum is inspired by the success of Bitcoin, an Internet currency that is decentralized, not administered by any single entity. The information about who owns how much Bitcoin is stored in a public ledger of transactions called a block chain. A block chain is a sophisticated technology for maintaining a record of all transactions that is updated and stored across the network of Bitcoin users. Distributing the ledger of transactions across the network is a good way to prevent mistakes and cheating. Ethereum uses a block chain method to allow collaboration via decentralized agreement of everyone involved in a project. The assumption is that information is safer if it is distributed across the community, preventing any one individual from having too much access. Access to information means control, and the goal of these collaboration platforms is to foster equity: to allow everyone to contribute according to their ability and to reap rewards according to their merit. The goal is to allow communities to divide up cognitive labor for any sort of project in a safe and secure way. Once one of these platforms becomes popular, it will create an entirely new way of doing business. If it becomes the norm to do business through teams that are constantly changing alliances of experts, we will have to redefine the notion of a company. It could lead to an entirely new kind of economy.

Predicting the Future

The power of crowdsourcing and the promise of collaborative platforms suggest that the place to look for real superintelligence is not in a futuristic machine that can outsmart human beings. The superintelligence that is changing the world is in the community of knowledge. The great advances in technology aren't to be found in creating machines with superhuman horsepower; instead, they'll come from helping information to flow smoothly through ever-bigger communities of knowledge and by making collaboration easier. Intelligent technology is not replacing people so much as connecting them. The web is demonstrating that real superintelligence resides in the community.

Our community of human-machine systems will continue to evolve. Technology continues to get more sophisticated at astonishing rates, and the role it plays in our community will become even greater. But it's a mistake to think about technology as a growing menace with an ever-growing power to impose its will on us. Technology for the foreseeable future will be missing a key element of the secret of human success: the ability to share intentionality. So technology will not be an equal partner in the community of knowledge; it remains a subservient tool. What we're seeing instead is that a key developing role of technology is to make our communities larger by managing crowdsourcing and collaboration. Crowds are composed of human beings, so the enlargement here is in the contribution of people. In a continuation of history and prehistory, the key developments in evolution involve an interaction between human beings and technology.

But technology is getting more sophisticated, and in that sense, it is getting even more remote from its users. If most of us don't know how a toilet works, think about how poorly we understand the various exotic electronics and Internet sites that pervade our lives these days. We'll be even more ignorant about how things work in the future. The irony is that successful technology is always easy to use; it always seems familiar. So we will continue to feel a sense of understanding even though our understanding of these increasingly complex systems will be weaker and weaker. Our illusion of understanding will get stronger and stronger. Managing your life or running a business today already requires constant access to machines and to the Internet. As technology becomes more sophisticated, we will become even more ignorant about what's under the hood. We will depend even more on experts to keep it all up and running. For the most part, this is fine. Until there's a problem. When the technology fails—because of neglect, war, or a natural disaster—the complacency induced by our illusion of understanding will come back to bite us. We'll be lost. Our dependence on experts will be on full display.

We may no longer be chiefs of our domains. We are more like cogs, working with systems that we do not fully understand and therefore do not have complete control over. This means we have to be even more vigilant and remind ourselves that we really don't know what's going on. The good news is that new technology will have countless benefits—increasing safety, reducing effort, and increasing efficiency. Even better, we will benefit by having at our disposal more and more of the world's expertise as we learn to take full advantage of the community of knowledge.

EIGHT

Thinking About Science

A cts of destruction are usually repellent. This makes it surprising that one young man's act of destruction turned him into a folk hero. This man was an apprentice in a knitting factory in Leicester, England, in the late eighteenth century, at the dawn of the industrial revolution. When a supervisor chastised him for poor work, he flew into a rage and smashed his knitting machine into pieces with a hammer. (At least that's how the story goes.) The young man's name was Ned Ludd, and he would become the patron saint of a group of protesters called the Luddites.

The Luddites were disturbed by the fast pace of technological change in England at the time, which they saw as threatening their livelihoods and values. Their favorite tool of protest was the "Great Enoch," a giant sledgehammer—crafted by a blacksmith named Enoch Taylor—and they used it to smash industrial machinery throughout England. They also clashed with police in scuffles that often turned deadly. The Luddites claimed to be led by a mysterious figure called King Ludd, Prince Ludd, or General Ludd. In reality, no such person existed. It was a merely a shout-out to Ned Ludd's act of defiance in Leicester.

Protest movements based on political and economic griev-ances usually fade fairly quickly from the public imagination, and the details of Ned Ludd's smashing of his machine are not that well known today, but the Luddites have been a cultural touchstone for centuries. The reason the Luddites made such a mark is because the act of smashing the most advanced technology of the day symbolizes a deep strain in human thinking. Some people have always looked upon science and technology with distrust and apprehension, and despite the astonishing scientific progress in the last century, antiscientific thought is still strong today. At the extreme are self-identified "neo-Luddites," like the participants in the Second Luddite Congress of 1996, a meeting organized around opposition to the "increasingly bizarre and frightening technologies of the Computer Age." But you don't have to look hard to find numerous mainstream examples, examples that represent serious danger to our future well-being. A reasonable skepticism toward science and technology is probably healthy for society, but antiscientific thinking can be dangerous when it goes too far.

Perhaps the most important issue of our day is climate change, a debate suffused with antiscientific rhetoric. James Inhofe, a senator famous for bringing a snowball to the Senate in 2015 to argue against the reality of climate change, has been a leading antiscience voice for many years. In 2003 he took direct aim at seventeen of the most influential climate scientists, threatening them with criminal prosecution and calling them out for deceit: "With all of the hysteria, all of the fear, all of the phony science, could it be that man-made global warming is the greatest hoax ever perpetrated on the American people? It sure sounds like it." Inhofe's claims have been discredited, but his message continues to resonate. He's been elected to the Senate by Oklahomans in four successive elections, most recently in 2014, with 68 percent of the vote.

One of the most transformative technologies of our time is genetic engineering, and it too has been a target of fierce opposition. Genetic engineering is a wonder of modern science, right on the cutting edge. Genetic engineering involves adding genes to (and once in a while removing genes from) an organism's DNA to create a new variety. Some varieties of tomatoes, soybeans, and corn have been genetically engineered to be more resistant to disease, to produce larger crops, or to have a longer shelf life.

Beta-carotene is a chemical that occurs naturally in foods like carrots and sweet potatoes. (It gives those foods their distinctive color.) Beta-carotene is broken down by the body and converted to vitamin A, a vitamin critical to important bodily functions, including vision. In many countries in the developing world, children do not get enough beta-carotene in their diets, leading to severe medical problems. By some estimates, half a million children go blind each year from vitamin A deficiency. In the early 2000s European scientists developed a genetically modified variety of rice that naturally produces beta-carotene. They called it "golden rice" due to the yellow color imparted by the beta-carotene. Rice is a staple food for many children afflicted with vitamin A deficiency, so golden rice has the potential to do a lot of good. Yet some opponents of genetically modified organisms (GMOs) do not see it that way. For instance, in 2013 a group of protesters swept through golden rice fields in the Philippines destroying the crop before it could be harvested. A sad irony is that these were scientific test fields that were to be used to test the safety and efficacy of golden rice. The act of destruction destroyed not only the crops but also the scientific knowledge that would have helped to evaluate whether the safety concerns that motivated the protesters had any merit.

Vaccination is another issue in which opposition can have negative consequences. Measles was essentially eradicated in the U.S. by the early 2000s, down to fewer than 100 cases per year. Due to decreasing vaccination rates, cases of measles spiked to over 600 in 2014. In Boulder, Colorado, a highly educated and wealthy city where the children of one of the authors of this book attend preschool, 10 percent of parents refuse to vaccinate their children, defying decades of unequivocal medical research. Vaccine opponents often use the language of science. They appeal to (discredited) scientific studies and statistics. But vaccine opposition is often suffused with anti-scientific sentiment, expressing mistrust of medical professionals and a rejection of scientific research. Here's a good example. A popular anti-vaccination website that lists "six reasons to say NO to vaccination" prefaces the article with the most important reason of all, that doctors are not to be trusted: "Don't just take your pediatrician's word for it that shots are safe. It is possible for doctors to be wrong. They are human, after all. In reality, your doctor is simply parroting the standard line about vaccination from the American Medical Association (AMA) playbook. If you think you are getting their honest assessment, think again."

The Public Understanding of Science

Walter Bodmer, a German-born geneticist, is a professor at Oxford University in the UK. In 1985 he was appointed by the Royal Society of London, the oldest scientific society in the world, to lead a team to evaluate the current state of attitudes toward science and technology in Britain. The Royal Society was concerned about antiscientific sentiment in Britain, seeing it as a serious risk to societal well-being. The team's results and recommendations were published in a seminal paper, now known as the Bodmer Report.

Previous research had focused primarily on measuring attitudes directly, but Bodmer and his team argued passionately for a simple and intuitive idea: that opposition to science and technology is driven by lack of understanding. Hence, by promoting better understanding of science, society can promote more favorable attitudes and take better advantage of the benefits afforded by science and technology.

The idea that science attitudes are determined by understanding is often called the deficit model. According to the model, antiscientific thinking is due to a knowledge deficit and will disappear once the deficit is filled.

The publication of the Bodmer Report was a seminal moment that inspired scientists around the world to step up research on the public understanding of science. In the United States, the National Science Board has led the charge. Every couple of years they summarize the state of research in the Science and Engineering Indicators report. It is a major challenge to figure out how to measure public understanding of science. Science is vast and complex and no simple test could possibly be perfect. One of the elements that the National Science Board focuses on is performance on a battery of basic factual questions.

Here are the questions that have been asked most often since the National Science Board began surveying Americans about scientific knowledge in 1979. The answers are at the bottom of page 158. See how many you can get right.

QUESTION	PERCENT CORRECT
1. True or false: The center of the Earth is very hot.	84
2. True or false: The continents have been moving their location for millions of years and will continue to move.	80
3. Does the Earth go around the Sun, or does the Sun go around the Earth?	73
4. True or false: All radioactivity is man-made.	67
5. True or false: Electrons are smaller than atoms.	51
6. True or false: Lasers work by focusing sound waves.	47
7. True or false: The universe began with a huge explosion.	38
8. True or false: The cloning of living things produces genetically identical copies.	80

9. True or false: It is the father's gene that decides whether the baby is a boy or a girl.	61
10. True or false: Ordinary tomatoes do not contain genes, while genetically modified tomatoes do.	47
11. True or false: Antibiotics kill viruses as well as bacteria.	50
12. True or false: Human beings, as we know them today, developed from earlier species of animals.[4]	47

Beside each question is the percentage of people who got it right in 2010. Questions 7 and 12 are controversial because getting them right requires some respondents to violate their religious beliefs. If the questions are prefaced with "according to astronomers" or "according to the theory of evolution," correct responses to both questions increase to about 70 percent. Still, overall performance on these questions may dismay you. If people were just guessing, they would get 50 percent correct. If you feel the urge to laugh at how ignorant Americans are, think again. Respondents from other countries including China, Russia, the EU, India, Japan, and South Korea do no better, and most do a little worse.

In addition to asking these knowledge questions, surveys often ask about people's attitudes and typically find that those who get more answers correct tend to be a little more favorably disposed toward science and technology. In one study we ran in 2013, we administered the science literacy quiz and then asked people for their feelings about a host of technologies, including genetically modified foods, stem cell therapy, vaccination, nanotechnology, nuclear power, and food irradiation. People who got more answers correct were a little more likely to report that the technologies were acceptable, that they had fewer risks, and that they had greater benefits for society.

So there does seem to be some relationship between knowledge

---

[4] 1. T. 2. T. 3. Earth around Sun. 4. F. 5. T. 6. F. 7. T. 8. T. 9. T. 10. F. 11. F. 12. T.

and attitudes, though the relationship is fairly weak. But here's the real problem with the deficit model. Decades of attempts to educate people about science have been ineffective at achieving the aspirations of the Bodmer Report: to promote positive views about science throughout society by fostering scientific literacy. Despite all the effort and energy that has gone into promoting public understanding of science, the millions and millions of dollars spent on research, curriculum design, outreach, and communication, we just do not seem to be making headway on that goal. Antiscientific beliefs are still pervasive and strong, and education does not seem to be helping.

Vaccine opposition is a good example where education has been ineffective at changing attitudes. Brendan Nyhan, a political scientist at Dartmouth, and his colleagues ran a study with parents to test whether providing information can increase acceptance of the MMR (measles, mumps, rubella) vaccine. Parents were given specific information in various formats and then asked what they believed about links between vaccination and autism, the likelihood of serious side effects from the vaccine, and the likelihood that they would vaccinate their children. In one case, the information given included a bunch of potentially negative outcomes of failing to vaccinate. In another, parents were shown images of children with measles, mumps, and rubella. In a third, parents read an emotional story about a child who contracted measles. Finally, some parents were given information from the Centers for Disease Control and Prevention debunking the link between vaccines and autism. The results were dismaying. None of the information made people more likely to say they would vaccinate. In fact, some of the information backfired. After seeing images of sick children, parents expressed an increased belief in the vaccine-autism connection, and after reading the emotional story, parents were more likely to believe in serious vaccine side effects.

So what's gone wrong? This is the question that has consumed

journal articles on the public understanding of science for the last
several years. The answer that has dominated thinking recently is
that nothing has gone wrong; the problem is with our expectations.
It is the deficit model that is wrong. Scientific attitudes are not based
on rational evaluation of evidence, and therefore providing information does not change them. Attitudes are determined instead by a
host of contextual and cultural factors that make them largely immune to change.

Committing to the Community

One of the leading voices in promoting this new perspective is Dan
Kahan, a law professor from Yale. Our attitudes are not based on a
rational, detached evaluation of the evidence, Kahan argues. This is
because our beliefs are not isolated pieces of data that we can take
and discard at will. Instead, beliefs are deeply intertwined with other
beliefs, shared cultural values, and our identities. To discard a belief
often means discarding a whole host of other beliefs, forsaking our
communities, going against those we trust and love, and in short,
challenging our identities. According to this view, is it any wonder
that providing people with a little information about GMOs, vaccines, evolution, or global warming has little impact on their beliefs
and attitudes? The power that culture has over cognition just swamps
these attempts at education.

Here's a powerful illustration of the influence of cultural values
on cognition. Mike McHargue is a podcaster and blogger who goes
by the moniker Science Mike. He grew up in Tallahassee, Florida, as
a member of a fundamentalist Christian church that supports many
beliefs that are counter to scientific consensus. The church interprets
the Bible literally, believes in Young Earth creationism, denies evo-

lution, and believes prayer can substitute for medical care. For most of his life, Science Mike firmly believed these things. However, in his thirties he began reading scientific literature and his faith in these beliefs began to waver. He read about randomized control trials that cast doubt on the healing power of prayer, physics research that identified the true age of the universe, and biology and paleontology studies that support evolution. His initial reaction was to completely lose his faith, but for a long time he hid his new beliefs from his community. Eventually a personal experience helped him rediscover his faith, and he is now a practicing Christian, but he continues to reject his fundamentalist church's antiscientific beliefs.

He hosts a podcast, "Ask Science Mike," which is a unique mix of science and religion. Much of the show focuses on detailed explanations of scientific topics, such as the theory of relativity, the cosmology of the big bang, and what happens when you die, but sometimes meanders into meditations on faith and the nature of God. In an episode discussing the taboo topics of masturbation and marijuana (both are deemed okay by Science Mike, in case you are wondering) a caller tells Science Mike about how he too has begun to question many of the beliefs of his fundamentalist church and asks for advice on how to deal with it. Here is Science Mike's response:

> Do I have advice on how to live when you're at odds with your community? Absolutely. Do not live at odds with your community . . . You are a time bomb right now. Because at some point you won't be able to pretend anymore and you will speak honestly, and there will be massive collateral damage and fallout in your church. It's time to move on. It's time to find a faith community that believes as you believe . . . When that happens, you're going to lose relationships. Some people cannot agree to disagree and those relationships can become abusive . . . There's

a lot of pain because there are some people who are dear to me that I can't talk to anymore . . . It is not possible for us to have the relationship we once had, and it's rough. I'm not gonna lie. It's rough.

When you listen to Science Mike talk about science, it's obvious that he is smart, thoughtful, and deliberative, and he has intellectual humility, expressing awareness of what he doesn't know and the complexity of the topics he grapples with. And yet for most of his life he maintained a host of beliefs that most scientists would say are completely outrageous. When he did begin to question those beliefs, the result was a complete upheaval of his life and the relationships that were most dear to him. This is the power of culture. Our beliefs are not our own. They are shared with our community. And this makes them really hard to change.

Science Mike's experience gives us a feel for where the knowledge illusion comes from. We typically don't know enough individually to form knowledgeable, nuanced views about new technologies and scientific developments. We simply have no choice but to adopt the positions of those we trust. Our attitudes and those of the people around us thus become mutually reinforcing. And the fact that we have a strong opinion makes us think that there must be a firm basis for our opinion, so we think we know a lot, more than in fact we do.

A good example of this comes from the study we described on page 157 where we asked people to answer the science literacy quiz and then asked about their attitudes to technologies. We also asked respondents to rate how much they knew about the technologies. There was no relationship at all between science literacy and people's evaluations of their own knowledge; those who got many answers wrong reported knowing just as much about the technologies as those who did well.

This confidence can seem pretty reasonable because it's never tested. We're surrounded by like-minded people who know equally little. We live in a community of knowledge, and unfortunately, communities sometimes get the science wrong. Attempts to foster science literacy cannot be effective if they don't either change the consensus of the community or associate the learner with a different community.

All of this should sound familiar by now. People tend to have limited understanding of complex issues and they have trouble absorbing details (like answers to factual questions). They also tend not to have a good sense of how much they know, and they lean heavily on their community of knowledge as a basis for their beliefs. The outcome is passionate, polarized attitudes that are hard to change.

Does all this mean we should give up on the deficit model? Is it really futile to try to educate people with an eye to making them more accepting of science and technology?

Causal Models and Science Understanding

One of the major limitations of science literacy research is the reliance on fact-based assessments of science knowledge. Fact-based science questions just don't do a good job of tapping the information that determines people's attitudes. Facts are hard to remember, especially when they are unsupported by deeper understanding. And very few of us have a deep understanding of scientific topics. As we discussed in chapters 1 and 2, the mind is just not designed to remember details, and our understanding of how things work is shallow.

Let's take one of the quiz questions as an example: True or False, antibiotics kill viruses as well as bacteria. When we assess science literacy using questions like this, it's natural to focus on the 50 percent of Americans who get the question wrong and ask ourselves how we can help them be more like the other 50 percent of Americans. Or if we are feeling less generous, we ask what the heck is wrong with these people? The media does not tend toward generosity. With the annual release of the Science and Engineering Indicators report, we expect a bevy of articles with headlines like "DUMB 101: 1 in 4 Americans is ignorant that Earth revolves around the Sun." But this misses the point. A different way to think about this result is to instead focus on the people who get the question right and ask whether they are really so different. The truth is that most people who know that antibiotics are effective only against bacteria know it as an isolated fact, unsupported by much detail. How many of us can explain in detail what the precise differences are between bacteria and viruses, what antibiotics do, and why they are effective against one but not the other? This should come as no surprise. It's just not realistic to imagine that ordinary people are going to retain a deep understanding of dozens of scientific topics. That's why we lean so heavily on our communities of knowledge.

In chapter 3, we showed that what the individual human cognitive system does is reason about causation. Humans construct and reason about causal models. Causal models are humanity's way of thinking and reasoning about the world, using our understanding of the mechanisms that make the world go round. In chapter 4, we saw that our individual models are often naive and inaccurate, biased to conform to our direct experience. These models also contribute to our attitudes.

Here's an example of how a common causal model leads to a false belief. Consumer researchers Veronika Ilyuk, Lauren Block, and David Faro have shown that most people believe that pharmacological products wear off faster when a person is engaged in a difficult task. For instance, a person who has consumed an energy-enhancing candy believes that its efficacy lasts a shorter time when he or she is working harder. In reality, how long most drugs work has nothing to do with how hard the user works. But the belief in rapid wear-off is very intuitive because our causal model for drug efficacy is learned from other domains in which greater effort does use up a resource faster. A car going uphill uses more gas than one traveling on flat ground, and a bicycle rider going uphill uses more calories than one going downhill. The error here is not just academic. This false causal model can lead people to consume more pharmaceuticals than they should.

Let's return to some of the examples of opposition to technology we talked about earlier in the chapter. Genetically modified foods are highly controversial, yet according to the American Association for the Advancement of Science, the science is clear: "crop improvement by the modern molecular techniques of biotechnology is safe." In the EU, opposition to GMOs is even stronger. Yet the European Commission declares: "The main conclusion to be drawn from the efforts of more than 130 research projects, covering a period of more than 25 years of research and involving more than 500 independent research groups, is that biotechnology, and in particular GMOs, are not per se more risky than e.g. conventional plant breeding technologies." So why does opposition persist?

The truth is that there are many reasons why people oppose GMOs, but it's clear that incorrect causal models of how genetic engineering technology works are partly to blame. Take a moment to ask yourself how much you know about genetic engineering. If you are like most people, you don't know very much. Yet many people have fairly specific fears when it comes to GMOs. A common concern is a fear of contamination. In one study we ran, about a quarter of respondents agreed that "a gene inserted into a food can migrate into the genetic code of humans who consume the food." Another quarter of respondents said they weren't sure, but this could be true. It's not true, but it sure is scary if you believe it. This explains why those who believed it also expressed the strongest opposition to GMOs in the study.

Even those who do not endorse the belief that GMOs can change their DNA seem to have other fears associated with contamination. In another study we asked people about their attitudes toward several different potential GM products. We asked them to rate both how acceptable the product was and how likely they would be to purchase it if there was also a conventional product available for a 20 percent higher price. We varied the amount of contact that the respondent was likely to have with the product. Some products were to be consumed, like yogurt and vegetable stock; others were put on the skin, like lotions; others sprayed in the air, like perfumes; and finally there were products participants would have little contact with, like batteries and home insulation. People would not accept a genetically modified product if it was consumable. They were a little more accepting of skin contact, even more accepting of products sprayed in the air, and quite willing to buy products they would have little contact with. Apparently, people think about genetic modification in the same way they think about germs.

Another important determinant of attitudes toward GMOs is the similarity between the modified organism and the organism the new gene comes from. Consider the search for a solution to citrus greening disease in the Florida orange crop. Citrus greening is a highly contagious bacterial infection that destroys citrus trees. It is fast moving and hard to eradicate. Fearing for the future of the Florida orange crop, producers have been experimenting with genetic engineering approaches that show promise in resisting the disease. One of the approaches that proved successful was to transplant a gene from a pig that encodes for a protein that conveys resistance. But the producers wouldn't move ahead with this solution because they believed that consumers would never accept a fruit that had a pig gene. They feared that consumers would think the modified organism would take on properties of the donor organism, beyond the properties conveyed by the specific protein the gene codes for. In this case, they might imagine that the orange would taste a little porky.

The orange producers were probably right. We replicated precisely this effect in a controlled lab study. People were much more accepting of a GMO product whose donor was similar to the recipient than one with dissimilar donor and recipient. In a separate study, nearly half of respondents said that a spinach gene inserted into an orange would make the orange taste like spinach. (It wouldn't.)

None of these concerns hold up if you know a little bit about how genetic engineering works. But they are certainly intuitive. People don't know much about how genetic engineering works, so they fill in the details using causal models learned from other domains. These concerns are not the only reason that people oppose GMOs. Some people respond to environmental concerns, others are nervous about large corporations wielding powerful technologies, and some people have diffuse worries ("This technology is so new, we just don't know what could happen"). But false causal models are an important part of the story.

Opposition to other controversial technologies may also stem from false causal models of how the technologies work. Take food irradiation, exposing foods to high-energy radiation to kill pathogens. Decades of testing have shown food irradiation to be safe and effective for decreasing food-borne illness and improving shelf life. But the technology has never caught on. Public opposition has hardened due in part to confusion between radiation and radioactivity. Radiation is the emission of energy, including things like visible light and microwaves. Radioactivity is the decay of unstable atoms, which gives off high-energy radiation that is dangerous to living things. When asked why they oppose food irradiation, many people report concerns that the radiation will "get stuck" in the food and contaminate it. Such a fear has no scientific basis.

Researchers Yanmei Zheng, Joe Alba, and Lisa Bolton have explored ways to mitigate such concerns. One approach that is relatively effective is to merely change the label for the technology so that it doesn't evoke radioactivity. When it is called cold pasteurization, people are much more accepting of the technology. Another technique is to use a metaphor to fix people's causal model. Comparing the technology to sunlight passing through a window improves evaluations, presumably because it is obvious that sunlight cannot get stuck in a window.

Vaccination is another case where false beliefs about mechanisms may lead to opposition. The most commonly cited reason for opposition to vaccination is a purported link between vaccines and autism. This claim has been debunked, but concern about it has persisted. Opponents usually blame thimerosal, a compound containing mercury, that is an ingredient in some vaccines. There is a grain of truth to this concern. Every child is taught that mercury is highly poisonous and can cause terrible injuries if consumed. The amount of mercury in vaccines is not enough to have detrimental effects, but it still feels scary to consume it.

Another claim often put forward by vaccine opponents is that a healthy lifestyle can take the place of vaccination. This too has a grain of truth. There is some evidence that lifestyle choices can boost the immune system, though the nature and magnitude of such effects is not well understood. However, the idea that lifestyle can take the place of vaccination is based on a vast oversimplification of how the immune system works. The immune system relies both on generalized protection mechanisms and a range of antibodies that target specific infections. Vaccines provide immunity to specific infections, and there is no evidence that lifestyle choices can provide such benefits.

Filling the Deficit

Beliefs are hard to change because they are wrapped up with our values and identities, and they are shared with our community. Moreover, what is actually in our own heads—our causal models—are sparse and often wrong. This explains why false beliefs are so hard to weed out. Sometimes communities get the science wrong, usually in ways that are supported by our causal models. And the knowledge illusion means that we don't check our understanding often or deeply enough. This is a recipe for antiscientific thinking.

Is there any way forward?

For the last few years Michael Ranney, a psychologist at the University of California, Berkeley, has been trying to find ways to educate people about global warming and make them more accepting of the scientific consensus. One of his first observations, which should come as no surprise to readers of this book, is that people have remarkably little understanding of how global warming works. In one study, he approached a couple of hundred people in parks in San Diego and asked a series of questions to gauge their understanding of the climate change mechanism. Only 12 percent of respondents were even partially correct, mentioning atmospheric gases trapping heat. Essentially no one could give a complete, accurate account of the mechanism.

Next, Ranney tried to inform people. In a series of studies, he showed participants a short, 400-word primer on the global warming mechanism. It dramatically increased their understanding and their acceptance of human-caused climate change. He is building on these results by creating a website that explains global warming in a short video. In fact, the video can be as short as you want: You can choose a "detailed" explanation that lasts a little less than five minutes or one of a series of shorter videos that go down to a brief fifty-two-second tour of the phenomenon. Preliminary tests have shown that these videos are having their intended effect.

Ranney's results are promising, but we are not naive enough to believe that there is a simple intervention that will instantly transform society into the science-loving utopia envisioned by Walter Bodmer. Still, perhaps it is too soon to give up on the deficit model. The lesson of this chapter is that to effectively influence scientific understanding and attitudes we need to understand the driving forces behind the deficits. New information that runs counter to our causal models is hard to absorb and easy to dismiss, especially when it contradicts the positions advocated by the people we trust. But it's harder to dismiss the discovery that one doesn't understand the mechanisms at play. This may be why Ranney's focus on the climate change mechanism has been so successful. The first step to correcting false beliefs is opening people's minds to the idea that they and their community might have the science wrong. No one wants to be wrong.

NINE

Thinking About Politics

F ew recent issues have excited Americans (and American political candidates) as much as the Affordable Care Act (more familiar as Obamacare) that became law in 2010. This law has been the subject of numerous debates and served as one of the pillars of the Republican attack on Barack Obama's presidency. The Republicans in Congress voted multiple times to repeal or change the law. Yet, even though it has engendered much excitement and posturing on both sides, few people actually understand the law. In fact, a survey by the Kaiser Family Foundation in April 2013, found that more than 40 percent of Americans were not even aware that the Affordable Care Act is law (12 percent thought that it had been repealed by Congress—it hadn't).

But this doesn't stop ordinary citizens from having strong opinions about it. In 2012, just after the Supreme Court ruled to uphold key provisions in the law, the Pew Research Center conducted a survey asking people whether they approved or disapproved of the ruling. Not surprisingly, responses were strongly divided: 36 percent in favor, 40 percent opposed, and 24 percent expressing no opinion. Pew also asked what the court ruled. Only 55 percent responded correctly. Fifteen percent said that the court struck down the law;

30 percent had no idea. So 76 percent expressed an opinion, but only 55 percent knew what they were expressing an opinion about.

The Affordable Care Act is just one example of a much broader problem. Public opinion is more extreme than people's understanding justifies. Americans who most strongly supported military intervention in the Ukraine in 2014 were the ones least able to identify the Ukraine's location on a map. Here's another example: A survey out of Oklahoma State University's Department of Agricultural Economics asked consumers whether the labeling of foods produced with genetic engineering should be mandatory. Some 80 percent of respondents thought it should. This seems like an excellent rationale to support such a law. The people deserve the information that they want and they have a right to it. But 80 percent also approved of a law stating that there should be mandatory labels on foods containing DNA. They believe that people have the right to know if their food has DNA. If you are scratching your head right now, note that most foods have DNA, just like all living things. According to the survey respondents, all meats, vegetables, and grains should be labeled "BEWARE: HAS DNA." But we would all die if we avoided foods that contain DNA.

How seriously should we take the vote to label genetically modified foods if it comes from the same people who believe we should label all foods that contain DNA? It does seem to reduce their credibility. Apparently, the fact that a strong majority of people has some preference does not mean that their opinion is informed. As a rule, strong feelings about issues do not emerge from deep understanding. They often emerge in the absence of understanding or, as the great philosopher and political activist Bertrand Russell said, "The opinions that are held with passion are always those for which no good ground exists." Clint Eastwood was more blunt: "Extremism is so easy. You've got your position, and that's it. It doesn't take much thought."

Why do people have such passion about issues they know so little about? Here is Socrates's answer in the guise of a response to a "political expert":

> I reasoned to myself, as I left him, like this—"I am actually wiser than this person; likely enough neither of us knows anything of importance, but he *thinks* he knows something when he doesn't, whereas just as I don't know anything, so I don't think I do, either. So I appear to be wiser, at least than him, in just this one small respect: that when I don't know things, I don't think that I do either." (Plato, *Apology*, 21d; trans. Christopher Rowe)

This guy, Socrates complained, just didn't know what he didn't know. Like so many of us, he knew less than he thought he did.

In general, we don't appreciate how little we know; the tiniest bit of knowledge makes us feel like experts. Once we feel like an expert, we start talking like an expert. And it turns out that the people we talk to don't know much, either. So relative to them, we are experts. That enhances our feeling of expertise.

This is how a community of knowledge can become dangerous: The people we talk to are influenced by us and—truth be told—we are influenced by them. When group members don't know much but share a position, members of the group can reinforce one another's sense of understanding, leading everyone to feel like their position is justified and their mission is clear, even when there is no real expertise to give it solid support. Everyone sees everyone else as justifying their view so that opinion rests on a mirage. Members of the group provide intellectual support for one another, but there's nothing supporting the group.

The social psychologist Irving Janis labeled this phenomenon *groupthink*. One common finding is that when people of like minds discuss an issue together, they become more polarized. That is, whatever view they had before the discussion, they are even more extreme in their support of it after the discussion. It's a kind of herd mentality. People arrive at dinner slightly concerned about health care or crime or guns or gun control or immigration or the amount of dog poop on the sidewalk. Everyone else at dinner feels the same way. By the time dinner is over, everyone's common feeling has been whipped up and everyone feels the right to demand action. This is a particularly noticeable problem today because the Internet makes it so easy to find like-minded people to confirm what we already believe while giving us a forum to complain about the stupidity and evil of those with a different world view. And those other guys don't want to interact with us anyway.

What makes the problem worse is that we're often unaware that we are inside a house of mirrors, and this insularity makes us even more ignorant. We fail to appreciate the other side's perspective. And on the rare occasion that we do hear what our opponent has to say, they seem ignorant because they fail to understand our perspective. They characterize us simplistically, without any appreciation for the nuance and depth of our position. The feeling that overwhelms us is "if only they understood." If only they understood how much we care, how open we are, and how our ideas could help, they would see things our way. But here's the rub: While it's true that your opponents don't understand the problem in all its subtlety and complexity, neither do you.

Taken to its extreme, the failure to appreciate how little we understand, combined with community support, can ignite really dangerous social mechanisms. You don't have to know much history to know how societies can become caldrons in an attempt to create a uniform ideology, boiling away independent thinking and political opposition through propaganda and terror. Socrates died because of a desire by ancient Athenians to rid themselves of contaminated thinking. So did Jesus at the hands of the Romans. This is why the first crusades were launched to free Jerusalem of the infidel, and why the Spanish Inquisition drove Jews and Muslims to convert to Christianity or leave Spain between 1492 and 1501. The twentieth century was shaped by the demons of ideological purity, from Stalin's purges, executions, and mass killings to Mao's Great Leap Forward: the herding of millions of people into agricultural communes and industrial working groups, with the result that many starved. And we haven't even mentioned the incarcerations and death camps of Nazi Germany.

The reasons for each of these events are multifaceted and complex, and we don't pretend to have offered any insight into the evil that permeated the first half of the twentieth century. We do note, though, that all the leaders of the time made use of a common and quite conscious justification for their barbarous acts: the need for ideological purity to enable the one true path to lead society into the future. It seems pretty safe to say in hindsight that none of the leaders who preached a rigid orthodoxy in that era turned out to be right. They all suffered from an illusion of understanding, and so did their followers. And the consequences of those illusions were appalling.

Shattering Illusions

The illusion of explanatory depth enables people to hold much stronger positions than they can support. To verify this point, we ran an experiment using the procedure that we introduced in chapter 1, Rozenblit and Keil's clever method to demonstrate the illusion of explanatory depth. But this time, instead of asking about everyday objects, as they did, we asked about various political issues. We asked participants whether they supported or rejected various policies that were hot-button issues at the time (2012):

- Whether there should be a national flat tax
- Whether there should be a cap-and-trade program on carbon emissions
- Whether there should be unilateral sanctions on Iran
- Whether the retirement age for Social Security should be raised
- Whether there should be a single-payer health care system
- Whether there should be merit-based pay for teachers

As in the standard procedure, we first asked people to rate their understanding of an issue on a scale of 1 to 7. Next we asked them to provide an explanation of all the effects that the policy would lead to. For instance, the instructions for the cap-and-trade issue read, "Please describe all the details you know about the impact of instituting a cap-and-trade system for carbon emissions, going from the first step to the last, and providing the causal connection between the steps." Finally, we again asked them to rate their understanding of the issue.

As in most experiments of this kind, participants were pretty bad at generating explanations. With very few exceptions, they simply had very little to say when we asked them to explain how a policy worked. They didn't know the mechanics of policies in a way that they could articulate. And consistent with their inability to explain, they rated their understanding the second time lower than their understanding the first time. They showed an illusion of explanatory depth. Their attempt to explain the issue revealed to them that they didn't understand it as well as they thought they had. We conclude that, just as people overrate their own understanding of toilets and can openers, they also overrate their understanding of political policies.

What we really wanted to know in this experiment was not whether people suffered from—or enjoyed—an illusion. What we wanted to know was whether the attempt to explain would make them less extreme in their position on the issue. We already knew that the attempt to explain had made them realize they didn't understand the issue as well as they thought they had. Would they incorporate this awareness into their attitude and modify their positions? In other words, would their failed attempt to explain increase their humility and decrease their confidence that their position was correct?

To find out, we asked them not only to rate their understanding, but also to rate their position on the issue, also on a 1–7 scale where 1 meant strongly for the policy and 7 meant strongly against. And again, we asked them both before and after they explained what the consequences of the policy would be. Then we measured how extreme their position was by seeing how far their judgment was from the midpoint of the scale (4), the value that indicates they had no opinion one way or the other. In this way, we combined scores of 1 (firmly in support of) and 7 (firmly against) because both are the most extreme scores possible.

We found that attempting to explain how a policy worked not only reduced our participants' sense of understanding, it also reduced the extremity of their position. If we consider the whole group together, the fact that people were on average less extreme means that the group as a whole was less polarized after the explanation exercise. The attempt to explain caused their positions to converge.

There is a counterintuitive aspect to these results. One interpretation of the findings is that asking people to think about an issue caused them to realize how little they understand and to consequently moderate their position. But other studies that have asked people to think about positions have actually made people more extreme, not less, presumably for the same reason that having people discuss their position in a group makes them more extreme. Usually when people think about their position on an issue, they recollect why they believe what they do and they generate arguments in favor of the position they already have. They don't engage in causal explanations about how the policy would lead to good or bad outcomes.

These are very different forms of thinking. Usually when people think about and talk about policies, they are not engaged in causal explanation. Most discourse about policy is about why we believe what we do: who agrees with us, why we hold whatever value the policy addresses, what we heard about it on the news the other day. Our experiment asked people to do something difficult and unusual, to causally explain the effects of a policy. That task requires engaging the details of the policy and spelling out how the policy would interact with a complicated world.

Causal explanation may be hard, but it has a benefit beyond the opportunity to learn. The beauty of causal explanation is that it takes explainers outside of their own belief systems. Imagine a new law came into effect tomorrow that limited everybody's water usage in your region to ten gallons a day. What consequences would arise in the short term? What about the long term? What would happen to real estate values where you live? What would happen to real estate values in regions close by? Would standards of cleanliness change? These are tough questions. But notice that the only way to answer them is to imagine a different world—one in which people use much less water—and to reason about what that world would be like. You have to think about your priorities (would you first wash yourself, your clothes, or your dishes?), but you can't focus entirely on yourself to answer the question. You have to think about how others would react and what would have to change.

You can't consider the implications of a policy by ruminating on how you feel about it. You are forced to think about the policy on its own terms, how it would actually be implemented and by whom and what would happen next in the world. This kind of thinking beyond yourself may be critical for moderating political opinion. Getting people to think beyond their own interests and experiences may be necessary for reducing their hubris and thereby reducing polarization. Causal explanation may be the only form of thinking that will shatter the illusion of explanatory depth and change people's attitudes.

To find out, we ran yet another experiment. This experiment included a group that was asked to do pretty much the same thing as the group in the first experiment, but instead of generating a causal explanation, they generated reasons they had for holding whatever position they had. They were asked to state precisely why they felt the way they did about the policy. Instead of getting outside their own interests by thinking about the policy on its own terms, we asked them specifically to think about the policy from their own perspective. In this way, we asked them to do what people normally do when thinking about political policy. Participants answered the same questions as those in the first experiment: They rated their understanding of the issue and their position on it both before and after generating reasons.

Generating reasons rather than a causal explanation led to quite different behavior: Participants showed no decrease in their sense of understanding, nor did they moderate their positions. Unlike generating a causal explanation, generating reasons had no effect on their illusion of understanding and left them just as extreme as they were before. Finding reasons is pretty easy. You can justify your position on cap and trade by appealing to your belief that it will help the environment. You can make this claim without appreciating how shallow your understanding of cap and trade is. In stark contrast, when you are asked to produce a causal explanation, you are forced to confront the gaps in your knowledge.

This suggests that causal explanation is special. People's positions can be moderated by having them think about the issue, but they cannot think about the issue in the usual way we think about political issues. Pondering your reasons for your position will do nothing but reinforce what you already believe. What you have to do is think about the issue on its own terms, think about exactly what policy you want to implement and what the direct consequences of that policy would be and what the consequences of those consequences would be in turn. You have to think more deeply about how things work than most people do.

You might not be too impressed by the fact that we got people to change a rating that indicated their attitude toward the policy. Their rating might not reflect their real attitude but just what they were willing to say to us. So in another experiment we pushed participants a little harder. We tested two groups. One gave causal explanations and the other gave reasons, as in the previous experiment. Then we gave them a decision to make. Instead of asking for a rating of their position, we offered both groups a small amount of money and gave them a choice. They had four options. They could:

1. Donate the money to an advocacy group in favor of their position.
2. Donate to an advocacy group against their position.
3. Keep the money.
4. Turn it down (thereby giving it back to the experimenters).

Not too surprisingly, few people chose either 2 or 4 (they neither donated it to an advocacy group against their position nor turned it down). The group who provided reasons acted as you would expect. Those who initially had a strong position on the issue were more likely to donate than those who were more moderate. But this difference disappeared in the group who tried to generate causal explanations. Those who were initially more extreme donated no more often than those who were initially more moderate. This suggests that causal explanation made the extremists more uncertain about their positions, and this uncertainty changed their behavior. Realizing the limits of their understanding made them less likely to want to take action to push their position forward.

People often have strong positions on issues, positions that are generally based on very little, certainly very little that they can articulate. But it doesn't have to be that way. Our research shows that shattering people's illusion of understanding by asking them to generate a detailed causal explanation also makes them less extreme. Given the negative consequences of extremism—including political deadlock, terror, and war—this seems like a good thing.

Values Versus Consequences

What does shape people's attitudes toward political policies? We've seen that careful analysis of the consequences of those policies matters a lot less than you might think and that the community one is embedded in matters a lot more. But it's important to recognize another critical driver of people's opinions: There are certain values that we hold sacred, and no amount of discussion is going to change them.

Jonathan Haidt argues that moral conclusions are rarely based on much reasoning but come instead from intuitions and feelings. His strongest evidence for saying this comes from cases that he calls *moral dumbfounding*. To demonstrate this, he offered the following scenario (beware: It's designed to cause discomfort):

Julie and Mark are brother and sister. They are traveling together in France on summer vacation from college. One night they are staying alone in a cabin near the beach. They decide that it would be interesting and fun if they tried making love. At the very least, it would be a new experience for each of them. Julie was already taking birth control pills, but Mark uses a condom too, just to be safe. They both enjoy making love, but they decide never to do it again. They keep that night as a special secret, which makes them feel even closer to each other.

Most people who read this scenario have two reactions: First, they are disgusted. Next, they condemn Julie and Mark, judging their behavior to be morally outrageous. So far, this isn't breaking news. Most societies have an incest taboo. What is more telling is that people cannot produce a reason to justify their response. Most people hem and haw and just appeal to the wrongness of incest or to the fact that it's taboo. But these are just restatements of their moral reactions; they don't say much more than "this action is wrong." Haidt has shrewdly constructed the scenario to rule out most reasons for moral outrage by eliminating the negative consequences of what Julie and Mark did. You might think they shouldn't have made love because babies born to siblings are likely to have birth defects. But this doesn't fly because Julie and Mark used two forms of contraception. You can't argue that it would ruin their relationship because it didn't. You can't complain that it would ruin their other relationships because nobody else knows. And yet most people have a strong negative reaction and stick to their guns. Reasons be damned.

Apparently, strong moral reactions don't require reasons. Strong political opinions don't, either. Sometimes whether or not we understand the consequences of a policy is irrelevant. Such attitudes are not based on causal analysis. We don't care whether the policy will produce good or bad outcomes. What matters are the values enshrined by the policy.

You might be like this yourself with regard to some policies.

Perhaps you're a supporter or a critic of any policy that would make it easier for women to get an abortion. Many people who are either strictly pro-choice or strictly pro-life have in common that they aren't concerned about what a policy concerning abortion would cost, what it would mean for women's health, or what the economic consequences would be. Abortion policy, such people would say, shouldn't be governed by a cost-benefit analysis based on projected outcomes. It should be governed by what's right or wrong. If you are pro-choice, your argument might be that women have a basic right to choose; nobody should be telling them what to do with their bodies. If you're pro-life, you might think that nobody has the right to end the life of an innocent fetus; that abortion is murder and murder is wrong. Either way, your attitude is not based on a causal analysis of a policy. It's based on a sacred value that governs how we should act regardless of consequences.

Many people's attitudes about assisted suicide are also based on sacred values, not consequences. One side believes that we all have the right when confronted with sufficient pain and desperation to ask a professional to end our life in a humane way. The other side believes that taking someone's life is murder regardless of whether that person wants to die and regardless of what the person's reason to die is. The effects of a right-to-die policy—the costs and savings, the suffering and guilt that would result and that would be avoided—all these consequences are irrelevant to everyone who bases his or her attitude on sacred values. For such people, the issue is one of right versus wrong.

Up to this point, we have focused on causal reasoning about consequences. We have argued that shattering the illusion of explanatory depth will reduce polarization because people will realize they don't understand the consequences of a policy as well as they thought they did, and that this will give them pause about taking an extreme position. But if people's positions are not consequentialist but based on sacred values, then shattering the illusion won't matter.

And it doesn't. We asked people about the two highly charged issues mentioned above that elicit perspectives based on sacred values. One concerned abortion (whether women should be permitted to terminate a pregnancy within the first three months) and the other assisted suicide (whether doctors should be able to give individuals experiencing extreme suffering assistance and approval to commit suicide). For these issues, we found no illusion of explanatory depth in that judgments of understanding were identical before and after causal explanation. We also found no moderation of opinions. People were just as extreme after causal explanation as they were before.

So our argument that causal explanation is an easy and effective way to moderate opinion applies only to certain issues, issues that elicit opinions based on outcomes as opposed to opinions based on values. That leaves us with plenty of issues—most opinions are driven by a consideration of outcomes. Opinions about everything from whether society should support nuclear power to education and health care are, for most people, a matter of how to achieve the best outcomes.

But they are not always talked about that way. Proponents of political positions often cast policies that most people see as consequentialist in values-based terms in order to hide their ignorance, prevent moderation of opinion, and block compromise. The health care debate is a perfect example of this. Most people just want the best health care for the most people at the most affordable price. The national conversation should be about how to achieve that. But such a conversation would be technical and boring. So politicians and interest groups make it about sacred values. One side asks whether the government should be making decisions about our health care, prompting their audience to think about the importance of limited government. The other side asks whether everybody in the country deserves decent health care, prompting an examination of the value of generosity and preventing harm to others. Both sides are missing the point. We all have roughly similar basic values: We want to be healthy, we want others to be healthy, and we want doctors and other medical professionals to be compensated, but we don't want to pay too much. The health care debate shouldn't be about basic values because in most people's minds basic values aren't the issue. The issue is the best way to achieve the best outcomes.

So why do politicians and interest groups so often take a sacred values position rather than thinking through the causal consequences of various policies? The most obvious answer is obfuscation: The policy preference that will earn them votes or money is not what a consequentialist analysis dictates, so they avoid the consequentialist analysis. The other answer is that thinking through the consequences of a policy is hard—very hard. It's much easier just to hide one's ignorance in a veil of platitudes about sacred values. It's an old politician's ploy. The secret that people who are practiced in the art of persuasion have learned over millennia is that when an attitude is based on a sacred value, consequences don't matter.

An evocative example of this kind of cynicism comes from research by Morteza Dehghani and his colleagues on Iranians' attitudes toward the pursuit of a nuclear program. As Iran antagonized much of the international community by doggedly developing their nuclear capabilities in the first decade of the twenty-first century, the leadership in Iran engaged in an active propaganda campaign to turn the issue into a sacred value for Iranians. The pursuit of nuclear power was pitched as a natural right of the Iranian people grounded in hundreds of years of national history and even religious dictates. They compared the current situation to previous experiences of foreign powers impinging on Iran's sovereignty, and they tried to turn the narrative into one about nationalism and self-determination. Dehghani's work shows, distressingly, how effective this kind of propaganda can be. Iranians who viewed nuclear power as a sacred value were opposed to any kind of a deal—even a really good deal—that would result in Iran giving up its nuclear ambitions. Fortunately, not all Iranians see the issue that way.

Examples can easily be found in the Western world as well. Americans' attitudes toward gay marriage have undergone a tectonic shift in recent years. According to the Pew Research Center, 60 percent of Americans opposed gay marriage in 2004 and only 31 percent were in favor of it. Fast-forward to 2015: 55 percent were in favor and only 39 percent opposed it. During this period, the debate shifted from being values-based ("gay marriage is wrong" versus "everyone has the right to marry") to a more consequence-based discussion about the benefits and harms of the institution of marriage. This shift in how the conversation got framed is not necessarily a cause of the changes in attitude. It could just as well be an effect: It could be that attitudes changed and this led people to talk about consequences rather than fundamental values. In all likelihood, it's both: Changing the frame of the conversation led some people to think differently about the issue and change their minds, while the number of people changing their position led to a shift in how people talked about the issue.

Whether we frame issues in terms of consequences or sacred values also influences the likelihood of achieving compromise in negotiation. Consider the Israeli-Palestinian conflict. Regardless of which side you come down on, most would admit that the situation is sad for both sides. Presumably there is an alternative world where both sides would be better off. Unfortunately, the dispute has become intractable, a conflict without a resolution in sight due to mutual distrust and antagonism. Negotiations seem to be stuck in an endless loop of moderate progress followed by recriminations and then collapse.

One reason for the lack of progress is that both sides have grievances that are construed as sacred values, making any compromise impossible. Jeremy Ginges, a psychologist at the New School in New York City, and his colleagues talked to both Palestinians and Israelis and asked them about their attitudes toward potential resolutions. On both sides, those who considered the conflict to hinge on sacred values reacted with outrage at any deal addressing grievances with material remuneration. A little consequentialism would go a long way in achieving a better world for Palestinians and Israelis. But consequences seem beside the point because both sides feel so deeply wronged by the other.

Sacred values perspectives are inviting because they simplify the field. All that nasty detailed causal analysis can be avoided. And sacred values can be correct. For instance, who are we to dispute the Golden Rule? We hold sacred that people should avoid harming others unless absolutely necessary. We're ready to affirm other sacred values as well. For instance, we agree that people are endowed with unalienable rights to life, liberty, and the pursuit of happiness. Sacred values have their place, but their place should not be to prevent causal reasoning about the consequences of social policy.

On Governance and Leadership

This discussion yields a variety of lessons about our political culture. One is simply a confirmation of an obvious fact about our political discourse: It's remarkably shallow. Citizens, commentators, and politicians frequently take a stand before engaging in a serious analysis of the pros and the cons of proposed legislation. TV shows often masquerade as news but in fact consist of participants screaming at one another. It doesn't have to be this way. As individuals, we tend to be ignorant. But our airwaves are an important medium to provide correctives and give thoughtful experts a voice. We don't expect shows not to be biased; all reporting has some bias. But the public does deserve an analysis; public voices should consider the actual consequences of proposed policy and not just overwhelm us with slogans and spin. If we encountered more detailed analysis, it might influence our decision-making.

We are definitely not insinuating that everybody should become an expert on every topic. That's not possible. It's hard enough to become an expert on just one topic. We've seen that the world is infinitely complex and beyond the grasp of any individual. People live in communities of knowledge, and to make the community work, there needs to be a division of cognitive labor. For knowledge to be shared within a community, the role of expert on any given issue must be filled by someone credible and informed. But not everybody needs to know everything. If the community is deciding how to provide health care to its members, then those people who know the most about the most efficient and effective method to distribute health care should be our guides. And if the community is deciding whether to build roads, then engineers are the people to ask, and they need to be trusted. Experts cannot tell communities what they want; that is something that communities have to decide for themselves. But experts can help communities understand what options are available and what the consequences are of taking one or another option.

Is this an elitist position? Is our appeal to experts just an appeal to an educated class that has its own self-interest at stake? Appealing to experts does open up a can of worms. Experts often have their own selfish interests on the very topics they know the most about.

The people who know the most about health care often work in the industry and thus have a financial interest in the way health care is distributed. Engineers might want to build roads because that's what they do; the more roads that are built, the more work there is for them. There are also more subtle interests at stake. Academics might provide advice that doesn't come from an objective, dispassionate analysis of a situation. Academics are famously wedded to their own theoretical perspectives. A professor of economics might advise signing a free trade agreement because the professor has published articles on the importance of open markets. A psychologist might give advice on parenting that comes from the latest theory of learning without any experience in actually bringing up children. A couple of cognitive scientists might write a book claiming that people live in an illusion of understanding to assuage their own feelings of ignorance.

Deciding on who has expertise and whether that expertise is biased is a difficult problem. But it's not insoluble. Indeed, society has many institutions in place to help. Experts come with recommendations that speak to their knowledge and credibility. They have histories that can be checked and reputations that can be assessed. Although information from the Internet does not come with a guarantee of accuracy, there is a fairly effective web industry that has developed to report clients' ratings of experts. As long as there are enough clients and the websites responsible for collecting and reporting the ratings are themselves credible, this can work well. Discovering the credibility of an expert is certainly a more manageable problem than asking everyone to become an expert and is, in fact, the only way to solve social problems.

The idea that decisions should be left to experts, that government should rely on technocrats, runs counter to a powerful force in American politics. At the turn of the twentieth century, one of the biggest problems the country faced was the concentration of wealth and power in the hands of a few corporations and trusts. Many state legislatures were beholden to these powerful interest groups. A movement arose to subvert the political influence of the legislatures' corporate masters using the tools of direct democracy. They developed a set of ballot measures that were voted on directly by the citizenry of a state or municipality, bypassing the legislature, thus taking power out of the hands of the politicians. The ballot measures came in various forms including initiatives, propositions, and referenda, and they remain very much alive in many states today.

Despite the auspicious origin of these democratic ballot measures, they have their detractors in large part, ironically, because the process of creating and promoting them has been usurped in some cases by special interests. A notorious 2015 ballot initiative, the California Sodomite Suppression Act, had several mandates. One was that any person who has sexual relations with someone of the same gender be "put to death by bullets to the head." Fortunately, that initiative was itself put to death in the courts. But the example demonstrates that direct democracy is vulnerable to manipulation just like other forms of governance.

There are a lot of reasons to be critical of ballot measures voted on directly by citizenry. Our main concern is that such measures neglect the knowledge illusion. Individual citizens rarely know enough to make an informed decision about complex social policy even if they think they do. Giving a vote to every citizen can swamp the contribution of expertise to good judgment that the wisdom of crowds relies on.

Reducing taxes sounds good in the abstract, but consider California's Proposition 13. This ballot measure, passed by a direct vote of the people of California in 1978, was designed to limit taxes on residential, business, and agricultural property, reducing them from an average of 3 percent to a cap of 1 percent of a property's sale value.

It also prevented increases in property taxes of more than 2 percent per year. The passage of Proposition 13 had a variety of effects. One was that homeowners living in areas with booming real estate markets were not forced to leave their homes by exploding tax debts. But not all effects were so positive. Many cities and towns rely on real estate taxes for their income. The ceiling on such taxes introduced by Proposition 13 has placed a huge financial burden on those municipalities. And it has distorted the real estate market in a number of ways. For one, it has discouraged owners from selling because, in many parts of the state with hot real estate markets, selling reduces the property's value by increasing its assessment and therefore the taxes that are owed on it. Proposition 13 has led to massive inequality between recent purchasers, who must pay large property tax bills, and old-timers, whose tax liability is capped.

The inequality resulting from Proposition 13 is a miscarriage of justice. In 1978, it would have been hard for an average person to see how the initiative would lead to this consequence. But an expert, someone who had studied the effects of changes to property tax rates, could have known. Changing the source of revenue of municipalities within a state is bound to have complex consequences, and very few people are in a position to predict those consequences in an informed way. Political representatives are elected to inform themselves and to consult with the experts. Individual citizens rarely have the time or interest to do so. They should not necessarily be the ones making the final decisions.

Winston Churchill surely went too far when he purportedly said, "The best argument against democracy is a five-minute conversation with the average voter." But he put his view in context when he echoed the verdict, "Democracy is the worst form of government, except for all the others." We too believe in democracy. But we think that the facts about human ignorance provide an argument for representative democracy, not direct democracy. We elect representatives. Those representatives should have the time and skill to find the expertise to make good decisions. Often they don't have the time because they're too busy raising money, but that's a different issue.

We have seen that a good way to reduce people's extremism and increase their intellectual humility is to ask them for an explanation of how a policy works. Unfortunately, the procedure does have a cost. Exposing people's illusions can upset them. We have found that asking someone to explain a policy that the person doesn't really understand does not improve our relationship with that person. Frequently, they no longer want to discuss the issue (and indeed, often they no longer want to talk to us).

We had hoped that shattering the illusion of understanding would make people more curious and more open to new information about the topic at hand. This is not what we have found. If anything, people are less inclined to seek new information after finding out that they were wrong. Causal explanation is an effective way to shatter the illusion, but people don't like having their illusion shattered. In the words of Voltaire: "Illusion is the first of all pleasures." Shattering an illusion can cause people to disengage. People like to feel successful, not incompetent.

A good leader must be able to help people realize their ignorance without making them feel stupid. This is not easy. One way is to demonstrate that everybody is ignorant, not just the person you're talking to. Ignorance has to do with how much you know, whereas being dumb is relative to other people. If everybody is ignorant, then no one is dumb.

Leaders also have the responsibility to learn about their own ignorance and effectively take advantage of others' knowledge and skills. Strong leaders make use of the community of knowledge by surrounding themselves with people who have deep understanding of specific issues. More important, strong leaders listen to those experts. A leader who spends significant time collecting information and talking to others before making a decision can be seen as indecisive, weak, and lacking vision. A mature electorate is one that makes the effort to appreciate a leader who recognizes that the world is complex and hard to understand.

TEN

The New Definition of Smart

You can't be a citizen in good standing of the North American community of knowledge without being familiar with Martin Luther King Jr. It's common knowledge that there was a civil rights movement in the 1950s and '60s, that King was one of its leaders and its chief orator, that he gave a stirring speech about a dream, and that he inspired millions before being ruthlessly gunned down in 1968 in Memphis, Tennessee. For good reason, he has become the primary symbol of equality and racial justice in the United States, and there is now an annual national holiday in his honor on the third Monday of January.

Sadly, that is pretty much the entirety of what many people know about Martin Luther King. We know he was a great man who made a speech. But most of us know little about the man, about the content of the speech, or about what specifically King was trying to achieve when he made it.

Perhaps an even bigger lacuna in our knowledge is what we know about the larger civil rights movement that propelled King to fame. He was certainly a seminal figure, but he was not alone in the Herculean effort that led to the civil rights legislation of the sixties. He was not even the only leader. Other great leaders included King's contemporaries who were also involved in founding the Southern

Christian Leadership Conference in 1957, an organization devoted to ending segregation. Among these activists were Bayard Rustin, Ella Baker, and Reverends C. K. Steele, Fred Shuttlesworth, Joseph Lowery, and Ralph Abernathy, all of whom demonstrated courage and determination. And civil rights depended on great men and women before King, like the abolitionist Frederick Douglass and suffragette leaders like Susan B. Anthony to name just two, as well as those on the front lines of the civil rights movement like Coretta Scott King, Rosa Parks, and the four African-American college students who jump-started the movement through a sit-in. They bravely took seats at the whites-only lunch counter at the Woolworth's in Greensboro, North Carolina, and were refused service but waited patiently in the face of threats and intimidation. These and many others were responsible for the tectonic shift that occurred in the legal position of minorities in America in the sixties. King operated in a rich historical context, receiving support and involvement even at the presidential level, from both John Kennedy and Lyndon Johnson.

The civil rights movement did not take place in a vacuum. The sixties was a time of significant cultural upheaval on many fronts, the best known being the country's attitudes toward war, drugs, and sex. After all, 1967 was the Summer of Love. The civil rights movement was only one component of the social revolution that took place in the sixties.

Martin Luther King Jr. was a primary activist in the civil rights movement and a great leader. But despite his cultural status, he did not single-handedly enact civil rights legislation. Yet he remains the face of the movement, as Mahatma Gandhi remains the face of Indian independence and Susan B. Anthony the face of women's suffrage in America. All three were great leaders, but they would have achieved nothing without supportive communities behind them; they did not operate alone.

The lionization of individuals, as well as our corresponding failure to appreciate the role of the communities they represent, is more than just a ruse to simplify complex histories. The images we retain of these individuals shape how we think about the events they participated in. Each leader has become a symbol for their respective movement and—in the popular imagination—each has come *to be* the movement. We say things like "MLK changed the face of America when he persuaded Congress to pass civil rights legislation" or "If it weren't for Gandhi, the queen would still reign over India." Statements like these are more than just figures of speech. The vast majority of people know little enough about the civil rights movement and about Indian independence that their understanding of each consists of not much more than the knowledge that these individuals made a huge difference. Cognitively speaking, the individual has become the movement and gets lone credit for complicated historical events involving millions of others.

Our tendency to mentally substitute individuals for complicated entities can be seen in how we talk about institutions. Americans talk about the Eisenhower administration or the Kennedy administration as if the president of the United States personally carries out all the functions of the executive branch of government. The Affordable Care Act runs to about 20,000 or so pages of legalese. It is commonly referred to as Obamacare. How much of it do you think Barack Obama himself wrote? Our guess is none. Our presidents may or may not be great leaders, but they are definitely human beings. It is certainly fair to hold them responsible for the actions of their administrations, but not because they actually performed those actions. For the vast majority of decisions, they are merely symbols, the faces of those administrations.

We don't just elevate individuals in politics. Hero worship dominates the entertainment industry. People tend to glamorize individuals and assign them credit and also blame them when things go bad. James Bond–type characters in Hollywood blockbusters don't only single-handedly prevent catastrophe but are often wine connoisseurs, formidable martial artists, and expert poker players, and of course, they always get the girl in the end. It goes without saying that their intelligence is off the scale. And people around the world love Hollywood films.

The truth is more boring. British secret agents actually need sleep, have to deal with anxiety, and (we suspect) aren't all candidates for *People* magazine's list of the most beautiful people. We have the utmost respect for Her Majesty's Secret Service; we're just skeptical that its missions are carried out by swashbuckling supermen. Though we don't have an inside view, we're guessing that the British Secret Intelligence Service is actually a community of mostly normal people doing a variety of specialized jobs.

The same bias can be seen in our understanding of science and philosophy. We tend to associate entire fields of study with a great man (rarely with a great woman). This man is pictured as having seen beyond the narrow mind-set and ethos of his era. He recognizes the limitations of his community's way of thinking and single-handedly develops a new paradigm that comes to revolutionize society by virtue of his staggering intelligence. Usually the great man succeeds only after a battle with the established interests and power elite. Popular history tells us that Socrates was forced to poison himself with hemlock to defend his right to freely espouse his beliefs, Copernicus shelved his theory that the earth revolves around the sun when the Church banned his treatise, and Galileo was banished to a small farmhouse in Arcetri, where he soon died.

These men may have been very smart, but they don't deserve all the credit for the accomplishments they are associated with. In every case, they were building on the work of others. Copernicus's heliocentric model of the solar system owed a huge debt to the ancient Greeks. They got a crucial fact wrong—that the solar system rotates around the earth—but Copernicus's theory is based upon the same observations and uses much of the same theoretical machinery that came down from Ptolemy. Copernicus proposed new trajectories for planetary bodies in a celestial system largely devised by the Greeks. Some great scientists have admitted that others plowed and fertilized the scientific field to make it possible to plant a theoretical seed. Einstein did. He said it would have been impossible to come up with the theory of relativity without the benefit of the great scientists that preceded him.

What seems so special about these great scientists is that they changed the world. Had they not lived, the world would not have benefited from their insights and we'd still be in the dark ages, busy trying to turn lead into gold. But it's not so clear that these individuals were critical. Had these scientists not been born, someone else might have made the same discovery. Over and over in the history of science, there are documented cases of different people working independently who came up with very similar findings or theories at roughly the same time. We all know the periodic table of the elements. Some of us have a love/hate relationship with it after having had to memorize it for chemistry class. The periodic table is the heart of modern chemistry. It is a table that lists all the elements—the building blocks of nature—in a way that reveals how they are related to one another and what their properties are. Most of us are taught that Dmitri Mendeleev formulated the periodic table, but there is wide agreement that Mendeleev did not do all the necessary work alone. He built upon the work of others, like the French chemist Antoine Lavoisier. But Mendeleev is given the lion's share of the credit. He was considered so important by other scientists that a new element was named after him, mendelevium.

A recent paper by Eric Scerri takes issue with the claim of Mendelevian priority. It introduces no less than five other scientists who came up with very similar periodic tables, all publishing their findings *before* Mendeleev's paper appeared in 1869. One (by the French geologist Alexandre-Émile Béguyer de Chancourtois) appeared *seven years* before Mendeleev's.

Our point is that Mendeleev did not develop the periodic table in a bubble. Mendeleev worked within a community, a community that was spread over Europe and perhaps beyond. It wrote letters, papers, and textbooks and had scientific meetings. Mendeleev surely made a grand contribution to this community, but without that community Mendeleev would have been nowhere. The periodic table has its roots in a community of knowledge.

This case is not unique. Simultaneous multiple discovery in science is startlingly common even today. At the time of this writing, there is a battle going on over who should have the rights to a patent for a process called CRISPR/Cas9 that is used to edit strands of DNA. What makes the case difficult is that two teams of scientists developed the basic ideas at roughly the same time.

Science seems to make progress not just because a genius comes along but also because conditions are right for particular discoveries. The right background theories have been formulated and the right data have been collected. Most important, the right conversations are already happening. The community of scientists is putting its combined wisdom together and focusing on the right questions, questions that are ripe for answering.

Human memory is finite and human reasoning is limited. Students of history can understand only so much. As a result, we tend to simplify. One way we simplify is through hero worship, by conflating significant individuals with the community of knowledge they represent. Instead of understanding the enormous complexity that goes along with multiple people pursuing multiple aims and trying to remember all of it—an impossible task—we wrap events up into a little ball and associate them with a single individual. Not only does that allow us to ignore vast amounts of gory detail, but also it allows us to tell a story. The story of the great individual's life becomes a surrogate for the complex web of interpersonal relationships and events that constitute a community. We do it when we think about politics, entertainment, and science. We substitute individual stories for the truth.

Intelligence

Upon encountering someone, our first impression is shaped by their personal attributes: their talents, skills, beauty, and intelligence. We may find out about their backgrounds and contexts: their upbringing, the help they've obtained from others, their home and work environments. But our initial focus is on personal attributes, qualities that the individual we're interacting with possesses. If we do pay attention to the individual's community and environment, we do so only as an afterthought. The individual captures the attentional field to create a first impression; learning about the person's context serves as a corrective to an impression that's already made.

Imagine you're interviewing someone for a job. You learn that the applicant was first in her graduating class. Do you infer that she had strict, disciplinarian parents that made her work really hard? Do you infer that she had an exceptional cohort of friends who helped her succeed and who inspired her? You might try to learn about these things, but what most people do is infer that she's smart. She came in first because she is capable; we jump to the conclusion that she is intelligent. This is hardly crazy. The conclusion is staring us in the face. She must have had some intelligence to have done so well. But what we will argue in the remainder of this chapter is that it's also unlikely to be the whole story. Significant successes require more than just individual intelligence.

What do we even mean when we talk about intelligence? It's easy to pick out good examples. Einstein was intelligent (very). We also sometimes agree on who has a screw loose and belongs at the bottom of the intellectual ladder (insert the politician you detest the most here). But do we really know what we're talking about when we talk about intelligence, or do we suffer from an illusion of explanatory depth? Once we try to spell it out, do we discover there's not much there?

Theories of intelligence tend to break it down into component parts. Unfortunately, there's little agreement about what the component parts are. One common and relatively old distinction is between fluid and crystallized intelligence. Fluid intelligence is what we're thinking when we say someone is "smart." The person has the ability to come to conclusions quickly whatever the topic and is able to figure new things out. Crystallized intelligence refers to how much information one has at one's disposal stored in memory. It includes the size of one's vocabulary and one's access to general knowledge.

Intelligence can also be broken down in terms of the skills that constitute it. One theory breaks it down into three separate skills: language ability, the speed and ability to perceive the world accurately, and the ability to manipulate spatial images in one's head. Another theory goes even further, arguing that there are eight distinct dimensions that underlie intelligence: linguistic, logical-mathematical, spatial, musical, naturalist, bodily kinesthetic, interpersonal, and intrapersonal. One researcher takes a practical perspective by arguing that intelligence reflects people's ability to formulate and attain their own goals. The basic skill set in this theory includes the ability to generate novel and creative ideas, analytic skills, practical skills, and skills related to wisdom that help to achieve a common good through the infusion of positive ethical values.

So different theorists break up the set of skills that compose intelligence in different ways and the debate among them continues. Psychologists have been studying intelligence for over a hundred years, and yet they haven't converged on a way to characterize it.

This does not bode well for the concept of intelligence as a deep and abiding property of human thought. It suggests that trying to identify the fundamental cognitive skills of individuals may not be the most productive way to understand the human mind.

A Brief History of Intelligence Testing

Psychologists like to define psychological concepts in ways that can be measured, in terms of actions that people can take in the real world. Psychologists like concepts that have an objective definition grounded in actual human behavior. That's why Freudian concepts like the id and the superego are largely out of favor. It's just not clear how to measure them in the real world. Intelligence is different; it can be measured. For modern psychology, a person's intelligence is just how well the person performs on an intelligence test, nothing more or less. Give people a test, score their performance, and define an individual's intelligence as that person's test score.

But which intelligence test? There are many of them, and if we're going to let them define what we're talking about, the choice could matter a lot. The first modern intelligence test was developed in 1904 by Alfred Binet and his student Theodore Simon. They gave children thirty tasks of increasing difficulty, from following simple instructions to recalling seven digits in their original order.

Generating a test this way sounds arbitrary. If we don't have a definition of intelligence to guide us, then we're just coming up with a test and ranking people according to their scores. And that's exactly what we're doing. In psychology, the study of intelligence is about how to rank individuals according to some cognitive ability. Binet was trying to identify struggling students to decide who should receive supplemental instruction. But this doesn't have to be arbitrary because we can choose tests according to how predictive they are. Psychologists are practical; they are looking for ways to predict who will succeed and who won't. Headhunters, human resources departments, graduate schools, and Ivy League admissions offices are all hoping to pick off the top few on the cherished spectrum of intelligence. The best test is the one that will do this job most effectively by predicting success most accurately.

What psychologists discovered as they tried to develop the best test is quite remarkable. It turns out that as long as you measure performance on a wide enough variety of mental abilities, the test you choose doesn't really matter. You'll get the same measurement—at least, one that's very close—regardless of which set of activities you use to grade performance. This is because all cognitive tests tend to be positively correlated, a fact that has been recognized since 1904 due to seminal work by Charles Spearman. Whether you ask people to solve difficult mathematical problems or test their ability to comprehend Virgil's *Aeneid* or test how quickly they can press a button when a light comes on (reaction time), as long as the task involves paying attention and thinking, there's a small but positive correlation in performance. That is, people who do well on one task are at least a little more likely than others to do well on another task, and people who do poorly on one task are more likely to do poorly on another. The fact that all tests are correlated implies that there's something in common to all tests; something that they are all picking up on that separates those who do well from those who do poorly. Spearman called this commonality general intelligence.

Spearman's real claim to fame is that he devised a sophisticated mathematical way to use an individual's test results to assign that person an intelligence score, using a method called factor analysis. Factor analysis takes everyone's score on each test and ferrets out the underlying dimension that all tests have in common. Your score on this dimension is your intelligence score.

The underlying dimension revealed by factor analysis is called *g* for—you guessed it—general intelligence. Psychologists like it because it satisfies their yearning to have numerical measurements. You can simply give people a battery of tests and then use factor analysis to deliver an intelligence score. Thus g is a statistical construct. It's not merely how well you do on one intelligence test, but it's close. It's how well you do overall on a *battery* of tests compared to other people. The beauty of it is that you can use just about any set of tests as long as they are distinct from one another and adequately cover the different kinds of thought (spatial, verbal, mathematical, analogical, simple, complex). Psychologists like g because it is grounded in performance, and because it has some power to predict various important life outcomes. People with higher g scores do better at school and perform better at their jobs. In some studies, g is one of the best predictors of job success. One report combined data from 127 studies that together tested over 20,000 people and found positive correlations between a simple measure of g and several measures of job success.

Other, much smaller studies have questioned whether intelligence is related to skilled cognitive performance in real life. A study of racetrack betting back in the eighties tested both experts and nonexperts, including men with more than twenty years of experience at the track. It included a measure of IQ, the most common measure of g. It turned out that knowing someone's IQ score offered no help in predicting the person's ability to pick the best horses in a series of races. IQ was not even related to the complexity of the process the gamblers used to make their decisions.

But such exceptions don't really challenge the conclusion that g predicts how people fare in real life. Caution is called for, though. It is important not to overrate any single person's intelligence score. Note that a score on a battery of tests is influenced by many things. It reflects how well you understood the questions, your degree of confidence, how much coffee you've drunk that day, whether your boyfriend just left you, and a million other random events. More-over, there's a lot more to an individual's worth than how well the person does on a battery of tests, such as the capacity to care for others (or how much the person will contribute to your company's soft-ball team).

Nevertheless, for those who want to sort people into bins, *g* is the gold standard. It is the best score currently available to decide who will succeed in fields that require mental horsepower.

Inspiration from the Community of Knowledge

Society takes *g* scores seriously. While there's strong evidence for *g*—for measurable differences among people in their mental abilities—it is not crystal clear what those abilities are. The *g* factor does help predict success in school and the workplace, but there remain a variety of open questions about intelligence and what it measures. Maybe this is because we've been thinking about intelligence the wrong way. The standard conception is that intelligence is a measure of a person's intellectual horsepower and measures of intelligence are a means to rank people according to the size of their engine.

Awareness that knowledge lives in a community gives us a different way to conceive of intelligence. Instead of regarding intelligence as a personal attribute, it can be understood as how much an individual contributes to the community. If thinking is a social entity that takes place in a group and involves teams, then intelligence resides in the team and not just in individuals. In the rest of this section, we will argue that the best way to assess intelligence is by assessing how much an individual contributes to a group's success. An individual contributes to a team, and it is the team that matters, because it is the team that gets things done. An individual's intelligence reflects how critical that individual is to the team.

If we think this way, intelligence is no longer a person's ability to reason and solve problems; it's how much the person contributes to a group's reasoning and problem-solving process. This will involve more than individual information-processing capacities like big memories and fast executive processing units. It will include the ability to understand the perspective of others, to take turns effectively, to understand emotional responses, and to listen. Intelligence becomes a much broader entity when conceived of in terms of the community of knowledge. People can contribute to a community in a variety of different ways: through creative insight but also through willingness to do drudge work for extended periods, by being great orators and by being great navigators.

The upshot is that an effective group doesn't need a lot of people with high g scores; it needs a balance of people with different skills. Whatever the task at hand, be it hunting for food, building a home, or navigating a ship, it's going to have different components that require different skills. Performance will be best whenever you have a team that has the full panoply of skills required to do the task. Those skills are more likely to be available if people are working together. A team with complementary skills is most likely to satisfy all the demands made by the division of cognitive labor. Therefore, when you're picking people to be part of that team, each person's ability to contribute to the group is more important than his or her g score. Instead of measuring intelligence by testing individuals alone in a room, we need to test teams of people working in groups.

Let's think about this through an analogy. We have been arguing throughout this book that we should think about the mind in terms of a division of cognitive labor: that the mind belongs to the community, not to individuals, and that different people play different roles in making the whole community productive. This can be compared to the different parts of a car participating in a division of transportation labor. Each car part has its role and together they make the car go. To measure the intelligence of an individual in this way is like measuring the quality of each car part. We might give each part a battery of sophisticated tests. Perhaps we would weigh the parts, measure their strength and their age and shininess, and price them. We could do that and we'd expect to find relatively high correlations for each part. That is, the better parts would be made of better materials than the inferior parts and they would probably be lighter, stronger, younger, shinier, and more expensive. Every test would be correlated with every other test, just as with intelligence. And we'd be measuring something meaningful, the quality of a car's parts. But would we be measuring what we care about the most? Presumably what we care about with a car are its properties as a car—its speed, mileage, and reliability. We don't care about the properties of the parts per se. We want good parts, not for their own sake, but because if we get them, we're more likely to end up with a better car.

Sometimes we'd expect those parts to show some deviations on the battery of tests. The best tires are not necessarily the shiniest, and the best hubcaps are not necessarily the most expensive (depending of course on what you're looking for in a hubcap). The best fuses shouldn't be too strong and the best radios are not always the lightest. So tests give a hint about what's good: On average you want your car parts to perform one way and not another. But it's just a hint: The best parts sometimes do the opposite. That's because the tests are not a direct measure of what you care about. You care about how well the car works. You want parts that contribute to the working of the car, not parts that individually all perform in the same way.

An identical principle applies to people working in groups. To perform most tasks, you want people who make different contributions. To run a company, you need some people who are cautious and others who are risk takers, some who are good with numbers and others who are good with people. It might even be a liability for someone who interacts with people to be really good at numbers; customers will be more comfortable with a salesperson who doesn't make them feel stupid by doing fancy calculations that they are unable to follow.

Because we mostly work in groups, what we care about the most is the group's ability to accomplish tasks. Whether we're talking about teams of doctors, mechanics, researchers, or designers, it is the group that creates the final product, not any one individual. And it is the final product that counts. So what we really need is a measure of group performance, not a measure of individual intelligence. A team led by Tepper School of Business professor Anita Woolley has offered one. Instead of testing people individually, they gave each of forty teams of three people a variety of tests that included brainstorming the possible uses for a brick, a spatial reasoning task called Raven's Advanced Progressive Matrices that is often used as a quick assessment of intelligence, a moral reasoning problem, a shopping trip planning task, and a group typing task. Each team did each task together.

What we know from work on individuals is that performance on any cognitive test is positively correlated with performance on any other cognitive test. The collective intelligence hypothesis is that an analogous correlation exists for groups: that performance on all group tasks will be correlated and that a factor analogous to g (the researchers called it c for collective intelligence) can therefore be extracted from an analysis of group performance. They found just that. Although some of the correlations were pretty low, all tasks were positively correlated in the sense that a group who did well on one task was more likely to do well on another task than a group who didn't do well on the first task. As a result, they uncovered the c factor.

They also conjectured that the c factor would be a better predictor of subsequent performance on a different group task than individual intelligence scores would be. In other words, they tested the hypothesis that the sum of a group's intelligence will be bigger than its parts. To test this hypothesis, they gave each group an unrelated task (computer checkers) and looked to see whether c was a better predictor of the team's performance against the computer than individual measures of intelligence. It was. While c was a good indicator of a team's likelihood of doing well at video checkers, individual intelligence scores were useless at making the predictions. To predict a group's performance, you need to look at the group. Individual intelligence scores are not that helpful. By way of an analogy, if you hire a company to renovate your kitchen, it's better to have a group of semiskilled workers who cooperate with one another than to have a group of prima donnas who do their separate tasks with finesse but fail to align the cupboards with the counter.

Now that we have a way to think about a measure of group intelligence c rather than a measure of individual intelligence g, we have come full circle: There's evidence that c has some reality in that it can be reliably measured, but we're back to our original question about intelligence: What is actually being measured? What characteristic distinguishes effective from ineffective teams and helps to predict how well they will do on a group task compared to other teams?

Woolley and her colleagues offered the beginning of an answer to this question. They made some additional measurements of each group and found that indicators of group cohesion, motivation, and satisfaction did not predict how well groups did. Other measures did: social sensitivity, how often groups took turns, and the proportion of females in the group. Their data suggest that having more females helps a group because it makes it more socially sensitive (this is not a surprise to anybody who has spent any time in a boys' locker room).

The idea of measuring collective intelligence is new, and many hard questions about it remain. While concepts like social sensitivity are bound to be very important to a group's functioning, they don't tell the whole story. What is it about a group's dynamics that encourages social sensitivity? Why is that important for playing checkers together? In addition to hearing what all group members have to say, you also need good ideas to play checkers and the whole team has to recognize which ideas are the best. There are a number of other ideas that have been proposed to explain when a group will perform well, and the jury is still out on what c is measuring. Nevertheless, data are starting to come in that suggest that the success of a group is not predominantly a function of the intelligence of its individual members. It's determined by how well they work together.

Collective Intelligence and Its Implications

The notion of intelligence has fostered a deep confusion: We think of intelligent acts as performed by individuals even when communities are really responsible. You can see this confusion in how we think about successful companies. Internet start-up entrepreneurs share a mistaken belief with the rest of us: that ideas matter. It is conventional wisdom that the key to a successful start-up is a good idea that can capture a market and produce millions of dollars. That's how Mark Zuckerberg of Facebook and Steve Jobs of Apple did it. Because we assign intelligence to individuals, we give the heroes all the credit by attributing their ideas to them alone. But that's not how it works, according to some of the venture capitalists who fund new start-ups. As one of them, Avin Rabheru, puts it: "Venture capitalists back teams, not ideas."

Consider the view of Y Combinator, one of the leading incubators of early-stage technology start-ups. Their strategy is based on the belief that successful start-ups rarely, if ever, capitalize on their initial idea. Ideas transform. So it's not ideas that matter the most. Far more important than the quality of an idea is the quality of the team. A good team can make a start-up successful because it can discover a good idea by learning how a market works and then do the work to implement the idea. A good team will divide and distribute the labor in a way that takes advantage of individual skills. Y Combinator avoids investing in start-ups that have a single founder not only because a single founder means there's no team to divide up the labor. They avoid single founders for a reason that isn't obvious and yet is fundamental to teamwork: Single founders lack the esprit de corps that prevents individuals from letting their friends down. Teams work harder when things aren't going well because members encourage one another; they do it for the team.

Once you accept that we live in a community of knowledge, it becomes clear that most researchers have been looking in the wrong place for a definition of intelligence. Intelligence is not a property of an individual; it's a property of a team. The person who can solve hard math problems can certainly make a contribution, but so can the person who can manage a group's dynamics or the person who can remember the details of an important encounter. We can't measure intelligence by putting a person alone in a room and giving him or her a test; we can measure it only by evaluating the production of groups that the person is a part of.

How can this be done? What's the right measure of an individual's contribution to group performance? This is not a question that has received a lot of attention. To begin trying to formulate an answer, let's make the simplifying assumption that different individuals do in fact consistently contribute more or less regardless of the group they happen to be in. One approach is to measure the individual's personal contribution across many groups in the same way ice hockey teams measure the contribution of each player, using a plus-minus score. The idea in hockey is that a team will score more goals when a good player is on the ice and the other team will score fewer. So the quality of a player is indicated by a plus-minus score, the number of goals that the player's team scored while the player was on the ice minus the number of goals that were scored against the player's team. One could measure the contribution of a thinker to a group's problem solving in a similar way. When the person is present, how often does the group succeed and how often does the group fail? A person who reliably contributes to group performance and therefore has a high plus-minus score is "intelligent" in a sense that matters. This is potentially a way to reduce collective intelligence to individual contributions in a way that's consistent with the community of knowledge.

A measure like this can be hard to put into practice. One problem is that success and failure are often not as clear as they are in hockey. Is building a widget that wins awards but doesn't sell a success or a failure? Another problem is that if two people tend to work together frequently, then one's success could reflect the contribution of the other one (in the same sense that a man might be perceived as a social success only because his partner is good at making friends).

But the principle holds nevertheless. An executive might seem bright and active, be a great speaker, and provide inspiration all around. But if projects that the executive is a part of tend to fail, then the person may not deserve a big bonus. And when a manager is reviewing employees, it's important not to confuse quick-wittedness and an engaging personality with contribution. The question an employer should ask is whether the projects that the employee is involved in tend to be successful or not relative to other employees.

Every farmer knows that the hard part is getting the field prepared. Inserting seeds and watching them grow is easy. In the case of science and industry, the community prepares the field, yet society tends to give all the credit to the individual who happens to plant a successful seed. Planting a seed does not necessarily require over-whelming intelligence; creating an environment that allows seeds to prosper does. We need to give more credit to the community in science, politics, business, and daily life.

Martin Luther King Jr. was a great man. Perhaps his greatest strength was his ability to inspire people to work together to achieve, against all odds, revolutionary changes in society's perception of race and in the fairness of the law. But to really understand what he accomplished requires looking beyond the man. Instead of treating him as the manifestation of everything great, we should appreciate his role in allowing America to show that it can be great.

ELEVEN

Making People Smart

The 1980s were a challenging time to live in the urban areas of Brazil. Hyperinflation quickly made money worthless. Inflation rates varied annually between 80 percent and 2,000 percent. In one year, the price of a cup of coffee could go from $1 in Brazilian currency to almost $2,000. Poor Brazilians did what they had to to survive. Many poverty-stricken urban children sold goods on the street in lieu of going to school. Young urban kids were selling anything they could, including candy, tangerines, and puffed wheat. How much did these kids know? They hadn't gone to school, so it would be strange if they were masters of Brazilian literature, world geography, or algebra. But they had certainly been active selling things. They had experience buying merchandise to sell, determining prices to ensure profit, and making change—activities that all require arithmetic. And because of inflation, it required dealing with large numerical values. Maybe these street sellers had mastered the rudiments of arithmetic? Perhaps, despite their lack of schooling, they were better at arithmetic than kids who had gone to school?

To find out, some clever education researchers talked to a bunch of ten- to twelve-year-old street vendors as well as other kids of the same age who were attending schools similar to those the street vendors would have attended if they had gone to school. They administered a series of tests dealing with arithmetic and numbers to all the children.

The first thing they found won't surprise anybody who has tried to teach math to kids: Neither group was very good at basic skills like simply reading out the value of a large number. They didn't really understand what the various digits in a large number represent. What they could do was compare numbers. Both groups could tell you which number of a pair was bigger. Where the groups differed was in their ability to do addition and subtraction. The street vendors shined; the schoolchildren struggled. The street vendors could even make sense of ratios of large numbers much better than the schoolchildren could. When it came to skills that their livelihoods depended on, it turned out that experience was better than formal education (at least, the formal education that poor kids were offered in Brazil).

People are primarily designed for action, not for listening to lectures, not for manipulating symbols, and not for memorizing facts. Educators have known this at least since the philosopher of education John Dewey advised in 1938:

> There should be brief intervals of time for quiet reflection provided for even the young. But they are periods of genuine reflection only when they follow after times of more overt action and are used to organize what has been gained in periods of activity in which the hands and other parts of the body beside the brain are used.

Skilled teachers and learners know that simply listening to lectures, mindlessly manipulating symbols, and memorizing facts are not the best ways to learn. Activity is required. We learn what we need to know to take the actions necessary to accomplish our goals. If your goal is to make change on a street corner and turn a profit, you'll learn the arithmetic required to do that. This is not to say that classrooms are useless. Classroom algebra is surely of great value to those who want to work in high finance, prove mathematical theorems, or figure out how to send a rocket to the moon.

But much classroom learning is divorced from goals that students care about. It is often difficult for students to know exactly how they are going to apply reading, writing, and arithmetic in their future lives, so they are commonly expected to learn for the sake of learning and not for the sake of acting. This could be part of why educators carp so often about students' failure to understand what they read. The discovery that they don't understand often comes as a shock to the students themselves, who believe they read carefully. What shocks students is how poorly they do on comprehension tests. They study and study and feel like they have achieved a deep understanding, yet they can't answer basic questions about the material. This phenomenon is so common that it has a name, the illusion of comprehension, reminiscent of the illusion of explanatory depth.

The illusion of comprehension arises because people confuse understanding with familiarity or recognition. When you pass your eyes over text, that text does seem familiar the next time you look at it. This is true even if it's been a long time since you read it last. In an extreme case, psychologist Paul Kolers had people read inverted text (each letter was upside down). More than a year later, he found that the same people could read the same text faster than different text that they hadn't read before. They had retained a memory over the course of a year for how to read specific text.

The problem that students have—that we all have, actually—is that this sense of familiarity can be confused with actual understanding of the material. It's one thing to be familiar with some text or even to know it by heart, and another to really get its meaning. Many American students can recite the U.S. Pledge of Allegiance by heart without any idea of what they're talking about. This is why you often hear odd versions. Instead of reciting "One nation, under God, indivisible," some students apparently think their country has disappeared: "One nation, under God, invisible," and others recite as if it's been taken over by supernatural forces: "And to the republic, for witches stand" rather than "the republic for which it stands." And every rock music aficionado has wondered why people don't do a double take when they sing along with Jimi Hendrix's "Purple Haze," "'scuze me while I kiss this guy." We have no idea if Jimi kissed a guy or two, but we do know he in fact sang "excuse me while I kiss the sky." Even memorized text isn't necessarily understood.

Comprehension requires processing text with some care and effort, in a deliberate manner. It requires thinking about the author's intention. This apparently isn't obvious to everyone. Many students confuse studying with light reading.

So the conclusion we have come to in previous chapters—that people are more superficial than they realize, that we suffer from a knowledge illusion—extends to education as well: Learning requires breaking common habits by processing information more deeply.

Knowing What You Don't Know

We also suffer from the knowledge illusion because we confuse what experts know with what we ourselves know. The fact that I can access someone else's knowledge makes me feel like I already know what I'm talking about. The same phenomenon occurs in the classroom: Children suffer from an illusion of comprehension because they can access the knowledge they need. It is in their textbook and in the heads of their teacher and the better students. Humans aren't built to become masters of all subjects; humans are built to participate in a community (another point suggested many years ago by the great John Dewey).

If our role is to participate in the community of knowledge by making our contribution to its shared cognitive labor, then we must avoid the mistaken belief that the purpose of education should be to give people the knowledge and skills to be independent thinkers. One might assume that we go to school to learn things we previously relied on others to do and know for us; that the purpose of education is to make people intellectually independent. For instance, if I want to be a car mechanic, I might assume that I should take a course to learn what it takes to fix a car. Once I'm done, I expect to be able to fix cars. I might need some resources—like tools, parts, and a garage—but otherwise I should be good to go. If I want to be a historian, then I might assume I should go to school and learn a bunch of history—facts, trends, and timelines—and I should emerge with, at minimum, the ability to answer questions about the past. If I want to be a scientist, I go to school and learn the theories and data in my domain. When I come out, I should be able to discover new things, develop new and better theories, teach what I learned, or perhaps apply my knowledge to build new and better widgets.

This idea that education is for increasing intellectual independence is not entirely correct because it rests on another problematic set of assumptions: that the purpose of education is to expand your personal knowledge and skills; that the set of concepts you have about whatever domain you're studying should be new and improved following an education; that there should be more and more accurate knowledge inside your head coming out of an education than there was going in; and that you should be able to do more things.

These ideas aren't wrong so much as incomplete. The idea that education should increase intellectual independence is a very narrow view of learning. It ignores the fact that knowledge depends on others. To fix cars, a mechanic needs to know who can provide parts and who can deliver them, how to find out which cars have been recalled, and how to learn about the latest design innovations. Cars these days depend on technology that comes from all around the world. A decent car mechanic will have access to knowledge distributed throughout the community of knowledge within the automobile industry. Learning therefore isn't just about developing new knowledge and skills. It's also about learning to collaborate with others, recognizing what knowledge we have to offer and what gaps we must rely on others to help us fill.

Imagine you're learning about the history of Spain. It's not good enough to just learn about what happened within the borders of Spain. You also have to be aware of the Roman Empire, the Crusades, the history of the Moors, and so much more. Part of knowing the history of Spain is knowing about the context surrounding that history. You don't need to know it in detail—you can't, there's just too much of it—but you need at least a skeletal understanding of Spain's historical context. When you have that skeletal understanding, you'll know what other information is available and who to get it from. You'll be able to make use of the community of knowledge.

A real education includes learning that you don't know certain things (a lot of things). Instead of looking in at the knowledge you do have, you learn to look out at the knowledge you don't have. To do this, you have to let go of some hubris; you have to accept that you don't know what you don't know. Learning what you don't know is just a matter of looking at the frontiers of your knowledge and wondering what is out there beyond the border. It's about asking why. Instead of learning to ask about events that occurred in Spain, it's learning to ask about other countries and how they influenced events in Spain. Instead of just learning long division, it's learning to ask what you don't know, like why long division works.

As individuals, we know little. There's not too much we can do about that; there's too much to know. Obviously we can learn some facts and theories, and we can develop skills. But we also have to learn how to make use of others' knowledge and skills. In fact, that's the key to success, because the vast majority of the knowledge and skills that we have access to reside in other people. In a community of knowledge, an individual is like a single piece in a jigsaw puzzle. Understanding where you fit requires understanding not only what you know but also what others know that you don't. Learning your place in a community of knowledge requires becoming aware of the knowledge outside yourself, what you don't know that touches on what you do know.

The Community of Knowledge and Science Instruction

We are hardly the first to appreciate the importance of knowing what you don't know. The idea has already gained some traction among science educators. Since 2006, a course entitled Ignorance has been taught at Columbia University. Guest scientists are invited to speak about what they don't know. The scientists come from a variety of disciplines to discuss what "they would like to know, what they think is critical to know, how they might get to know it, what will happen if they do find this or that thing out, what might happen if they don't." The course focuses on all that is not in the textbooks and thus guides students to think about what is unknown and what could be known. The idea is to focus not on what students themselves don't know, but what entire fields of science don't know, with the aim of provoking and directing students to ask questions about the frontiers of a scientific field. This course requires that students ponder not just some set of scientific theories and associated data; it requires that they begin to understand what the entire community has and hasn't mastered.

A good way to learn about what one doesn't know is to learn about a discipline by doing the work of the discipline. Scientists work at the frontiers of their fields. Their job is to change what is unknown into what is known. So learning to act like a scientist entails finding out what is unknown. Associations representing a variety of fields advocate this approach to science education. The National Council for the Social Studies advocates learning history by doing history like historians do. The U.S. National Research Council (NRC) promotes a philosophy to teach science called "nature of science" instruction: Science education should mirror actual science; students should learn about science in a way that conforms to how science is actually done. But these ideas are more easily proposed than followed. The NRC's directives have largely been ignored. According to the editor in chief of the primary journal of science in the world—aptly named *Science*—even college-level introductory science classes privilege fact retention over learning how science is actually done. The problem is even greater at elementary and high school levels. "Science texts have grown fat with superficial and disconnected information," according to education theorist David Perkins, in part because everyone has an agenda: A smorgasbord of interest groups and scholars each insist that their particular hobbyhorse gets mentioned. By trying to satisfy everyone's taste for what's important, textbooks become litanies of facts and ideas without any soul—without any deep integrative principle—so that no one in the end is satisfied.

Let's focus more closely on science, an area your authors claim to know something about. How is science actually done? It turns out that scientists don't spend their time alone in their labs uncovering nature's mysteries. Science is done by a community. There is a division of cognitive labor: Different scientists are experts in their own domain and scientific knowledge is distributed across the community of scientists. This division doesn't just mean that each scientist has a little bit of knowledge and that the sum total of knowledge depends on everybody. The division of cognitive labor is a constant presence; the community infiltrates everything that a scientist does. Every technique the scientist employs, every theory a scientist appeals to, every idea a scientist has is made possible by the community.

Imagine you're a modern-day molecular biologist trying to figure out, say, how plants reproduce: how the DNA from a mommy and a daddy plant gets combined and replicated over and over to produce baby plants. You read about a new finding involving the role of a molecule called RNA in transferring information around the cell. Do you go out and replicate the finding before you believe it? Very rarely. If you did, you would spend all your time and resources replicating the work of others. Instead, you just believe it (while keeping in the back of your mind the possibility that what you read is wrong). Similarly, if you're taught a new fancy method to analyze your data, you're not likely to derive the method yourself, checking every proof and approximation. That would require more time than it would take to rewrite every book that was ever written. If your community tells you that a method is a good one, normally you'll just run with it.

Science is all about justification—coming to only those conclusions that can be justified. Justifications come in various forms. One way is through direct observation (using a microscope, we can actually see a father's set of chromosomes pairing with a mother's at conception). Another way is through inference (the original geneticist Gregor Mendel inferred the existence of chromosomes by observing how traits are passed from parents to offspring).

But most conclusions in science aren't based on either observation or inference. Instead, they are based on authority, on what is written down in a textbook or journal article or what your expert friend tells you. That's one role of the community of knowledge, to supply facts when direct justification would take too much time or be too costly or difficult. The community of knowledge fills in the vast majority of the details in our knowledge. Everyone's understanding—that of scientists and nonscientists alike—is dependent on what others know, so it is more important for students to understand what is known and what can be justified by others than to know the facts and the justifications themselves. A molecular biology lab will make progress only if those working in it are willing to use tools and methods that they don't fully understand, but that are accepted by the larger community of molecular biologists. Because most knowledge is not maintained inside their own heads, scientists operate on trust, as we all do. We drive cars with little comprehension of the incredible technology that makes them go, and we turn on the light without fully understanding how switches work (modern switches are more sophisticated than you might think). Much of what scientists hold true is a matter of faith—not faith in a supreme being, but faith that others are telling the truth. What distinguishes this faith from religious faith is that there is a higher power to appeal to: namely, the power of verification. Scientific claims can be checked. If scientists are not telling the truth about a result or if they make a mistake, eventually they are likely to be found out because, if the issue is important enough, someone will try and fail to replicate their result.

Scientists care about the truth, but what drives their day-to-day behavior isn't the search for truth as much as the social life entailed by a community of knowledge. Jane Doe's success as a researcher is only indirectly related to how many important findings she discovers in her laboratory. She'll get tenure at Harvard and be allowed to stay there only if she publishes those findings in high-profile outlets. So her job is as much to persuade others of the importance of her work as it is to actually do the work. To get published, she has to write papers that convince peer reviewers and editors to print them in high-profile outlets. In this way, scientists are constantly evaluating the quality of one another's contributions, and like it or not, evaluation is a social process.

Scientists also must obtain funding and other resources to do their work, to pay students and assistants, and to travel to various venues to participate in community events such as conferences and workshops. Resources come from other people, people in government agencies, foundations, and other institutions. Some of the people making decisions about who gets resources are other scientists (other people include politicians and business interests). So these people also need to be persuaded that funding a scientist will benefit the larger community (or the donor's private interest). This is another way in which a scientist depends on the community.

So if you believe that science education should reflect science itself, then science education needs to train people to rely on the knowledge of others. This would help develop thoughtful individuals who are in tune with their environments. It's also important for legal reasons. Individuals, even nonscientists, can be held responsible for negligence even though scientific knowledge was necessary to foresee the harm that was done. In our youth, one of us heard about a guy who sold a white powdered household cleaning product as cocaine. Despite our youth, we recognized that such an act was not only illegal but pure evil. We knew nothing of biochemistry, but we knew enough to know that any reasonable person would assume that snorting cleaning crystals would likely be fatal (or worse). Similarly, it is not obvious to the naif why disposing of engine oil down the drain is so bad for the environment, but it is. Pleading ignorance is not a defense. Understanding certain consequences of our actions takes a scientist, but we're responsible for those consequences even if we're not scientists. In that sense, our everyday actions depend on the knowledge of scientists to stay within the law. In every domain of life, knowledge is interdependent. The knowledge that I'm legally responsible for is not necessarily in my head.

The interdependence of knowledge is truer today than it has ever been. Many scientific fields have become so interdisciplinary that the breadth of knowledge encompassed makes it impossible to master all the knowledge required to do scientific research. More than ever, scientists depend on one another to work. Our field of cognitive science offers a perfect illustration. Many of the recent innovations in the field have come from a variety of places. Computer science has always played a role in cognitive science, for reasons we spelled out earlier. Many cognitive scientists are using methods developed in neuroscience. Physics has made important contributions to the machinery used to measure brain function and has also provided sophisticated mathematical models of learning and the flow of information. This book represents the assimilation by cognitive scientists of ideas from anthropology and cultural and social psychology. We also hope this book spawns the opposite direction of flow: that the ideas we discuss here are read and assimilated by people in many other fields.

One indication of this trend toward larger and more diverse communities is that the average number of authors on published journal articles has not only grown but has increased at an astounding rate. MEDLINE is a database of millions of published papers in the biomedical sciences. The average number of authors per article has nearly quadrupled from about 1.5 in 1950 to almost 5.5 in 2014. This means that the average publication today requires the effort and expertise of almost 6 scientists. Like so many other disciplines, the community of science operates via teamwork.

Teaching science requires more than teaching scientific theory and facts. It also requires that students pay attention to the limits of their knowledge and learn how to fill in the gaps by working within a community. This entails learning about who to trust and where the real expertise is. When someone makes a scientific claim, should we believe that person? This is a critical question for everyone—

scientists and nonscientists alike—because it is often more responsible to defer to experts than to trust ourselves. If you pick a mushroom and have to decide whether or not to eat it, you could go with the rules of thumb suggested by a mushroom-picking friend, such as avoid mushrooms that are shaped like parasols, or you could ask an expert. You really should ask an expert. And if your child is going to eat it, then it's your responsibility to ask an expert. There are many situations in life in which obtaining expert advice is the only sane thing to do: when you can't identify a weird flat discoloration on your skin; when the brakes on your car are smoking; when you're considering spending your life savings to purchase stock in an exciting new company (or a bridge in Brooklyn); or when you're thinking about mixing Diet Coke and hydrochloric acid to clean the rust off your cutlery.

How do you know when the advice you're getting is coming from an expert? If you understand the science behind the claim, then you're golden. You can evaluate the claim directly. But usually you don't have the necessary knowledge. Then you can ask if the claim is based on replicable evidence or if it's wisdom that comes from a friend of a friend. Was it published in a peer-reviewed scientific journal, in the *New York Times*, or in a supermarket tabloid? Learning about the nature of science—about the scientific process, about cases of scientific fraud, about the nature of peer review, and about scientific change and uncertainty—is critical to obtain the skills to evaluate scientific claims.

It's also critical to understand the economics of science. Who profits from doing bad science? The answer isn't merely nutritional supplement companies that claim their products are effective based on questionable studies. People can profit from science in many ways. Profit-making media outlets sensationalize scientific claims (the love center in the brain has not actually been located) and almost always oversimplify. Practicing scientists are frequently disappointed by media pieces about their work. Rarely do the news outlets get it right, and often they get it wrong in bizarre and inexplicable ways. As a result, practicing scientists tend to view news pieces about science with a grain of salt. One goal of education should be to allow nonscientists to also be critical of what they see in the media. If enough of their audience was critical, news organizations might make a more concerted effort to get it right.

An important part of an education consists of learning whether a claim is plausible, who would know, and whether that person is likely to tell the truth. There's no simple answer to making any of these judgments, but an educated person should be better at them than an uneducated one. This isn't just true in science; it's true of everything we teach, be it the law, history, geography, literature, philosophy, or anything else.

Communities of Learning

What does all this mean for the classroom? It means that we should take Dewey's advice to heart and instead of teaching to the "person-solo," we should teach to human beings who rely on the world and others to learn, to figure things out interactively, and to retain information.

One education researcher, Ann Brown, who held positions at several institutions over a short but illustrious career, figured out one way to do this. In a program that she called Fostering Communities of Learners, she focused on the importance of teamwork in learning. In this program, a grade school class is presented with a topic, such as how animals live. The class is divided into research groups that each focus on a separate component of the issue. One group might focus on the animal's defense mechanisms, another on predator-prey relations or protection from the elements or reproductive strategies. Each research group draws on a variety of resources—teachers, visiting experts, computers, and written materials—but are ultimately responsible for their own research. They receive only limited guidance from the teachers. Their job is to master their subject area, to learn as much about the component as they can.

Then the division of cognitive labor kicks in: The class reorganizes into teaching groups that each includes one member of each research group. They call this the jigsaw method because each student gets slotted into a role like a piece in a puzzle. And they are given a puzzle to complete. An example would be to *design an animal of the future.* Each student is now an expert on one topic, the topic that the student did research on in the first phase. So each teaching group in phase two is composed of a set of experts, one on each relevant component for the puzzle the group must solve.

This group/regroup strategy is implicitly a model of the community of knowledge. As Ann Brown puts it:

Expertise is deliberately distributed but is also the natural result of students majoring in different areas of knowledge. Learning and teaching depend heavily on creating, sustaining, and expanding a community of research practice. Members of the community are critically dependent on each other. No one is an island; no one knows it all; collaborative learning is necessary for survival. This interdependence promotes an atmosphere of joint responsibility, mutual respect, and a sense of personal and group identity.

The strategy is successful not only in coming up with first-rate outputs—the students invent interesting animals—but also in teaching the students about animal life. Jigsaw puzzle students learn more about the concepts they are studying than students who read the same materials but don't participate in the research aspect. Participation in a research group allows individuals to share ideas and to seed one another in ways that elicit new ideas. Group thinking creates a richer intellectual environment that individual thinkers can steep themselves in.

These are impressive results, and Ann Brown probably would have come up with many more if she hadn't died prematurely in 1999 at the age of fifty-six. One implication of these results that was important to her is that they provide an argument for diversity in the classroom. Learning and performance benefit from having a greater range of expertise. Having a diverse group of people of different backgrounds, classes, genders, and races can only increase that range.

There's no reason in principle that this sort of communal learning could not be applied well beyond grade school level. It would have to be adapted for older students and for adults—at minimum we'd recommend different jigsaw puzzle topics—but the same basic idea of first developing an expertise and then applying that expertise in a group composed of people who have developed other sorts of expertise seems generally applicable. Imagine asking college students to take classes in different basic sciences and then assigning students who have taken different courses to each group. Each group could then be given a different problem to solve—like reducing water usage or designing a better computer interface. Such groups might be more productive and creative than groups that self-organize in the usual way, according to common interests and friendship.

A variety of communal learning techniques other than the jigsaw method have been tried with some success. They often come under the title "peer education" and include peer tutoring, cooperative learning, and peer collaboration. They work best when the group of peers shares a common workspace and resources. This facilitates the sharing of attention and collaboration. There's no reason other principles of learning could not also be employed. For instance, we know that learning is better when people generate explanations, so those could be put on record too.

It's futile to try to teach everything to everyone. Instead, we should play to individuals' strengths, allowing people to blossom in the roles that they're best at playing. We should also value skills that enable people to work well with others, skills like empathy and the ability to listen. This also means teaching critical thinking skills, not focusing just on facts, to facilitate communication and an interchange of ideas. This is the value of a liberal education, as opposed to learning what you need to get a job.

The purpose of such educational strategies would be to make us not just better consumers of science, but better consumers of information in general. We all need to be skeptical when deciphering the media. Besides all the usual sensationalist and ignorant reporting, there's been alarming news of purveyors of false information with more evil intentions. Adrian Chen writes in the *New York Times Magazine* of a Russian "troll farm," a business whose employees are assigned pro-Kremlin viewpoints and putative information to propagate by blogging, posting on social media sites, and flooding comment sections of news sites, often using multiple false identities. The sad truth is that this sort of thing goes on all the time in both the political and the commercial domains. Marketing agencies post positive feedback for the products of their clients. What *is* new is that Chen links the company, the Internet Research Agency, to several recent hoaxes, including an explosion at a chemical plant in St. Mary Parish, Louisiana, on September 11, 2014, that never actually happened. Reports of the supposed explosion spread quickly through a diverse portfolio of sources: text messages, including one sent to the local director of Homeland Security, tweets to journalists and politicians, and most startling, screen shots of CNN's website showing national coverage of the event, a YouTube video of a man watching a television report that had ISIS claiming responsibility, functioning mirror sites of local TV news organizations, and a Wikipedia page about the disaster—all of them fabricated. Fortunately, the sources of the information we consume are rarely so nefarious. But enough of them are unreliable that we should be vigilant.

Being dependent on others for what we know makes us vulnerable to those who would exploit this fact in order to spread falsehoods. Making students scientifically literate and more able to distinguish accurate statements from garbage and noise has implications beyond teaching better strategies for writing papers.

TWELVE

Making Smarter Decisions

Susan Woodward is a financial economist who served as the chief economist of the U.S. Securities and Exchange Commission and of the U.S. Department of Housing and Urban Development. She has spent much of her career studying how to help people make better financial decisions.

She started in academia teaching finance and has taught at Stanford, UCLA, and the University of Rochester. Coming from a finance and economics background, she generally believed that consumers were well informed and tended to make choices in their best interest. That started to change when she moved into public service at the Department of Housing and Urban Development and began to interact with everyday consumers. Her first clue that something was amiss came from looking at interest rates on government-backed mortgages called Federal Housing Administration loans. These loans offer similar benefits, so there should not be large differences in the rates charged to borrowers, but there were. Susan attributes these differences to the fact that many borrowers don't understand mortgages and lenders take advantage of this. Lenders appear to assess how well informed a borrower is, and offer worse terms to those who are less informed.

As she moved to different roles in government and the private sector, she studied other financial industries such as mutual funds, and the evidence continued to pile up that people's understanding of all types of financial decisions is extremely limited. She summarized her overall assessment for us: "At the SEC [Securities and Exchange Commission], I started getting involved in not just focus groups, but survey research on who understood [these issues], and the answer was—almost no one."

Susan's insight is backed up by experimental evidence. One of the most important elements of financial decision-making is evaluating how a quantity like savings or debt will change over time. Our decisions today should depend on our expectations for the future. We start saving now because we think it will position us well in the future, when we need the money. We feel comfortable taking on a mortgage or a car loan because we anticipate paying it off in a reasonable amount of time. People tend to be pretty good at thinking about how quantities will change when the change is simple. When something changes in a constant way, we call it linear because you could draw the change as a straight line on a graph. If you took twenty dollars every month and put it under your mattress, it's easy to see you will have $240 under your mattress after a year (a linear increase of $20 for each of twelve months). But finances often behave in a nonlinear way, and in such cases people tend to have a hard time understanding. This can lead to really bad decisions.

Savings behavior is a good example. People typically don't save enough and don't start saving soon enough. There are many reasons why people don't save, but one important factor is failure to understand the power of compound interest. When a savings account earns interest, interest accrues on the savings and the savings grow larger. Now the larger savings earn even more interest, which causes the savings to grow even larger. Because of this, the growth of savings is nonlinear. After a few years, the compounding interest really adds up. But people tend not to understand this. Instead they treat savings growth as a linear change. In a study by Craig McKenzie, a psychologist at the University of California, San Diego, and Michael Liersch, currently the head of behavioral finance for Merrill Lynch Wealth Management, people were asked the following question:

> Assume that you deposit $400 every month into a retirement savings account that earns a 10 percent yearly rate of interest. (You never withdraw any money.) How much money do you think you will have in your account (including interest earned): After 10 years, 20 years, 30 years, and 40 years.

What do you think the answer is? After forty years, the median participant guessed $223,000. In fact the right answer is almost $2.5 million. That's the power of compounding and the value of saving early and often.

Here's another example of how linear thinking leads to mis-understanding finances. Do you have credit card debt? If so, you probably receive a statement every month and have to make a deci-sion about how much to pay. One piece of information on the state-ment is the minimum payment. That is the smallest payment you can make and stay in good standing with the credit card company. Many people choose this level of payment. Take a minute to think about how long it will take to pay off your debt if you were to choose the minimum.

Research by Jack Soll, professor of management at Duke Uni-versity, and his colleagues suggests that you probably drastically underestimated the time required due to misunderstanding the non-linear nature of the problem. Imagine you have $10,000 in debt at 12 percent annual interest and you decide to pay $110 per month. How long until you are out of debt? The answer may surprise you: 241 months, or just over 20 years. Here's why it takes so long. In the first month, the $110 covers $100 interest on the loan (1/12 of the total interest of $1,200) plus $10 of principal. In month two the math is similar, but the principal is now slightly lower and the interest on the principal is also slightly lower. The fact that your payment level is only barely more than the interest makes payoff times really drag out. As the amount of principal you pay gets closer to 0, payoff time goes toward infinity. As you increase payments, payoff time decreases dramatically. If you increased your payment by $10 to $120 per month, you would be debt free 5 years sooner.

Now, 241 months is a long time, but it's shorter than infinity. Up until 2003, credit card companies were allowed to set minimum payments as low as they wanted. Guess what happened? Many people paid the minimum and it sometimes didn't even cover interest. They stayed in debt indefinitely. Sometimes the debt even grew! Many well-meaning people who happen not to understand nonlinear functions must have been exasperated to "do their share" one month and see the same credit card bill in the mailbox the next.

In 2003, a law was passed obligating credit card companies to set minimum payments such that the debt will be paid off "over a reasonable period of time." Banks choose different rules for setting the minimum. Chase, for instance, makes sure that the minimum covers interest plus at least 1 percent of the principal.

Mortgages are another case of nonlinearity that is hard to understand. Mortgages are typically structured so that the monthly payment stays the same over the course of the loan, typically fifteen or thirty years. Each month, part of the payment goes to interest and part to principal. Longer loan terms require smaller monthly payments, and less pay-down of the principal each month means more interest has to be paid on the remaining principal the next month. Imagine you take out a $250,000 mortgage at 5 percent interest. If you pay it off over fifteen years, you will end up paying the bank a total of $355,000—$250,000 for the loan and about $105,000 for interest. If you chose a thirty-year mortgage instead, you would pay the bank a total of $483,000, with $233,000 in interest, more than twice as much as with the fifteen-year loan. In reality the difference would probably be larger because you typically get a better interest rate with a shorter loan term. The magnitude of the difference is surprising to many people, because again it's a nonlinear problem. Many people who own mortgages don't have a good grasp of how they work. Instead they tend to choose using simple heuristics like trying to minimize their monthly payment.

Explanation Fiends and Foes

Understanding is shallow, and not just when making financial decisions. People fail to care about details when buying any kind of product. Imagine you go to the store to look for Band-Aids and see a box on the shelf that advertises a cool new feature:

> Bubbles in the padding help cuts heal faster.

Would you pay extra for these bandages? Maybe, but one question you might ask is: How do they work? If you're given a little bit of explanation, perhaps you would be more of a believer and pony up the extra cash. It turns out that almost everyone appreciates a little explanation. When we added the following detail to advertisements, people liked the Band-Aids more:

> Bubbles increase air circulation around the wound, thereby kill-
> ing bacteria. This causes cuts to heal faster.

Being told why the bubbles are there gave people a sense of causal understanding. But this explanation is actually pretty shallow. It doesn't tell us how the bubbles increase air circulation or why air circulation kills bacteria. As it happens, most people did not want the answers to these detailed questions. When we added a little more explanation that answered them:

> Bubbles push the padding away from the wound, allowing air to circulate. Oxygen in the air interferes with the metabolic processes of many bacteria, killing them and allowing the wound to heal faster.

most people's evaluations of the product actually decreased. Too much causal explanation actually turned them off.

Most of us are *explanation foes* when it comes to our decisions. We are like Goldilocks: We have a sweet spot for explanatory detail, not too little and not too much. The truth is that we all know a few people who are exceptions. They do try to master all the details before making a choice. They spend days reading everything they can find, learning the ins and outs of all the new technology. We call such people *explanation fiends*.

What explains the difference between explanation foes and fiends? The answer is cognitive reflection, discussed in chapter 4. People who get high scores on the Cognitive Reflection Test tend not to fall for trick questions because they naturally mull over how well they understand. Similarly, highly reflective people have a higher threshold for satisfactory explanation. A shallow explanation like the first one and even the second one is not enough. They want to know more. But most people are explanation foes. They are satisfied long before getting to the third explanation. Adding too much detail only makes the product feel more complex. Who knew that bacteria's metabolic processes are relevant to assessing a simple box of Band-Aids? And who cares?

Is it better to be a fiend or a foe? There's no right answer. Both orientations have benefits and drawbacks. The world is complex and it is impossible to know everything. Spending reams of time mastering details that don't matter too much—as explanation fiends do—can be a waste of time. Moreover, even people who are explanation fiends in their domains of expertise—housewares or classic cars or audio equipment—are often explanation foes when it comes to things they don't care about as much.

The marketplace is set up to take advantage of explanation foes' abhorrence of detail. Most advertising relies on the vaguest of justifications. Ads tend to focus the viewer on an individual that the advertiser hopes the viewer can relate to (like an average-looking construction worker) or one that the viewer sees as a role model (like a hunk with bedroom eyes) and to say vague things about how the product will improve your life, while avoiding fraudulent claims. One TV ad for an antidepressant medication devotes five seconds to the evidence for its clinical benefits and fifty-five seconds to its possible side effects, with background images of a girl-next-door type seeing the light and discovering the joy in little things. Another merely says it "can help," along with forty-five seconds of possible side effects, again played over images of women regaining their lives, though this time the women are middle-aged. Even this is more informative than beer commercials that merely show sexy young people having a great time.

Skin care is an egregious example of an industry built on appeals to explanation foes. Beauty companies make their money by charging incredible prices for tiny vials of cream that promise to "repair your DNA" or "make you look twenty years younger," with little clinical evidence to back up the claims. How do they get away with it? By giving the appearance of evidence in the form of pseudo-scientific jargon. A whole industry has sprung up around pseudoscience. "Skin science clinics" offer impressive-seeming technology like fancy imaging devices and "complexion-analysis software," with no evidence of any clinical value. It's all a marketing ploy to move skin cream.

In some ways, our vulnerability to misleading claims and bad explanations is unavoidable. Many of our decisions require reasoning about how the world works. We have to guess which diet plan will be most effective, which tires will be best in the snow, or which investment will set us up best for retirement. The world is dauntingly complex, so the range of decisions each of us faces is far too broad for any individual to master all the details. If we had to research the metabolic processes of bacteria every time we wanted to buy a package of Band-Aids, many of us would just walk around with festering wounds. So we mostly just grab the option that looks good, and it works fine most of the time.

The Solution Is Not More Information

The standard response to the superficiality of consumers is to try to reduce ignorance through education. The hope is that if you teach people what they need to know, they will make wiser decisions.

This has been tried many times in an effort to improve people's financial decision-making, because such decisions are among the most important we make throughout our lives—buying a home, saving for retirement, paying for college. Given the amount of wealth in our society, it is shocking how many people live their lives on the brink of financial calamity. Here's a scary statistic showing the financial fragility of many American households: only a quarter of U.S. households report being confident they could come up with $2,000 in thirty days. What happens when an accident or illness occurs, or the head of the household gets laid off? Here's another scary statistic: The median American household heading to retirement has only enough savings to live on for three years. Obviously, that is not close to enough.

In attempts to solve the problem, governments and advocacy groups around the world have poured billions of dollars into financial education programs. But these have gotten nowhere. By 2014, there had been at least 201 studies exploring the effect of financial education on nurturing positive financial actions such as saving for retirement, having a rainy-day fund, avoiding bounced checks and late credit card payments, and improving creditworthiness. These education programs have had almost no effect. What little benefit they did provide disappeared within months of the educational interventions. This is reminiscent of the failed attempts to increase science literacy based on the deficit model we talked about in chapter 8.

Here's where we think these efforts have gone wrong: They put all the weight of a decision on the individual. Individuals make decisions, and therefore the individual must be educated to make wise decisions. If things go wrong, the individual is to blame.

But this is the same faulty reasoning that we've seen throughout this book. Individuals don't make decisions by themselves. Other people formulate options for them, other people present those options, and other people give them advice. Moreover, people sometimes copy decisions that are made by others (for example, when stock market guru Warren Buffett makes a decision to buy a stock, many people copy him). We should be thinking about decision-making from a communal perspective. The knowledge required for decision-making is not merely in individuals' heads but depends heavily on the community of knowledge.

Misleading claims and bad explanations also depend on the community of knowledge. They work because we tend to let others do our thinking for us. Just pointing to the community is often sufficient to make us feel we understand, at least enough to make a decision. As a result, we're susceptible to product appeals that sound good without making any actual substantive claim about how the product provides benefits. Terms like "natural" and "organic" can be misleading when they are applied to products that aren't any more natural or organic than comparable products. Similarly, in this era hallowing all foods gluten-free, the "gluten-free" label can be found on foods that never did contain gluten. And how many people know how being "probiotic" benefits a dietary supplement?

Failure to appreciate the role of the community of knowledge can be subtle. When people are thrust into a marketplace with hundreds of complex options described with technical terms in small print, they can get overwhelmed and give up.

Consider a puzzle in economics called the annuity paradox. One kind of annuity can be thought of as an insurance policy. You pay in a lump sum and you get a guaranteed fixed payment each month for the rest of your life. The size of the payment depends primarily on how much you pay in and how old you are when you start receiving benefits. Many economists believe annuities are really good investments, but few people buy them. A lot of research has focused on trying to explain why consumers don't find them more attractive. One of the reasons is that consumers don't understand them.

In a study in collaboration with colleagues at the University of Colorado, we brought people who were near retirement into the lab and asked them to evaluate a brochure for an annuity on a computer screen. We used a device called an eye tracker to figure out where they were looking as they were reading the brochure. To mimic the distractions of everyday life, we had web pages with various content rotating on the other side of the screen, and we were interested in seeing how often people's attention diverted from the annuity brochure. One group of participants saw a real brochure taken directly from a large financial services company. The other group saw a simplified version that reduced the length by providing fewer details.

If you look at what passes for a standard annuity brochure you could probably anticipate our results. The brochure is long (twenty-one pages) and filled with technical jargon and includes reams of intimidating numerical information. The eye-tracking data revealed a sad pattern. You could see that our participants were trying really hard to concentrate at the outset. They spent a lot of time inspecting the brochure's first few pages and hardly looked at the distracting websites. But as time wore on, their attention started to flag, and then it collapsed completely. By the end of the brochure they were spending hardly any time at all on each page, and their attention kept shifting to the websites. Participants who viewed the simplified version of the brochure did a lot better, but even they struggled.

It's hard to accuse these people of being lazy or ignorant. They really wanted to pay attention and absorb the information, but their attention failed them.

This idea goes far beyond annuities. One of us recently received a letter from a former employer. It reads, in part:

> You have 5 year (s) of vesting service and are 100% vested in the retirement contributions made by XXX on your behalf. This means that 0% of the contributions are forfeitable. Forfeitable funds will be swept from your account after at least one year has passed in which you have not performed any service. The sweep is expected to occur in the near future. Please note that the vesting service includes service on the student and limited duration payrolls as well as the regular payroll, and that the calculations of your vesting service may not equal your actual calendar years of service at XXX.

It goes on like this for another couple of paragraphs. Do you know what it means? We have no clue. We could try to find out, but instead we did what most people do: We threw it in the trash and turned our attention to more pressing matters. Hopefully we won't find out that ignoring the letter was a big mistake.

A lot of the kind of legalese one comes across reflects a lack of appreciation for the role of the community of knowledge in decision-making. Communications are written by experts. Those experts feel like everyone must understand what they write because the expert does. This is the curse of knowledge. It is a result of participation in the community of knowledge—the failure to separate what is in one's own head from what is in the heads of others.

On top of that, most people are not inclined to master the details. Most of us are explanation foes. Our lives are filled with situations where we are confronted with things we don't really understand. Sometimes we don't even realize there are gaps in our understanding. Even when we do, we are often too uninterested or embarrassed to ask for help.

The Hive Economy

Financial decision-making is a good place to point out the relevance of the community of knowledge because the value of financial assets depends on the community in the most fundamental way. Economies are dreadfully complex (that's why economics is known as the "dismal science"). Most individuals have only the most superficial understanding of them. Yet economies chug along merrily because they don't depend on individuals' understanding. An economy works because we each do our own little part. The economy is a great example of the hive mind, an incredibly complex system that emerges from the cooperation of many individual minds. Here's what the Peruvian economist Hernando de Soto has to say about the underpinnings of an economy: "Remember, it is not your own mind that gives you certain exclusive rights over a specific asset, but other minds thinking about your rights in the same way you do. These minds vitally need each other to protect and control their assets."

In chapter 8 we talked about how the beliefs of a community are powerful, strong enough to make intelligent people believe outrageous things. But there is a limit to the power of these beliefs. Those outrageous things don't become true by virtue of the community believing in them. Even if everyone in the world believed the earth was flat, it wouldn't make it so. Economies are different.

Rai stones are large, doughnut-shaped pieces of limestone that the Yapese people of the small island of Yap in Micronesia use as currency. The stones can be really big, up to twelve feet across, and can weigh several tons. Some are so big that when ownership changes, the new owner doesn't move the stone. It remains in the same spot, but everyone accepts that it now belongs to the new owner. In one story, a large rai stone fell out of a canoe and sunk to the seafloor. The stone was never seen again, but it retained its value and continued to be traded. The Yapese couldn't see it, but reasoned that it must still be there.

To Western ears, this story sounds odd. How can a hunk of stone at the bottom of the sea have value? But the odd thing is not the economy of the Yapese. It is the nature of economies in general. Up until the 1930s our economy was also based on hunks of rock that we couldn't see. Our rocks were made of gold instead of limestone and hidden in Fort Knox instead of at the bottom of the sea, but still, the parallel is obvious.

Today we no longer use the gold standard, but it's still the case that the only reason the dollar bill in your pocket is worth anything is because other people believe it is worth something. If amnesia for the meaning of a dollar bill suddenly beset everybody, that dollar wouldn't offer much but fuel for a fire, and not much fuel at that. Money gets its value from the communal belief that it has value; its worth depends on a social contract. Someone else might agree to give you an item of substance, like a chocolate bar, in return for the dollar. But that person is only willing to do that because that person believes that other people will in turn give something of substance in return for the dollar. And those third parties are willing to do it only because they know that others will trade them for it too. Money has value because the community deems it valuable through its willingness to trade with it. Even something as fundamentally individualistic as money depends on a community of knowledge.

This isn't just academic. The state of the economy depends on what people believe. When people believed they could get a lot of money for tulip bulbs in seventeenth-century Holland, a single bulb could be sold for many times the annual income of a solid middle-class household. And when they stopped believing this, the market crashed. Most economic bubbles have a similar flavor. Leading up to the crash of 2008, house prices skyrocketed because people believed housing would continue to increase in value and they wanted to get in on it. Compounding the problem, homeowners used complex vehicles like adjustable rate mortgages to buy houses they couldn't afford. Buying a mortgage is perhaps the most consequential financial decision most of us will ever make, and yet we've already seen that most people don't understand simple mortgages, let alone exotic types. We rely on a belief that we don't need to grasp the details because the community of knowledge is there for us. We have advisers we can turn to if we ever do need details, a marketplace where the best financial products should float to the top because others have done the research, and laws that are presumably written to protect people like us, those who are not financial virtuosos. The community of knowledge makes us feel like we understand more deeply than we do, and this gives us the necessary confidence to make this complicated decision.

Just as the economy depends on a division of cognitive labor, households divide their cognitive financial labor. Many people go through their lives ignoring as much financial information as they can. A revealing illustration comes from studies looking at how couples divide responsibility for financial decision-making led by Adrian Ward from the University of Texas. He asked people in relationships how long they had been with their partner and how much of the couple's financial decision-making they are responsible for. Next the researchers assessed the couples' financial literacy with a battery of quiz questions about common financial topics. Not surprisingly, people responsible for financial matters got more financially literate as the length of the relationship increased. People learn, and practice makes perfect. More surprising was that the partner not responsible for financial matters actually got *less* financially literate. Apparently this is a case of "use it or lose it." Ward told us that his biggest takeaway from these studies is how the division of cognitive labor affects what we learn, with the result that we become even more entrenched in our roles. "For me, the story is about how relying on others affects attention, which feeds into learning and knowledge, which feeds into decision-making and downstream outcomes . . . if you are bad at finances but are tasked with financial responsibility, you pay attention to financial stuff in the environment and that helps you get better. If you offload financial responsibility, you don't even notice financial information."

We think it is inevitable that people will continue to make decisions—even very consequential decisions—without deep understanding. So how can we help people to make wiser choices?

Nudging Better Decisions

The University of Chicago economist Richard Thaler and the Harvard legal scholar Cass Sunstein have developed a philosophy that they call *libertarian paternalism*. Although the name is a mouthful, the idea is simple and compelling. The main observation is that people don't always make the best possible decisions; they don't always choose the option that makes it most likely that they will achieve their own goals. Examples abound: We choose the large pizza instead of the salad and regret it as we're leaving the restaurant. We decide to go on a date with somebody who is very attractive but has no sense of humor. That one we regret even before leaving the restaurant. We buy pants that would have fit us ten years ago because we're not ready to admit how much we've expanded. We decide that we have only a short drive home, so the fact that we've had one too many isn't a reason to call a cab. Or we believe in organ donation and want to be organ donors but never took the time to sign the back of our driver's license so our organs will not be donated if something tragic happens to us. In each of these cases, humans are being human: making choices that are regretted in hindsight, or would be if they were reconsidered.

The libertarian paternalist believes that behavioral science can be made a force for good, that it can be used to improve our decision-making. Behavioral science can be used to identify the reasons we make decisions that we regret and change the process of decision-making so that better decisions are made in the future. Such changes are referred to as nudges. The idea is that behavioral science can be used to nudge decisions to make them better in the sense that they are more aligned with what decision makers actually want. A nudge for the overeating example mentioned above would be to alter the order of choices so that you first choose a salad before choosing whether to have pizza. The order in which food choices are made can make a big difference to what people choose; items earlier in the cafeteria line tend to get picked more often than if the same item appears later. A nudge for organ donation is to change the law so that everyone is an organ donor by default. You can choose not to be, but that requires a little action. The simplest way is to change the system so that, instead of signing the back of your driver's license to be an organ donor, you have to sign the back of your driver's license in order *not* to be an organ donor, in order to opt out. This simple change turns out to have enormous consequences, drastically increasing the number of organ donors. Making people opt out rather than opt in increases enrollment in a variety of plans. In order to increase retirement savings, the U.S. Department of Labor is encouraging small businesses to create retirement plans for their employees that they would be automatically enrolled in.

Nudges are libertarian in the sense that they don't reduce people's ability to choose. Nobody is preventing you from eating a large pizza or from being an organ donor or not. But they are paternalistic in the sense that somebody else decides which options are going to be encouraged. Somebody else has put the pizza later in the cafeteria line so that you're more likely to choose the salad. The main argument for this kind of paternalism is that the choice has to be made one way or another. Something has to be earlier in the cafeteria line, so why not make it the item that people feel most attracted to when they are not in the heat of the moment, when they can think dispassionately about what the best food options are?

The big lesson of the nudge approach is that it is easier and more effective to change the environment than it is to change the person. And once we understand what quirks of cognition drive behavior, we can design the environment so that those quirks help us instead of hurt us.

We can apply this lesson to how we make decisions as part of a community of knowledge. We have to appreciate that people are explanation foes—that we usually don't have the inclination or even the capability to master the details of all our decisions. What we can do is try to structure the environment to help ourselves make good decisions despite our lack of understanding.

Lesson 1: Reduce Complexity

Because so much of our financial knowledge is possessed by the community and not by us individually, we need to radically scale back our expectations of how much complexity people can tolerate. We need to give people the opportunity to understand and evaluate products and then decide for themselves. They can do this only if they have the wherewithal to absorb the information in the decision-making environment. On Reddit you can find a discussion forum called "Explain Like I'm 5." People post questions, often about difficult topics like particle physics or finance, and forum members try to provide a satisfying explanation that is easily understood. The popularity of this forum speaks to how enjoyable it is to read explanations that we can actually make sense of. It also highlights how rare these are in our day-to-day lives.

Lesson 2: Simple Decision Rules

Richard Thaler, one of the fathers of the libertarian paternalism approach, has thought a lot about financial decision-making. He agrees that attempting to give people a deep understanding of financial topics is unlikely to work. The financial world is just too complex and people's abilities are too limited. He argues that rather than trying to educate people, we should give them simple rules that work pretty well and can be applied with little knowledge or effort, rules like "Invest as much as possible in your 401(k) plan," "Save 15 percent of your income," or "Get a fifteen-year mortgage if you are over fifty."

This is a great starting point, but the challenge we see with implementing the idea is that people are not very good at sticking to rules. Imagine a fifty-year-old shopping for mortgages who has the best intention to follow Thaler's rule, but then sees what seems like an amazing deal on a thirty-year mortgage, a deal so good, the mortgage broker assures him, it only comes along once in a generation. There's a decent chance the decision rule goes out the window.

Decision rules might be more effective if they are supplemented with a short, clear explanation that gives people an understanding of why the rule is a good one. Giving people a correct intuition about the benefit of diversifying, the power of compound interest, or other core financial principles might make them more likely to apply rules correctly and stick to them.

Lesson 3: Just-in-Time Education

Here's one more idea. John G. Lynch Jr., the director of the Center for Research on Consumer Financial Decision Making at the University of Colorado, advocates for an approach he calls "just-in-time" financial education. The idea is to give people the information they need just before they need it. A class in high school that teaches the basics of managing debt and savings is just not that useful. As we've argued throughout the book, people are bad at remembering details. By the time that high school student is faced with a consequential financial decision, he or she will likely have long forgotten about the power of compounding or the benefits of asset diversification. Giving people education just before they use it means the information is fresh and that they will have the opportunity to practice what they have learned, increasing the chance that it is retained.

Lynch offers a great example of a case where this could really help. Getting laid off is a terrible experience, its horror compounded by its tendency to cause people to make bad financial decisions. For instance, it often leads people to take money out of their retirement account. They may do it to cover expenses they anticipate while being unemployed, or they may roll it into a different investment account. The problem is that this is a complex decision that most people don't understand well. Withdrawals from retirement accounts that aren't repaid result in penalties, and there are complicated tax implications. Making matters worse, when people lose their job they often get approached by financial services companies—Lynch calls them "vultures"—that try to sell them on bad investment vehicles with high fees. The solution, says Lynch, is to provide education at the moment of termination that lays out the options and gives people an understanding of the pros and cons of each one.

Just-in-time education can be applied to many complex decisions. For instance, new parents are inundated with complex health decisions for their newborn. One of us recalls having to make a decision about the costs of banking cord blood while his wife was in bed with contractions. If you haven't had a baby (or maybe if you have) you probably don't know what cord blood is or why you might be interested in banking it. Prospective parents could benefit from just-in-time education on many aspects of neonatal health.

Lesson 4: Check Your Understanding

These ideas are all things society can do for individuals. What can individuals do to help themselves? One starting place is to be aware of our tendency to be explanation foes. It's not practical to master all the details of every decision, but it can be helpful to at least have some awareness of the gaps in our understanding. If the decision is important enough, we might pause and gather more information before jumping into a choice that we later regret.

In the last chapter, we saw that real understanding requires knowing what you don't know. Knowing what you don't know allows you to get help and fill in the gaps when the need arises. It brings you down to earth and prevents you from allowing intellectual arrogance to drive important decisions, decisions that you might regret later. Knowing what you don't know about your credit, new house, potential spouse, and little red sports car can be the trigger to cause you to obtain solid advice from someone who isn't trying to profit from your bad decisions.

In the financial sector, knowing what you don't know can even make you a better investor. This is the advice given by Ray Dalio, founder and cochief investment officer of Bridgewater Associates, a hedge fund. "My success is . . . due to how I deal with not knowing . . . How I go look for where I might be wrong . . . I love to find people who could disagree with me . . . I can see it through their eyes and I can consider, is that right, is that wrong? That learning experience helps me learn more and it also helps me make better decisions. So it's dealing with what one doesn't know that's more effective than knowing." By knowing what he doesn't know, Dalio has learned to take advantage of the community of knowledge. This has proven quite the successful strategy. Bridgewater is currently the largest hedge fund in the world. It's a piece of advice that we can all use when making all kinds of decisions.

Conclusion:
Appraising Ignorance and Illusion

When academics encounter a new idea that doesn't conform to their preconceptions, there's often a sequence of three reactions: first dismiss, then reject, and finally declare it obvious. The initial reaction to an idea that challenges an academic's world view is to ignore it: Assume it's not worthy of one's time and consideration. If that doesn't work, if community pressure forces the idea to be confronted, academics come up with reasons to reject it. Academics are terrific at justifying their opposition to an idea. Finally, if the idea is just too good to reject, if the idea hangs on in the community, academics find reasons to claim they knew it all along because it's self-evident.

Our hope is that you jump to the conclusion that the ideas in this book are self-evident. Isn't it apparent that individuals are ignorant in the sense that they know little compared to what could be known? Obviously, the world is complicated and there's too much to know. It's a little more surprising that we think we know more than we do, but you may already have an inkling of even that about yourself. After all, it's evident every time you think you know the answer to a question but don't. The claim that thought is an extension of action almost goes without saying, and our proposal that reasoning is primarily causal is not exactly shocking, given how broad a category that is. The fact that we live in a community of knowledge is hardly revolutionary; every time you ask someone else a question, you are relying on the fact that you depend on others for knowledge. All the ramifications and details that we have discussed are certainly not obvious. But the main ideas are consistent with what most people already believe. We've shown through the course of the book that the ideas have been around a long time. Moreover, none of them defy common sense.

Why write a book stating the obvious? Why offer ideas that we don't expect people to think are really new?

It's because the ideas are obvious only when you think about them. When you don't, when you go about your daily life and are not conscious of them, you think very differently. People tend to live in an illusion of understanding, and we focus on individuals—their power, talents, skills, and achievements—instead of appreciating that we are citizens of a community of knowledge. Worse, we make decisions—minor and major life decisions as well as decisions about how to structure our society—that overestimate our knowledge and that fail to acknowledge how much our knowledge depends on others. We've seen examples of this that concern how people make choices about what they eat, how they will invest their retirement income, how they will vote, what political positions they will support, how they will interact with technology, how they will choose employees, and how they will educate the young. It's important not to just know the obvious, but to be aware of it: to use it to craft decisions that concern both the individual and society.

This book has three central themes: ignorance, the illusion of understanding, and the community of knowledge. We have no illusion that the lessons we can draw from our discussion are simple. Those lessons are decidedly *not* to reduce ignorance, live happily within your community, and dispel all illusions. On the contrary, ignorance is inevitable, happiness is often in the eye of the beholder, and illusions have their place.

Is Ignorance to Be Avoided at All Costs?

Ignorance is not bliss, but it doesn't have to be misery. For humans, ignorance is inevitable: It's our natural state. There's too much complexity in the world for any individual to master. Ignorance can be frustrating, but the problem is not ignorance per se. It's the trouble we get into by not recognizing it.

David Dunning is a psychologist who spent much of his career at Cornell University. He has been shocked by how much ignorance he has seen in daily life and in scientific surveys, and he has documented much of it. What alarms Dunning is not the amount of human ignorance, but that ignorant people don't know how ignorant they are. He points out that "we're not very good at knowing what we don't know."

The problem, according to Dunning, occurs when the only way to evaluate how much you know is via your own knowledge. How good a driver are you? If you know a lot about driving, then you're probably a reasonable judge of your own skills. You have a good sense of what driving skills are out there and how many of them you've mastered. But if you're a lousy driver, not only do you not have skills, you also don't know what the range of possible driving skills is. So you think you're better than you are. Say you've spent twenty years driving in the suburbs. If you're relatively accident free, then you might think you're a pretty darn good driver because you're unaware that some people can also drive in the city, in emergency situations in all kinds of weather, in mud, on ice, and even on the beach. Relative to people with such broad experience driving, your skills may be quite limited. Expertise means that you have skills as well as knowledge about what constitutes being skilled. Ignorance means you have neither.

This pairing explains what is commonly known as the Dunning-Kruger effect, that those who perform the worst overrate their own skills the most. The effect is found by giving a group of people a task to do and then asking them how well they think they've done on the task. Poor performers overestimate how well they've done; strong performers often underestimate their performance. The effect has been found many times both in the psychological laboratory and in many real-world environments: among students, in offices, and among doctors. And Dunning has collected an impressive amount of evidence that the reason it happens is that those who lack skills also lack the knowledge of what skills they're missing. So they think they're pretty good. Those who have skills have a better sense of what the terrain looks like: They know what skills they could improve on.

The unskilled just don't know what they don't know. And, according to Dunning, it matters because all of us are unskilled in most domains of our lives:

> Our ignorance, in general, shapes our lives in ways we do not know about. Put simply, people tend to do what they know and fail to do that which they have no conception of. In that way, ignorance profoundly channels the course we take in life . . . People fail to reach their potential as professionals, lovers, parents, and people simply because they are not aware of the possible.

This is a fact of life. We can't choose what we don't know about. Most of the time, this isn't a problem. We won't miss Disneyland if we don't know it's there. It's only knowledge of enticing possibilities that makes us miss them. That's why winning the lottery can be more of a burden than a pleasure: Once we've tasted getting what we want, we can't go back to our state of ignorance. This is the best argument we've encountered both for staying away from addictive substances and—for those of us with limited budgets—from expensive consumer items. The less you know about them, the less you'll miss them and the happier you'll be.

But ignorance has costs. If we don't know about birth control, then we won't use it. If we remain ignorant about the horrors that are going on next door, we won't do what's necessary to stop them. And if we are ignorant about the dangerous things our children are getting into, disaster can follow.

A Saner Community

Some Eastern philosophies encourage adherents to appreciate their own ignorance: to accept that they know little and to respect what others know. Indeed, some traditions go further, encouraging people to have gratitude for the knowledge of others. We take this as a lesson of cognitive science too. We can learn and conceive only a finite amount as individuals; to achieve greater things we need a community. In the most fundamental way—in terms of how we think— we're all in it together.

Intelligence resides in the community and not in any individual. So decision-making procedures that elicit the wisdom of the community are likely to produce better outcomes than procedures that depend on the relative ignorance of lone individuals. A strong leader is one who knows how to inspire a community and take advantage of the knowledge within it, and who can delegate responsibility to those with the most expertise.

But despite living within a community, we must retain the responsibility for our decisions. Others can be wrong, and sometimes communities come to extremist and misguided views. People can deceive themselves and groups can jointly deceive one another. If they couldn't, we wouldn't see the bizarre tragedies that occur when cults with charismatic leaders go off the deep end, as Jim Jones's Peoples Temple did in Jonestown, Guyana, in 1978. After attacking the entourage of Congressman Leo Ryan and killing the congressman, the group participated in a mass murder-suicide that left 909 men, women, and children dead, mostly of cyanide poisoning. Fortunately, this kind of event is extraordinarily rare, but it is not isolated. David Koresh led the Branch Davidian cult into a skirmish with the FBI in 1993 that ended in a fire that killed Koresh and 79 others. And in 1997, 39 members of the Heaven's Gate cult committed suicide because they believed that doing so was necessary to reach an extraterrestrial spaceship following comet Hale-Bopp. All of these groups developed insane beliefs that led to their own destruction. Communities can have an insidious effect on what people believe and consequently on their decisions and actions.

So we're not championing faith in whatever a community believes or whatever a credentialed expert says. Along with faith must come a healthy dose of skepticism and a keen eye for charlatans and those who are confidently wrong. When your community gives you bad advice, it's your responsibility not to take it. Nazi prison guards are not excused because they were just following orders, and terrorists are certainly not excused because they are members of an ideological community.

But most of us have the freedom to choose communities that do their best to avoid false statements and lies. Society has come as far as it has because most people are cooperative most of the time. We try to surround ourselves with people who report only what they know, and tell us if they're not sure. And we mostly succeed. We can almost

always trust the people we interact with; that's what makes community living possible.

Appraising Illusion

We live with the illusion that we understand things better than we do. Is this illusion something we necessarily need to dispel? Should we always strive to have beliefs and goals that are as realistic as possible? This is the choice that confronts Neo, Keanu Reeves's character in the film *The Matrix*: Take the red pill and live in the real world or take the blue pill and maintain the comfort of illusion. If he chooses the red pill, he'll have to face the world as it is, including the pain, sorrow, and robot overlords that accompany reality. If he chooses the blue pill, he'll return to the collective delusion of human existence.

By avoiding illusion, you're more likely to be accurate. You'll know what you know and what you don't know, and this can only help you achieve your goals. You won't take on projects that are beyond you and you will be less likely to disappoint others. You'll be better positioned to deliver on your promises.

But illusion is a pleasure. Many of us spend a significant part of our lives living in illusion quite intentionally. We entertain ourselves with fictional worlds that offer no pretense of being real. And we fantasize, for the pleasure of it and also to enhance our creativity. Illusions can stimulate creative products by inspiring us to imagine alternative worlds, goals, and outcomes. And they can motivate us to attempt things we wouldn't otherwise attempt. Is that wrong? Should we really be minimizing our illusions?

One of us, Steve, has two daughters. Let's call them S and L. L knows a lot. She also has a pretty good sense of what she knows. She even knows what she doesn't know. Because she has a good sense of how much she knows relative to how much there is to know, let's say that she is *calibrated*. She is calibrated in the sense that a scale is calibrated if it tells you what your true weight is. S, in contrast, is not so well calibrated. S strives to understand everything. She also knows a lot but believes she knows even more. Like most of us, she tends to live in an illusion of understanding.

L is a happy, well-adjusted person who is reasonably confident when she speaks. She can talk in detail about what she knows, she knows when to stop, and she knows when to say, "I don't know." She pursues realistic goals and she tends to accomplish them. She comes across as calm and relaxed (though who knows what's going on inside). L reads what interests her and has a few hobbies, but her focus is really on her area of expertise.

S is also well adjusted though perhaps a little less happy-go-lucky. She doesn't draw sharp boundaries between her expertise and that of others. She thinks beyond her own limited domain of knowledge. She has big dreams: She wants to solve big problems, not just the ones she has the expertise to solve, and she does everything she can to make her dreams reality. She works very hard and she accomplishes a tremendous amount. But because she's focused on the big picture, she's often disappointed in the outcome: Reality rarely meets her lofty expectations. She experiences more frustration than L. S also reads very widely and is willing to discuss anything. Learning is her greatest pleasure, whatever the subject. She has several hobbies that she pursues with gusto.

Who is the better role model, calibrated L or less calibrated S? From a father's perspective, the answer is obvious: They are both perfect. And that may be right. Living in an illusion of understanding certainly has its pitfalls. In this book, we have pointed out how the illusion of understanding can lead to war, nuclear accidents, partisan gridlock, rejection of science, lack of fairness, and other misfortunes. But we have also shown that the illusion results from an incredible feature of mind. The knowledge illusion is a result of living within a community of knowledge; it arises because we fail to distinguish what's in our own heads from what's in other people's heads. It arises because, cognitively speaking, we're a team. You don't have to have an illusion to be a team player, but having the illusion is a sign that you are.

Those who live in a knowledge illusion are overconfident about how much they know. This has some benefits. For one, it opens doors. It provides the strength to make bold statements and take bold actions. In 1961, John F. Kennedy had no right to predict that an American would land safely on the moon by the end of the decade. His prediction came directly from hubris that can only be described as illusory. Then the incredible happened: America came through. Likely they would not have even tried had JFK not had such chutzpah.

The knowledge illusion gives people the self-confidence to enter new territory. Great explorers must believe they know more than they do to undertake novel adventures. This explains great catastrophes such as Robert Scott's doomed adventure to the South Pole, in which he refused to use dogs because he knew better. All his men died along with the ponies that accompanied them. But it is also necessary for great successes. The teams led by men like Marco Polo, Christopher Columbus, and Vasco da Gama, each of whom were the first Europeans to explore new continents, displayed a kind of courage and perseverance that have turned them into historical heroes. We have not met these men personally, but we suspect that they maintained a self-confidence that could come only from a lack of appreciation of how vast their ignorance was. Many great human achievements are underwritten by false belief in one's own understanding. In that sense, the illusion may have been necessary for the development of human civilization.

The illusion that we understand things better than we do is why we fix our own bicycles and electric train sets and build our own porches (or at least try to). We do many of these things because we don't appreciate what we're getting into. We discover only after we've taken our bicycle apart or bought all the necessary tools that we wish we knew more about what we're doing. Sometimes we give up and take the bike to the shop or call a carpenter, but sometimes we persevere. When we do persevere, we have to credit the knowledge illusion for motivating us to start in the first place.

A similar point can be made about human relationships: If we're having a problem in a relationship, our belief that we understand what's going on can serve as motivation to try to fix the problem. Generally, we find out that what's going on is more complicated than we thought, but at least we're trying.

Illusion may be pleasant, but like ignorance, it is not bliss. The flip side of our illusion of understanding human relationships is that sometimes we don't try to mend relationships because we believe we already know what's going on. We cut ourselves off out of hubris or fear in the belief that we can pinpoint the other person's failings. Inevitably, we fail to understand the full social dynamics; we are part of the problem ourselves. More broadly, we have described a number of human foibles and catastrophes throughout this book that result from the knowledge illusion.

So L's virtue as a role model is that she gets things right. She has a calm certainty that stems from her awareness of what's inside her domain of understanding and what's outside of it, what she's not responsible for. She also has a confidence and openness in working with others that come from her ability to delimit her own expertise. She welcomes contributions from others and she appreciates their knowledge because she knows the limits of her own.

S is just as virtuous a role model. She projects enthusiasm about everything she encounters and is constantly breaking new ground, finding new conceptual links, and exploring uncharted waters (sometimes quite literally, to her parents' chagrin). She is a pleasure to talk to because she is so full of ideas and willing to engage on any topic. Her willingness to see herself as knowledgeable means that she can be combative, and she's certainly exhausting. She does live in a bit of an illusion. But it's her parents' impression that whatever is causing this illusion also has the potential to cause her to achieve great things. Thank heaven for little illusions.

Acknowledgments

The story of this book starts with the work of Frank Keil; we are merely following up on his insights about the nature of cognition. Once we began, Sabina Sloman kept us going, pointing out connections we hadn't seen, sharing observations, uncovering our contradictions, and editing our text. Critical edits were also provided by Linda Covington, who patiently went over the book more than once, improving our prose and focusing our thinking. Jessamyn Hope and Nick Reinholtz also contributed to the readability of the text. Samantha Steiner is responsible for the artwork that you can find in the Introduction and at the beginning of chapter 4. Her generosity and flair are deeply appreciated.

The ideas for this book were incubated while working with Craig Fox, Daniel Walters, and Todd Rogers on a project supported by a grant from the Thrive Center for Human Development and the John Templeton Foundation. In addition, this publication was made possible through grants from the Varieties of Understanding project at Fordham University, also funded by the John Templeton Foundation.

Several colleagues contributed important ideas and acted as intellectual compasses: Michael Shiner, Nathaniel Rabb, Bill Warren, Mark Johnson, Uriel Cohen-Priva, Andy Horwitz, David Over,

Patrick Mulligan, Richard Florest, Susan Woodward, Adrian Ward, John Lynch, Pete McGraw, Bart de Langhe, and Donnie Lichtenstein.

Steven would also like to thank Leila Sloman for her help and willingness to be a sounding board. His parents, Valerie and Leon Sloman, provided critical encouragement, insights, and housing.

Phil would like to thank his extraordinarily supportive family: Joan and Joe, Bruce and Joyce, Rachel, Alex, and the rapidly growing clan of Gagers and Edelsteins. He hopes that the two lights of his life, Andrea and James, soon learn to read, so they can tell him about all the mistakes he made in the book. Most important, nothing would work without Anna, his partner in life.

Finally, this book would not have been written without the faith of our agent, Christy Fletcher. It would have been unreadable without the patience and expertise of our editor, Courtney Young.

Notes

INTRODUCTION: IGNORANCE AND THE COMMUNITY OF KNOWLEDGE

1 *Castle Bravo:* A complete recounting of the Castle Bravo accident is provided in C. Hansen, ed. (2007). *The Swords of Armageddon.* Chukelea Publications. Also see B. J. O'Keefe (1983). *Nuclear Hostages.* Boston: Houghton Mifflin.

2 *Hiroshima:* An excellent history of the development of the atomic bomb up to the end of World War II is provided in R. Rhodes (1986). *Making of the Atomic Bomb.* New York: Simon & Schuster.

14 *division of cognitive labor:* P. Kitcher (1990). "The Division of Cognitive Labor." *The Journal of Philosophy* 87(1): 5–22.

ONE. WHAT WE KNOW

17 *Slotin:* The story is recounted in M. Zeilig (1995). "Louis Slotin and 'The Invisible Killer.'" *The Beaver* 75(4): 20–27.

21 *Rozenblit and Keil:* L. Rozenblit and F. Keil (2002). "The Misunderstood Limits of Folk Science: An Illusion of Explanatory Depth." *Cognitive Science* 26(5): 521–562.

23 *Rozenblit and Keil quote:* ibid., 10.

23 *what people know about bicycles:* R. Lawson (2006). "The Science of Cycology: Failures to Understand How Everyday Objects Work." *Memory & Cognition* 34(8), 1667–1675.

25 Can machines think?: A. M. Turing (1950). "Computing Machinery and Intelligence." *Mind* 59: 433–460.

25 *Landauer:* T. K. Landauer (1986). "How Much Do People Remember? Some Estimates of the Quantity of Learned Information in Long-term Memory." *Cognitive Science* 10(4): 477–493.

26 *They learned at approximately the same rate:* For those familiar with information

theory, the rate of acquisition Landauer estimated was roughly two bits per second.

27   Jeopardy!: A popular American game show that tests participants' ability to quickly answer general knowledge questions.

27   *early days of computer science and cognitive science*: Parallel, distributed computation is becoming the norm in the age of the Internet and powerful graphics engines.

28   *30,000 parts*: www.toyota.co.jp/en/kids/faq/d/01/04.

29   *cancer:* A story told in S. Mukherjee (2010). *The Emperor of All Maladies: A Biography of Cancer.* New York: Scribner.

30   *weather forecasting*: www.bbc.com/news/business-29256322.

30   *The weather in your location today depends:* www.scholastic.com/teachers/article/weather.

32   *the more likely ones*: These issues are discussed in Nassim Nicholas Taleb (2007), *The Black Swan.* New York: Random House.

34   *Gould quote*: S. J. Gould (1989). *Wonderful Life: The Burgess Shale and the Nature of History*, 1st ed. New York: W. W. Norton, 320–321.

TWO. WHY WE THINK

37   *Borges quotes*: J. L. Borges (1964). "Funes the Memorious." *Labyrinths: Selected Stories and Other Writings*. Trans. James E. Irby. Ed. Donald A. Yates and James E. Irby. New York: New Directions, 59–66. Quotes from pp. 63–64. Story originally published in 1942.

38   *AJ*: E. S. Parker, L. Cahill, and J. L. McGaugh (2006). "A Case of Unusual Autobiographical Remembering." *Neurocase* 12(1): 35–49.

39   *1-terabyte*: aimblog.uoregon.edu/2014/07/08/a-terabyte-of-storage-space-how -much-is-too-much.

40   *National Public Radio*: www.npr.org/sections/health-shots/2013/12/18/2552 85479/when-memories-never-fade-the-past-can-poison-the-present.

40   Paris japonica: J. Pellicer, M. F. Fay, and I. J. Leitch (2010). "The Largest Eukaryotic Genome of Them All?" *Botanical Journal of the Linnean Society* 164(1): 10–15.

41   *Venus flytrap*: A. G. Volkov, T. Adesina, V. S. Markin, and E. Jovanov (2008). "Kinetics and Mechanism of *Dionaea muscipula* Trap Closing." *Plant Physiology* 146(2): 694–702.

42   *jellyfish*: T. Katsuki and R. J. Greenspan (2013). "Jellyfish Nervous Systems." *Current Biology* 23(14): R592–R594.

42   *horseshoe crab numbers*: news.nationalgeographic.com/news/2014/06/140617-horse shoe-crab-mating-delaware-bay-eastern-seaboard.

43   *Hartline*: H. K. Hartline, H. G. Wagner, and F. Ratliff (1956). "Inhibition in the Eye of Limulus." *The Journal of General Physiology* 39(5): 651–673.

44   *Barlow*: R. B. Barlow, L. C. Ireland, and L. Kass (1982). "Vision Has a Role in *Limulus* Mating Behavior." *Nature* 296(5852): 65–66.

45 *Danny DeVito yearbook photo*: i.imgur.com/njXUFGa.jpg.

46 *Face perception*: D. Maurer, R. L. Grand, and C. J. Mondloch (2002). "The Many Faces of Configural Processing." *Trends in Cognitive Sciences* 6(6): 255–260.

46 *Humans can detect*: N. D. Haig (1984). "The Effect of Feature Displacement on Face Recognition." *Perception* 13(5): 505–512.

THREE. HOW WE THINK

50 *Pavlov's bell*: There's been some dispute about whether he actually used a bell, a dispute that seems to have been resolved in his favor by R. Thomas (1994). "Pavlov's Dogs 'Dripped Saliva at the Sound of a Bell.'" *Psycoloquy* 5(80).

51 *one of Garcia's studies*: J. Garcia and R. A. Koelling (1966). "Relation of Cue to Consequence in Avoidance Learning." *Psychonomic Science* 4(1): 123–124.

54 Modus ponens *and causal considerations*: D. D. Cummins, T. Lubart, O. Alksnis, and R. Rist (1991). "Conditional Reasoning and Causation." *Memory & Cognition* 19(3): 274–282.

54 *We excel at casual analysis*: An introduction to this literature can be found in B. F. Malle and J. Korman (2013). "Attribution Theory." In ed. D. S. Dunn, *Oxford Bibliographies in Psychology*. New York: Oxford University Press.

58 *Reasoning backward*: See, for example, A. Tversky and D. Kahneman (1978). "Causal Schemata in Judgments Under Uncertainty." *Progress in Social Psychology*. Hillsdale, NJ: Lawrence Erlbaum.

59 *error in predictive reasoning*: P. M. Fernbach, A. Darlow, and S. A. Sloman (2011). "Asymmetries in Predictive and Diagnostic Reasoning." *Journal of Experimental Psychology: General* 140(2): 168–185; P. M. Fernbach, A. Darlow, and S. A. Sloman (2010). "Neglect of Alternative Causes in Predictive but Not Diagnostic Reasoning." *Psychological Science* 21(3): 329–336.

61 *No evidence for diagnostic reasoning in animals*: D. C. Penn, K. J. Holyoak, and D. J. Povinelli (2008). "Darwin's Mistake: Explaining the Discontinuity Between Human and Nonhuman Minds." *Behavioral and Brain Sciences* 31(2): 109–130.

62 *Crow study*: A. H. Taylor, G. R. Hunt, F. S. Medina, and R. D. Gray (2009). "Do New Caledonian Crows Solve Physical Problems Through Causal Reasoning?" *Proceedings of the Royal Society B: Biological Sciences* 276(1655): 247–254.

63 *Storytelling*: See R. Hastie and N. Pennington (1995). "The Big Picture: Is It a Story?" in *Knowledge and Memory: The Real Story*. Ed. R. S. Wyer Jr. and J. K. Srull. Hillsdale, NJ: Lawrence Erlbaum, 133–138.

64 *Heider and Simmel video*: You can see the film on Youtube: www.youtube.com/watch?v=76p64j3H1Ng.

66 *identities as stories*: A major proponent of this view is Jerome Bruner.

FOUR. WHY WE THINK WHAT ISN'T SO

69   *naive understanding of physics*: M. McCloskey (1983). "Intuitive Physics." *Scientific American* 248(4): 122–130.

71   *Andrea diSessa*: A. A. diSessa (1983). "Phenomenology and the Evolution of Intuition." In ed. D. Gentner and A. L. Stevens. *Mental Models*. Hillsdale, NJ: Lawrence Erlbaum.

72   *People understand electricity*: D. Gentner and D. R. Gentner (1983). "Flowing Waters or Teeming Crowds: Mental Models of Electricity." In *Mental Models*.

72   *Quote from an experimental participant*: W. Kempton (1986). "Two Theories of Home Heat Control." *Cognitive Science* 10: 75–90.

76   Thinking, Fast and Slow: D. Kahneman (2011). *Thinking, Fast and Slow*. New York: Farrar, Straus.

76   *associative versus rule-based thinking*: S. A. Sloman (1996). "The Empirical Case for Two Systems of Reasoning." *Psychological Bulletin* 119(1): 3–22.

76   *System 1 versus System 2*: K. E. Stanovich and R. F. West (2000). "Individual Differences in Reasoning: Implications for the Rationality Debate." *Behavioral and Brain Sciences* 23(5): 645–726.

77, 78   *Aristotle and Plato quotes*: We thank Tamar Gendler for these quotes.

81   *Frederick refers*: S. Frederick (2005). "Cognitive Reflection and Decision Making." *Journal of Economic Perspectives* 19(4): 25–42.

82   *They make fewer errors and are less likely to fall for tricks*: K. Stanovich (2011). *Rationality and the Reflective Mind*. New York: Oxford University Press.

83   *Profound versus random words*: G. Pennycook, J. A. Cheyne, N. Barr, D. J. Koehler, and J. A. Fugelsang (2015). "On the Reception and Detection of Pseudo-profound Bullshit." *Judgment and Decision Making* 10(6): 549–563.

83   *bigger reward*: S. Frederick (2005). "Cognitive Reflection and Decision Making." *Journal of Economic Perspectives* 19(4): 25–42.

83   *Dark versus milk chocolate*: Shane Frederick, personal communication.

83   *Belief in God*: A. Shenhav, D. G. Rand, and J. D. Greene (2012). "Divine Intuition: Cognitive Style Influences Belief in God." *Journal of Experimental Psychology: General* 141(3): 423–428. For a review, see G. Pennycook (2014). "Evidence That Analytic Cognitive Style Influences Religious Belief: Comment On." *Intelligence* 43: 21–26.

83   *CRT predicts illusion of explanatory depth*: P. M. Fernbach, S. A. Sloman, R. St. Louis, and J. N. Shube (2013). "Explanation Fiends and Foes: How Mechanistic Detail Determines Understanding and Preference." *Journal of Consumer Research* 39(5): 1115–1131.

FIVE. THINKING WITH OUR BODIES AND THE WORLD

86   *Minsky quote*: *Wired Magazine*, Issue 11:08, August 2003. archive.wired.com/wired/archive/11.08/view.html?pg=3.

86 *GOFAI*: J. Haugeland (1989). *Artificial Intelligence: The Very Idea.* Cambridge, MA: MIT Press.

89 *Frame problem*: For a philosophical analysis, see H. L. Dreyfus (2007). "Why Heideggerian AI Failed and How Fixing It Would Require Making It More Heideggerian." *Philosophical Psychology* 20(2): 247–268.

90 *Rodney Brooks's tic-tac-toe game*: www.bostonmagazine.com/news/article/2014/10/28/rodney-brooks-robotics.

93 *Reading text with an eye tracker*: Reviewed in P. S. Churchland, V. S. Ramachandran, and T. J. Sejnowski (1994). "A Critique of Pure Vision." In ed. C. Koch and J. L. Davis, *Large-Scale Neuronal Theories of the Brain.* Cambridge, MA: MIT Press, 23–60.

95 *"outside memory store"*: J. K. O'Regan (1992). "Solving the 'Real' Mysteries of Visual Perception: The World as an Outside Memory." *Canadian Journal of Psychology/Revue canadienne de psychologie* 46(3): 461–488.

96 *What experimenters were wearing*: E. S. Parker, L. Cahill, and J. L. McGaugh (2006). "A Case of Unusual Autobiographical Remembering." *Neurocase* 12 (1): 35–49.

97 *calculating trajectories*: A strategy like this for catching balls (to solve what vision scientists call the outfielder problem) was proposed by B. V. H. Saxberg (1987). "Projected Free Fall Trajectories. I. Theory and Simulation." *Biological Cybernetics*: 56(2–3): 159–175.

97 *angle is always increasing at a constant rate*: A strategy first suggested by S. Chapman (1968). "Catching a Baseball." *American Journal of Physics* 36(10): 868–870.

98 *chasing virtual balls*: P. W. Fink, P. S. Foo, and W. H. Warren (2009). "Catching Fly Balls in Virtual Reality: A Critical Test of the Outfielder Problem." *Journal of Vision* 9(13): 14.

98 *players catching real balls*: P. McLeod and Z. Dienes (1993). "Running to Catch the Ball." *Nature* 362(6415): 23; P. McLeod and Z. Dienes (1996). "Do Fielders Know Where to Go to Catch the Ball or Only How to Get There?" *Journal of Experimental Psychology: Human Perception and Performance* 22(3): 531–543.

100 *the side with the faster flow*: A. P. Duchon and W. H. Warren Jr. (2002). "A Visual Equalization Strategy for Locomotor Control: Of Honeybees, Robots, and Humans." *Psychological Science* 13(3): 272–278.

100 *Bees . . . slower optic flow*: M. V. Srinivasan, M. Lehrer, W. H. Kirchner, and S. W. Zhang (1991). "Range Perception Through Apparent Image Speed in Freely Flying Honeybees." *Visual Neuroscience* 6(5): 519–535.

101 *it's in the brain*: We were inspired to ask this question and present the material this way by a talk entitled "Cognitive Ethnography" by Edwin Hutchins at the Cognitive Science Society conference that took place in Boston in 2003. A more recent articulation of Hutchins's views about the relation between cognition, culture, and the environment can be found in E. Hutchins (2014). "The Cultural Ecosystem of Human Cognition." *Philosophical Psychology* 27(1): 34–49.

101 *Experiment to judge orientation*: M. Tucker and R. Ellis (1998). "On the Relations Between Seen Objects and Components of Potential Actions." *Journal of Experimental Psychology: Human Perception and Performance* 24(3): 830–846.

102 *memorization techniques*: C. L. Scott, R. J. Harris, and A. R. Rothe (2001). "Embodied Cognition Through Improvisation Improves Memory for a Dramatic Monologue." *Discourse Processes* 31(3): 293–305.

102 *embodiment*: These ideas took on prominence due to the work of a number of people, including Lawrence Barsalou and Arthur Glenberg.

102 *Oksapmin people*: G. B. Saxe (1981). "Body Parts as Numerals: A Developmental Analysis of Numeration Among the Oksapmin in Papua New Guinea." *Child Development* 52(1): 306–316.

103 *unified with the objects that we're thinking about and with*: A fuller presentation of these ideas can be found in M. Wilson (2002). "Six Views of Embodied Cognition." *Psychonomic Bulletin & Review* 9(4): 625–636.

103 *somatic markers*: This idea is spelled out in A. R. Damasio (1994). *Descartes' Error: Emotion, Reason and the Human Brain*. New York: G. P. Putnam's.

105 *moral reactions*: This is an idea made popular by J. Haidt (2001). "The Emotional Dog and Its Rational Tail: A Social Intuitionist Approach to Moral Judgment." *Psychological Review* 108(4): 814–834.

SIX. THINKING WITH OTHER PEOPLE

109 *Speth describes communal bison hunts*: J. D. Speth (1997). "Communal Bison Hunting in Western North America: Background for the Study of Paleolithic Bison Hunting in Europe." *L'Alimentation des Hommes du Paléolitique* 83: 23–57, ERAUL, Liége.

112 *brain mass of modern humans*: S. Shultz, E. Nelson, and R. I. Dunbar (2012). "Hominin Cognitive Evolution: Identifying Patterns and Processes in the Fossil and Archeological Record." *Philosophical Transactions of the Royal Society B: Biological Sciences* 367(1599): 2130–2140.

112 *physically weaker to compensate*: www.nytimes.com/2014/05/28/science/stronger -brains-weaker-bodies.html?_r=0.

112 *snowball effect*: A. Whiten and D. Erdal (2012). "The Human Socio-Cognitive Niche and Its Evolutionary Origins." *Philosophical Transactions of the Royal Society of London B: Biological Sciences* 367(1599): 2119–2129.

113 *Hunting . . . instrumental to human evolution*: R. Ardrey (1976). *The Hunting Hypothesis: A Personal Conclusion Concerning the Evolutionary Nature of Man*. New York: Atheneum.

113 *Robin Dunbar, social brain hypothesis*: R. I. Dunbar (1992). "Neocortex Size as a Constraint on Group Size in Primates." *Journal of Human Evolution* 22(6): 469–493.

115 *reasoning about intentionality*: For a penetrating analysis of what this kind of rea-

soning requires, see B. F. Malle and J. Knobe (1997). "The Folk Concept of Intentionality." *Journal of Experimental Social Psychology* 33(2): 101–121.

116 *Tomasello, shared intentionality*: This and the other work on shared intentionality reviewed here are discussed in M. Tomasello and M. Carpenter (2007). "Shared Intentionality." *Developmental Science* 10(1): 121–125.

117 *Tomasello quote*: Ibid., p. 123

118 *not . . . getting smarter:* Though they are doing better and better on intelligence tests. J. R. Flynn (2007). *What Is Intelligence? Beyond the Flynn Effect.* New York: Cambridge University Press.

120 *couples divide cognitive labor*: D. M. Wegner (1987). "Transactive Memory: A Contemporary Analysis of the Group Mind." In ed. B. Mullen and George Goethals, *Theories of Group Behavior.* New York: Springer, 185–208.

122 *more credit than they deserve*: Reviewed in M. R. Leary and D. R. Forsyth (1987). "Attributions of Responsibility for Collective Endeavors." In ed. C. Hendrick, *Review of Personality and Social Psychology*, vol. 8. Newbury Park, CA: Sage, 167–188.

122 *household chores*: M. Ross and F. Sicoly (1979). "Egocentric Biases in Availability and Attribution." *Journal of Personality and Social Psychology* 37(3): 322–336.

123 *glowing rocks study:* Sloman, S. A., & Rabb, N. (2016). Your understanding is my understanding: evidence for a community of knowledge. Psychological science, 27(11), 1451–1460. Some of you might be worried that these results just reflect either task demands or judgments about the understandability of the phenomena. Sloman and Rabb controlled for both of these types of alternative explanations.

125 *placeholders*: There is a view in philosophy that claims this is true of certain aspects of language. This "meaning ain't in the head" view is called "essentialism" and was articulated with great insight by Hilary Putnam and a related view by Saul Kripke.

126 *compatibility of communal knowledge:* Frank Keil has done a lot of work on this topic—for example, F. C. Keil and J. Kominsky (2013). "Missing Links in Middle School: Developing Use of Disciplinary Relatedness in Evaluating Internet Search Results." *PloS ONE* 8(6), e67777.

127 *George Bernard Shaw quote*: gutenberg.net.au/ebooks02/0200811h.html.

128 *curse of knowledge*: C. Camerer, G. Loewenstein, and M. Weber (1989). "The Curse of Knowledge in Economic Settings: An Experimental Analysis." *Journal of Political Economy* 97(5): 1232–1254.

128 *shocked that others don't recognize the tune*: C. Heath and D. Heath (2007). *Made to Stick: Why Some Ideas Survive and Others Die.* New York: Random House, 2007.

128 *hindsight bias*: B. Fischhoff and R. Beyth (1975). "'I Knew It Would Happen': Remembered Probabilities of Once-Future Things." *Organizational Behavior and Human Performance* 13(1): 1–16.

129 *few people today read* Alice in Wonderland: A fact bemoaned by Anthony Lane in "Go Ask Alice," *The New Yorker*, June 8 and 15, 2015.

SEVEN. THINKING WITH TECHNOLOGY

131 *commuting a little less*: www.governing.com/topics/transportation-infrastructure/how-america-stopped-commuting.html.

132 *attendance at movie theaters*: www.slashfilm.com/box-office-attendance-hits-lowest-level-five-years.

132 *Vernor Vinge*: V. Vinge (1993). "The Coming Technological Singularity." *Whole Earth Review*, Winter.

132 *Ray Kurzweil*: R. Kurzweil (2005). *The Singularity Is Near: When Humans Transcend Biology.* New York: Penguin Books.

132 *Nick Bostrom*: N. Bostrom (2014). *Superintelligence: Paths, Dangers, Strategies.* Oxford, UK: Oxford University Press.

133 *Ian Tattersall*: As told to Dan Falk in the online magazine *aeon*: http://aeon.co/magazine/science/was-human-evolution-inevitable-or-a-matter-of-luck.

134 *extensions of our bodies*: A. Clark (2004). *Natural-Born Cyborgs: Minds, Technologies, and the Future of Human Intelligence.* New York: Oxford University Press; J. H. Siegle and W. H. Warren (2010). "Distal Attribution and Distance Perception in Sensory Substitution." *Perception* 39(2): 208–223; R. Volcic, C. Fantoni, C. Caudek, J. A. Assad, and F. Domini (2013). "Visuomotor Adaptation Changes Stereoscopic Depth Perception and Tactile Discrimination." *The Journal of Neuroscience* 33(43): 17081–17088.

136 *when we search the Internet*: D. M. Wegner and A. F. Ward (2013). "How Google Is Changing Your Brain." *Scientific American* 309(6): 58–61; and M. Fisher, M. K. Goddu, and F. C. Keil (2015). "Searching for Explanations: How the Internet Inflates Estimates of Internal Knowledge." *Journal of Experimental Psychology: General* 144(3): 674–687. See also A. F. Ward (2013). "Supernormal: How the Internet Is Changing Our Memories and Our Minds." *Psychological Inquiry* 24(4): 341–348.

138 *WebMD*: Adrian F. Ward (May 2015), "Blurred Boundaries: Internet Search, Cognitive Self-Esteem, and Confidence in Decision-Making." Talk presented at the annual meeting of the Association for Psychological Science, New York, New York.

141 *fifty microprocessors each*: auto.howstuffworks.com/under-the-hood/trends-innovations/car-computer.htm.

141 *Elon Musk*: fortune.com/2015/12/21/elon-musk-interview.

142 *compromise overall safety*: S. Greengard (2009). "Making Automation Work." *Communications of the ACM* 52(12): 18–19.

143 *pilots . . . didn't know what to do*: www.popularmechanics.com/technology/aviation/crashes/what-really-happened-aboard-airfrance-447-6611877.

143 *GPS master*: Examples can be found at www.straightdope.com/columns/read/3119/has-anyone-gotten-hurt-or-killed-following-bad-gps-directions.

143 Royal Majesty: The story is described in much greater detail in chapter 8 of A. Degani (2004). *Taming HAL: Designing Interfaces Beyond 2001.* New York: Palgrave Macmillan.

147 *more than on financial incentives*: E. Bonabeau (2009). "Decisions 2.0: The Power of Collective Intelligence." *MIT Sloan Management Review* 50(2): 45–52.

147 *OED . . . is still doing so*: For an engaging history of the OED, see S. Winchester (1998). *The Professor and the Madman: A Tale of Murder, Insanity, and the Making of the Oxford English Dictionary.* New York: HarperCollins.

148 *PK-35*: The story and conclusion come from E. Bonabeau (2009). "Decisions 2.0: The Power of Collective Intelligence." *MIT Sloan Management Review* 50(2): 45–52.

148 *Amazon ratings are not all they're cracked up to be*: B. De Langhe, P. M. Fernbach, and D. R. Lichtenstein (2015). "Navigating by the Stars: Investigating the Actual and Perceived Validity of Online User Ratings." *Journal of Consumer Research* 42: 817–830.

148 The Wisdom of Crowds: F. Galton (1907). *Vox Populi (the Wisdom of Crowds).* First published in *Nature* 75(1949): 450–451. The topic is discussed in detail in J. Surowiecki (2005). *The Wisdom of Crowds.* New York: Doubleday Anchor.

148 *within 1 percent of the ox's true weight of 1,198 pounds*: Despite frequent reports saying otherwise, he did not find that the mean weight was within 1 pound of the ox's true weight. Nor did he find that the average was better than any individual guess.

149 *prediction market*: K. J. Arrow, R. Forsythe, M. Gorham, R. Hahn, R. Hanson, J. O. Ledyard, S. Levmore, et al. (2008). "The Promise of Prediction Markets." *Science* 320(5878): 877–878.

EIGHT. THINKING ABOUT SCIENCE

153 *a giant sledgehammer*: smithsonianmag.com/history/what-the-luddites-really-fought-against-264412/?all.

154 *increasingly bizarre*: Ibid.

154 *James Inhofe's snowball*: washingtonpost.com/news/the-fix/wp/2015/02/26/jim-inhofes-snowball-has-disproven-climate-change-once-and-for-all.

154 *Inhofe quote*: nytimes.com/2003/08/05/science/politics-reasserts-itself-in-the-debate-over-climate-change-and-its-hazards.html.

155 *cases of measles spiked*: cdc.gov/measles/cases-outbreaks.html.

156 *10 percent of parents*: dailycamera.com/news/ci_19848081.

156 *doctors are not to be trusted*: www.thehealthyhomeeconomist.com/six-reasons-to-say-no-to-vaccination.

158 *increase to about 70 percent*: These results are summarized in the 2014 version of the Science and Engineering Indicators report.

159 *MMR vaccine*: B. Nyhan, J. Reifler, S. Richey, and G. L. Freed (2014). "Effec-

tive Messages in Vaccine Promotion: A Randomized Trial." *Pediatrics* 133(4): e835–e842.

160 *Science Mike*: kernelmag.dailydot.com/issue-sections/headline-story/14304/ science-mike-mystical-experience-podcast.

161 *Science Mike quote:* mikemchargue.com/blog/2015/1/11/new-podcast-ask-science -mike.

164 "*Earth revolves around the Sun*": www.techtimes.com/articles/3493/20140216/dumb -101-1-in-4-americans-is-ignorant-that-earth-revolves-around-the-sun.htm.

165 *consume more pharmaceuticals*: V. Ilyuk, L. Block, and D. Faro (2014). "Is It Still Working? Task Difficulty Promotes a Rapid Wear-Off Bias in Judgments of Pharmacological Products." *Journal of Consumer Research* 41(3): 775–793.

165 *AAAS conclusion*: Statement by the AAAS Board of Directors on Labeling of Genetically Modified Foods. American Association for the Advancement of Science, October 20, 2012. www.aaas.org/sites/default/files/AAAS_GM _statement.pdf.

165 *European Commission conclusion*: A Decade of EU-funded GMO Research, 2001–2010. European Commission: Food, Agriculture and Fisheries, Biotech- nology. ec.europa.eu/research/biosociety/pdf/a_decade_of_eu-funded_gmo _research.pdf.

166 *Florida orange crop*: http://www.nytimes.com/2013/07/28/science/a-race-to-save -the-orange-by-altering-its-dna.html?pagewanted=all&_r=0.

168 *sunlight cannot get stuck in a window*: Y. Zheng, L. E. Bolton, and J. W. Alba (working paper). "How Things Work: Production Matters in Technology Acceptance."

168 *oversimplification of how the immune system works*: www.health.harvard.edu/ staying-healthy/how-to-boost-your-immune-system.

168 *antibodies that target specific infections*: www.biologymad.com/resources/Immunity %20Revision.pdf.

168 *Generalized versus specific immunity*: This idea was inspired by a conversation with Joanna Arch.

169 *global warming in a short video*: www.howglobalwarmingworks.org.

NINE. THINKING ABOUT POLITICS

171 *Kaiser Family Foundation*: http://kff.org/health-reform/poll-finding/kaiser-health -tracking-poll-april-2013/.

172 *Ukraine's location*: www.washingtonpost.com/blogs/monkey-cage/wp/2014/04 /07/the-less-americans-know-about-ukraines-location-the-more-they-want -u-s-to-intervene.

172 *Oklahoma State University survey*: Food Demand Survey, Oklahoma State De- partment of Agricultural Economics, 2(9), 2015. www.washingtonpost.com/

news/volokh-conspiracy/wp/2015/01/17/over-80-percent-of-americans
-support-mandatory-labels-on-foods-containing-dna.

172 *Clint Eastwood quote*: Interview, *Time*, February 20, 2005.

173 *groupthink*: I. L. Janis (1983). *Groupthink: Psychological Studies of Policy Decisions and Fiascoes*, 2nd ed. Boston: Houghton Mifflin, 349.

173 *Polarization from discussion*: An early paper showing this effect is D. Pruitt (1971). "Choice Shifts in Group Discussion: An Introductory Review." *Journal of Personality and Social Psychology* 20(3): 339–360. A review of the literature can be found in D. J. Isenberg (1986). "Group Polarization: A Critical Review and Meta-Analysis." *Journal of Personality and Social Psychology* 50(6): 1141–1151.

175 *illusion of explanatory depth with political issues*: P. M. Fernbach, T. Rogers, C. Fox, and S. A. Sloman (2013). "Political Extremism Is Supported by an Illusion of Understanding." *Psychological Science* 24(6): 939–946.

177 *Thinking increases extremism*: A. Tesser, L. Martin, and M. Mendolia (1995). "The Impact of Thought on Attitude Extremity and Attitude-Behavior Consistency." In ed. R. E. Petty and J. A. Krosnick, *Attitude Strength: Antecedents and Consequences*. Mahwah, NJ: Lawrence Erlbaum, 73–92.

181 *intuitions and feelings*: J. Haidt (2001). "The Emotional Dog and Its Rational Tail: A Social Intuitionist Approach to Moral Judgment." *Psychological Review* 108(4): 814–834.

181 *Incest scenario*: Ibid., 814.

182 *Causal analysis versus values*: For a rich discussion of these issues, see J. Greene (2014). *Moral Tribes: Emotion, Reason, and the Gap Between Us and Them*. New York: Penguin Books.

185 *Iranians' attitudes*: M. Dehghani, R. Iliev, S. Sachdeva, S. Atran, J. Ginges, and D. Medin (2009). "Emerging Sacred Values: Iran's Nuclear Program." *Judgment and Decision Making* 4(7): 930–933.

186 *gay marriage*: Changing attitudes on gay marriage, Pew Research Center, July 29, 2015. www.pewforum.org/2015/07/29/graphics-slideshow-changing-attitudes -on-gay-marriage.

187 *material remuneration*: J. Ginges, S. Atran, D. Medin, and K. Shikaki (2007). "Sacred Bounds on Rational Resolution of Violent Political Conflict." *Proceedings of the National Academy of Sciences* 104(18): 7357–7360.

192 *Not more open to new information*: In a 2014 Brown University honors project by Julia Shube.

TEN. THE NEW DEFINITION OF SMART

195 *Martin Luther King Jr.*: As Henry Louis Taylor Jr., professor of urban and regional planning at the University of Buffalo, says, "Everyone knows, even the

smallest kid knows about Martin Luther King, can say his most famous moment was that 'I have a dream' speech. No one can go further than one sentence. All we know is that this guy had a dream. We don't know what that dream was." Reported by Deepti Hajela, Associated Press, January 21, 2008.

198 *Popular history*: History is never so simple. See B. Hughes (2011). *The Hemlock Cup: Socrates, Athens, and the Search for the Good Life*. New York: Alfred A. Knopf; and M. Singham (2007). "The Copernican Myths." *Physics Today* 60(12): 48–52.

198 *Copernicus*: D. J. Boorstin (1985). *The Discoverers*. New York: Vintage Books.

199 *Einstein*: G. Holton (1981). "Einstein's Search for the 'Weltbild.'" *Proceedings of the American Philosophical Society* 125(1): 1–15.

199 *documented cases*: D. Lamb and S. M. Easton (1984). *Multiple Discovery: The Pattern of Scientific Progress*. Amersham: Avebury Publishing Company, 70. The authors conclude that "multiple discovery is a normal feature of science."

199 *Scerri*: E. Scerri (2015). "The Discovery of the Periodic Table as a Case of Simultaneous Discovery." *Philosophical Transactions of the Royal Society A* 373(2097): 20140172.

200 *CRISPR/Cas9*: www.wired.com/2015/10/battle-genome-editing-gets-science-wrong.

202 *fluid versus crystallized intelligence*: R. R. Cattell (1943). "The Measurement of Adult Intelligence." *Psychological Bulletin* 40: 153–193; J. L. Horn (1976). "Human Abilities: A Review of Research and Theory in the Early 1970's." *Annual Review of Psychology* 27(1): 437–485.

202 *three separate skills*: W. Johnson and T. J. Bouchard (2005). "The Structure of Human Intelligence: It Is Verbal, Perceptual, and Image Rotation (VPR), Not Fluid and Crystallized." *Intelligence* 33(4): 393–416.

202 *eight distinct dimensions*: H. Gardner (1999). *Intelligence Reframed: Multiple Intelligences for the 21st Century*. New York: Basic Books.

202 *The basic skill set*: Ed. R. J. Sternberg and S.B. Kaufman (2011). *The Cambridge Handbook of Intelligence*. New York: Cambridge University Press.

203 *objective definition:* They call these operational definitions.

203 *The first modern intelligence test*: M. Alfano, T. Holden, and A. Conway (2017). "Intelligence, Race, and Psychological Testing." *Oxford Handbook of Philosophy and Race*. New York: Oxford University Press.

204 *Charles Spearman*: C. Spearman (1904). "'General Intelligence,' Objectively Determined and Measured." *The American Journal of Psychology* 15(2): 201–292. More recent evidence comes from an exhaustive survey by J. B. Carroll (1993). *Human Cognitive Abilities: A Survey of Factor-Analytic Studies*. New York: Cambridge University Press.

205 *best predictors*: I. J. Deary (2001). "Human Intelligence Differences: A Recent History." *Trends in Cognitive Sciences* 5(3): 127–130.

205 *data from 127 studies*: N. R. Kuncel, S. A. Hezlett, and D. S. Ones (2004). "Ac-

ademic Performance, Career Potential, Creativity, and Job Performance: Can One Construct Predict Them All?" *Journal of Personality and Social Psychology* 86(1): 148–161.

205 *gamblers*: S. J. Ceci and J. K. Liker (1986). "A Day at the Races: A Study of IQ, Expertise, and Cognitive Complexity." *Journal of Experimental Psychology: General* 115(3): 255–266.

209 *Anita Woolley*: A. W. Woolley, C. F. Chabris, A. Pentland, N. Hashmi, and T. W. Malone (2010). "Evidence for a Collective Intelligence Factor in the Performance of Human Groups." *Science* 330(6004): 686–688.

211 *what c is measuring*: J. Salminen (2012). "Collective Intelligence in Humans: A Literature Review." arxiv.org/pdf/1204.3401.pdf.

211 *Avin Rabheru*: www.theguardian.com/media-network/media-network-blog/2014/jun/05/good-ideas-overrated-investor-entrepreneur.

212 *esprit de corps*: www.paulgraham.com/startupmistakes.html.

ELEVEN. MAKING PEOPLE SMART

215 *Brazilian inflation*: www.inflation.eu/inflation-rates/brazil/historic-inflation/cpi-inflation-brazil.aspx.

215 *administered a series of tests*: G. B. Saxe (1988). "The Mathematics of Child Street Vendors." *Child Development* 59(5): 1415–1425.

216 *Dewey quote*: J. Dewey (1938). *Education and Experience*. New York: Macmillan, 63.

217 *students care about*: A rich discussion can be found in D. Perkins (1995). *Smart Schools: Better Thinking and Learning for Every Child*. New York: The Free Press.

217 *illusion of comprehension*: W. Epstein, A. M. Glenberg, and M. M. Bradley (1984). "Coactivation and Comprehension: Contribution of Text Variables to the Illusion of Knowing." *Memory & Cognition* 12(4): 355–360; A. M. Glenberg, A. C. Wilkinson, and W. Epstein (1982). "The Illusion of Knowing: Failure in the Self-Assessment of Comprehension." *Memory & Cognition* 10(6): 597–602.

217 *inverted text*: P. A. Kolers (1976). "Reading a Year Later." *Journal of Experimental Psychology: Human Learning and Memory* 2(5): 554–565.

218 *Jimi Hendrix*: For many more examples, see www.kissthisguy.com.

219 *John Dewey*: Dewey, *Education and Experience*, 56.

219 *the mistaken belief*: A point made by philosophers Rom Harré and John Hardwig and by education theorists Stephen Norris, David Perkins, and Neil Postman. See, for instance, S. Norris (1995). "Learning to Live with Scientific Expertise: Toward a Theory of Intellectual Communalism for Guiding Science Teaching." *Science Education*, 79(2): 201-217.

221 *Ignorance course*: S. Firestein (2012). *Ignorance*. New York: Oxford University Press.

222 *National Council for the Social Studies: National Curriculum Standards for Social*

Studies: A Framework for Teaching, Learning and Assessment. National Council for the Social Studies, 2010.

222 *NRC:* National Research Council (1996). *National Science Education Standards.* Washington, D.C.: National Academies Press; H. A. Schweingruber, R. A. Duschl, and A. W. Shouse, ed. (2007). *Taking Science to School: Learning and Teaching Science in Grades K-8.* Washington, D.C.: National Academies Press.

222 *a philosophy to teach science:* N. G. Lederman (2007). "Nature of Science: Past, Present, and Future." Ed. S. K. Abell and N. G. Lederman. *Handbook of Research on Science Education.* New York: Routledge, 831–879.

222 *"nature of science":* B. Alberts (2009). "Redefining Science Education." *Science* 323(5913): 437. In direct support of this complaint, a study looked at the exams and quizzes used in a variety of introductory biology courses at the college level and concluded "that introductory biology courses emphasize facts more than higher-order thinking." J. L. Momsen, T. M. Long, S. A. Wyse, and D. Ebert-May (2010). "Just the Facts? Introductory Undergraduate Biology Courses Focus on Low-Level Cognitive Skills." *CBE Life Sciences Education* 9(4): 435–440.

222 *David Perkins:* Perkins, *Smart Schools,* 33.

223 *based on authority:* Philosophers call this epistemic dependence.

226 *1950–2014:* U.S. National Library of Medicine. www.nlm.nih.gov/bsd/authors1.html.

227 *trust ourselves:* This is another point emphasized by Stephen Norris (1995), 211.

228 *"person-solo":* A term used by Perkins, *Smart Schools,* 132, to argue in favor of attending to social learning, to distributed cognition in the classroom.

228 *to figure things out interactively:* This view is argued for by R. Pea (1993). "Practices of Distributed Intelligence and Designs for Education." In ed. G. Salomon, *Distributed Cognitions: Psychological and Educational Considerations.* New York: Cambridge University Press, 47–87.

229 *Ann Brown quote:* A. L. Brown (1997). "Transforming Schools into Communities of Thinking and Learning About Serious Matters." *American Psychologist* 52(4): 399–413.

230 *diversity in the classroom:* A. L. Brown and J. C. Campione (1994). *"Guided Discovery in a Community of Learners."* In ed. Kate McGilly, *Classroom Lessons: Integrating Cognitive Theory and Classroom Practice.* Cambridge, MA: MIT Press, 229–270.

230 *"peer education":* See, for instance, E. Phelps and W. Damon (1989). "Problem Solving with Equals: Peer Collaboration as a Context for Learning Mathematics and Spatial Concepts." *Journal of Educational Psychology* 81(4): 639–646.

230 *sharing of attention:* Perkins, *Smart Schools.*

231 *generate explanations:* J. J. Williams and T. Lombrozo (2013). "Explanation and Prior Knowledge Interact to Guide Learning." *Cognitive Psychology* 66(1): 55–84.

231 *what you need to get a job:* A point made by F. Zakaria (2015). *In Defense of a Liberal Education.* New York: W. W. Norton; and by N. Postman (1995). *The End of Education.* New York: Alfred A. Knopf.

231 *"troll farm":* A. Chen, "The Agency." *New York Times Magazine,* June 2, 2015.

TWELVE. MAKING SMARTER DECISIONS

235 *Craig McKenzie:* C. R. M. McKenzie and M. J. Liersch (2011). "Misunderstanding Savings Growth: Implications for Retirement Savings Behavior." *Journal of Marketing Research* 48: S1–S13.

236 *Jack Soll:* J. B. Soll, R. L. Keeney, and R. P. Larrick (2013). "Consumer Misunderstanding of Credit Card Use, Payments, and Debt: Causes and Solutions." *Journal of Public Policy & Marketing* 32(1): 66–81.

236 *Chase:* www.creditcards.com/credit-card-news/minimum-credit-card-payments -1267.php.

237 *a little explanation:* P. M. Fernbach, S. A. Sloman, R. St. Louis, and J. N. Shube (2013). "Explanation Fiends and Foes: How Mechanistic Detail Determines Understanding and Preference." *Journal of Consumer Research* 39(5): 1115–1131.

239 *skin care:* T. Caulfield (2015). "The Pseudoscience of Beauty Products." *The Atlantic.* www.theatlantic.com/health/archive/2015/05/the-pseudoscience-of-beauty -products/392201/; Z. Liu (2014). "How Cosmetic Companies Get Away with Pseudoscience." *Pacific Standard.* www.psmag.com/nature-and-technology/cosmetic -companies-get-away-pseudoscience-placebo-week-92455.

240 *$2,000 in thirty days:* A. Lusardi, D. J. Schneider, and P. Tufano (2011). *Financially Fragile Households: Evidence and Implications.* National Bureau of Economic Research Working Paper No. 17072.

241 *enough savings to live on for three years:* D. Rosnick and D. Baker (2014). *The Wealth of Households: An Analysis of the 2013 Survey of Consumer Finances.* Center for Economic and Policy Research. www.scribd.com/doc/245746907/The -Wealth-of-Households.

241 *educational interventions:* D. Fernandes, J. G. Lynch Jr., and R. G. Netemeyer (2014). "Financial Literacy, Financial Education, and Downstream Financial Behaviors." *Management Science* 60: 1861–1883.

244 *de Soto quote:* H. de Soto (2001). *The Mystery of Capital: Why Capitalism Triumphs in the West and Fails Everywhere Else.* London: Bantam Press, 186.

249 *cafeteria line:* B. Wansink (2007). *Mindless Eating: Why We Eat More Than We Think.* New York: Bantam.

249 *organ donors:* E. J. Johnson and D. G. Goldstein (2003). "Do Defaults Save Lives?" *Science* 302: 1338–1339.

249 *Small business retirement plans:* https://www.dol.gov/ebsa/publications/auto maticenrollment401kplans.html.

250 *simple rules:* R. H. Thaler. "Financial Literacy, Beyond the Classroom." *New York Times*, October 5, 2013.

253 *Ray Dalio quote:* Interview with Fareed Zakaria, April 27, 2015.

CONCLUSION: APPRAISING IGNORANCE AND ILLUSION

257 *ignorance documentation:* D. Dunning (2011). "The Dunning-Kruger Effect: On Being Ignorant of One's Own Ignorance." Ed. J. M. Olson and M. P. Zanna, *Advances in Experimental Social Psychology* 44: 247–296.

257 *"We're not very good":* David Dunning in interview with Errol Morris, *New York Times* Opinionator, June 20, 2010.

258 *Dunning-Kruger effect:* J. Kruger and D. Dunning (1999). "Unskilled and Unaware of It: How Difficulties in Recognizing One's Own Incompetence Lead to Inflated Self-Assessments." *Journal of Personality and Social Psychology* 77(6): 1121–1134.

258 *Dunning quote:* David Dunning in interview with Errol Morris, *New York Times* Opinionator, June 20, 2010.

Index